D1209943

SOUTHERN HOMECOMING TRADITIONS

SOUTHERN HOMECOMING TRADITIONS

RECIPES AND REMEMBRANCES

CAROLYN QUICK TILLERY

CITADEL PRESS
Kensington Publishing Corp.
www.kensingtonbooks.com

CITADEL PRESS BOOKS are published by

Kensington Publishing Corp.
850 Third Avenue
New York, NY 10022

All Kensington titles, imprints, and distributed lines are available at special quantity discounts for bulk purchases for sales promotions, premiums, fund-raising, educational, or institutional use. Special book excerpts or customized printings can also be created to fit specific needs. For details, write or phone the office of the Kensington special sales manager: Kensington Publishing Corp., 850 Third Avenue, New York, NY 10022, attn: Special Sales Department; phone 1-800-221-2647.

First printing: November 2006

10 9 8 7 6 5 4 3 2 1

Printed in the United States of America

Library of Congress Control Number: 2006929663

ISBN 0-8065-2683-1

To Richard: You are the iron to my stone. Words cannot express my thanks for your vision and dedicated efforts.

To Margaret and Bruce—who provided both the roots and wings of this series. You will be missed, but never forgotten.

As always, I first give all honor to God
and Jesus Christ, my Lord and Savior,
who goes before me as my Jehovah Nissi
or "Banner of Victory" and comes behind
as my strong rear guard!

CONTENTS

PREFACE:
ATLANTA AND THE CIVIL WAR

"A House divided against itself cannot stand. I believe this government cannot endure permanently half slave and half free. I do not expect the Union to be dissolved—I do not expect the house to fall—but I do expect it will cease to be divided."

—Abraham Lincoln, U.S. Senate nomination acceptance speech,
Springfield, Illinois, June 16, 1858

On January 19, 1861, Georgia seceded from the Union, declaring itself to be "a free and independent State." And by the time of the Civil War the city of Atlanta was a major Southern arsenal and rail terminus, making it a primary war target of the federal government. Because of its importance to the Confederate war effort, General Ulysses S. Grant ordered General William Tecumseh Sherman to "[inflict] all the damage you can against their war resources." Those resources were many and varied because Atlanta was prospering as a war supplier of the South, manufacturing railroad cars, revolvers, cannon, knives, saddles, spurs, buttons, belt buckles, tents, and canteens.

Total annihilation of this southern war machine would be the hard-won trophy Sherman presented to Lincoln, virtually guaranteeing Lincoln's reelection. It also served as the key to Lincoln's "divide and conquer" strategy.

The Battle of Atlanta, on July 22, 1864, nearly destroyed the city; more than 10,000 people perished. Almost four months after seizing the city, Sherman ordered it burned and Federal troops left only 400 of almost 4,000 buildings standing. The next day Sherman began his "march to the sea." Cutting himself off from Union supply lines, he intended to live off the land and proceeded to cut a swath of death and destruction 300 miles in length and 60 miles wide through Georgia, destroying factories, bridges, railroads, and public buildings. Pursuing a strategy of total war, Union troops not only broke the will of the people to fight, but also deprived them of any resources with which to attack. The Mayor of Atlanta led a city delegation to the corner of Marietta and Northside Drive where they surrendered what remained of the city to the Union on September 2, 1864.

Racial Division Unites Black Atlanta

By the 1870s, newly emancipated African Americans constituted almost half of Atlanta's population but after federal troops withdrew from the city in 1877, they lost all political power, including the right to vote, and saw the reemergence of legislatively mandated racial segregation.

In the face of these setbacks, African Americans did what they did best—they turned inward and formed their own communities, helping one another survive and eventually thrive by effectively harnessing polarizing social forces to their advantage. The divisive social segregation in effect following reconstruction led former slaves to begin purchasing property east of the city in the area of Wheat Street (now Auburn Avenue) and Butler Street (now Jesse Hill Jr. Drive). By 1881, the year Spelman College was founded, Butler Street was central to a largely African-American community derisively known as "Darktown."

This community prospered, especially along a social and commercial artery that became known as Sweet Auburn Avenue. Prosperity and pride were the keys to racial progress in Atlanta and led to the establishment of several powerful churches, such as Ebenezer Baptist Church, which provided their members with religious, financial, and political educations. And within the sanctuary walls of activist churches such as Friendship Baptist and Big Bethel Baptist, early homes were provided to historic black colleges that were founded in Atlanta or relocated there in their infancy.

In the case of Morehouse College, which moved from the basement of Atlanta's Friendship Baptist Church in 1879, the church provided for the school; and in turn the school produced preachers as the community leaders and social activists, which graced the church's pulpit. The largesse of its well-off membership's offerings funded facilities, furnishings, and books, among other needs.

This increasingly affluent and educated black populace then began to push for equal rights and the ballot. Although the push began in the churches, the banner was carried by the students. The Atlanta University Center, founded in 1929, became home to the emerging student-led protest movement fighting for the civil rights of oppressed and disenfranchised African Americans. They were urged on by ministers and activists such as Dr. Martin Luther King, Jr., who in delivering the Founders' Day address at Spelman College in 1960 proclaimed, "The students have taken passionate longings of the ages and filtered them in their own souls and fashioned a creative protest. It is one of the glowing epics of the time and I predict that it will win. . . . "

Three unique attributes of black Atlanta, the ABCs, generated the birthplace of the civil rights "dream": A—Auburn Avenue; the three Bs—bucks, books, and the ballot; and C—the powerful black churches. The ABCs also helped ensure the survival and success of the five historic black colleges and the university in the city of Atlanta when most states where historic black colleges existed could boast of only one. The Atlanta schools attracted the best and brightest students from across the nation. They came for the education but stayed for the economic opportunity.

> *"It's almost like you can see a great hand reaching down and lifting Atlanta up,*
> *because of these colleges."*
>
> —Maynard Jackson

In large part, it was the graduates of Atlanta's historic black colleges who finally brought post-Reconstruction freedom and healing to Atlanta and the nation. The Atlanta student civil rights movement was born at the University Center. Advocates such as W.E.B. Du Bois and Whitney Young nursed it. Morehouse College, Spelman College, Atlanta University, and Morris Brown were all active participants in this historic civil rights movement where students such as Lonnie King, Julian Bond, and Ruby Doris Smith Robinson attended college, mentored by movement leaders such as Morehouse graduate Dr. Martin Luther King, Jr., and pastor of West Hunter Street Baptist Church Reverend Ralph Abernathy.

A: Auburn Avenue—What's in a Name?

Auburn Avenue was the main social and commercial artery of Atlanta's African-American community, a "grand lady" in her prime—courted, respected, and loved by everyone. The two-mile stretch offered black-owned nightclubs where Cab Calloway and Duke Ellington performed. "There were big churches, fancy restaurants, clean hotels and black-owned shops, ranging from

John Wesley Dobbs
(Courtesy Spelman College Archives)

beauty salons to clothing stores to funeral parlors. . . . Verily, the sons and daughters of Ham are applying themselves to the useful arts and professions of life."—Reverend E. R. Carter, *The Black Side of Atlanta.*

Early civil rights leader and the unofficial mayor of Auburn Avenue John Wesley Dobbs dubbed the street "Sweet Auburn Avenue," perhaps inspired by the financial opportunities the street afforded to the emerging black middle- and upper-classes, even in the face of oppressive segregation laws. Or perhaps the name was inspired by the fact that on Auburn Avenue people knew each other by name. And within her graceful social and commercial folds they could meet and greet each other with the personal and political news of their insulated community. Regardless of the inspiration for the name, today "Sweet Auburn Avenue" is a name symbolic of the post-Reconstruction development of black business in Atlanta.

B: Bucks

By the turn of the century, Auburn Avenue, the thriving economic and commercial epicenter of African-American life in Atlanta, hosted 64 black-owned businesses and the offices of several black professionals. Money earned outside the community was almost always brought to and circulated within the community. Atlanta Life Insurance, the first black-owned life insurance company founded by former slave Alonzo Franklin Herndon, and black-owned Citizens Trust Bank flourished on Sweet Auburn Avenue. Herndon's success was a brilliant reflection of all that The Avenue represented, a place where a poor country boy could lift himself up and bring others along for the ride. And oh, what a ride it was!

Born into slavery just seven years before the Civil War ended, Herndon began training as a barber at age 20 in Senoia, Georgia. He moved to Atlanta upon being offered a position by the black proprietor of Dougherty Hutchins's barbershop, which catered to a wealthy, white clientele, and he became a partner less than a year later (and the shop's name was officially changed to Hutchins & Herndon). In 1893, he married Adrienne Elizabeth McNeil, a graduate and faculty member of Atlanta University, where she taught elocution and drama.

In 1902, he opened a barber shop at 66 Peachtree Street, around the corner from Auburn Avenue. One of Atlanta's most elegant establishments, it featured crystal chandeliers, gilt-framed mirrors and fittings, massive front doors of solid mahogany, and beveled plate glass. Known from Richmond all the way to Mobile as "the best barbershop in the South," it became an unofficial city attraction visited by local Atlantans as well as tourists who reveled in its opulence. Despite his success, however, Jim Crow laws in Georgia forced Herndon to ride in the back of the streetcar that took him to work. When he arrived at the Crystal Palace, where he served a white clientele, Jim Crow legislation forced Herndon to enter his own establishment through the back door; and he was not permitted to be served on its premises during business hours. His bold response was to create a back entrance to the Crystal Palace that was the same as the front.

Herndon rose above the inherent inequities of segregation to build a real estate and business empire that included the Atlanta Life Insurance Company, one of the nation's premier African American businesses. Through it, Herndon earned money from rich white patrons who came through the front door of his palatial, racially segregated barbershop, and took those earnings out through the back door and invested it in the black community, such as his acquisition of over a hundred residential houses, along with a large commercial block of properties.

In addition to Herndon's barbershop, Sweet Auburn Avenue boasted several other precedent-setting black businesses, as enumerated by civil rights leader John Wesley Dobbs who was born just 17 years after the Civil War. He would later recall arriving in Atlanta in 1897, "when the old artesian well still stood at Five Points," and living to see Atlanta and the state of Georgia "rise above the ruin and devastation of war to places of power and importance in this nation of ours."

During an address to the Atlanta Metropolitan Planning Commission in 1952, he recounted the contributions made by African Americans to Atlanta's rapid growth, saying,

Mr. and Mrs. John Wesley Dobbs
(Courtesy Spelman College Archives)

"Negroes own at least 90 percent of the property on Auburn Avenue . . . where they erected churches, brick buildings and substantial businesses. . . . It is true that we are a poor people, liberated only 85 years ago, without education or money; and yet in the last 50 years we have acquired property along Auburn Avenue, built businesses like the Atlanta Life Insurance Company, which now has more than $25,000,000 in assets; the Citizens Trust Company, a member of the Federal Reserve Banking System, with more than $5,000,000 in assets; the Atlanta Daily World, the only Negro Newspaper in America; a broadcasting station, WERD 860 on your dial, if you please."

In Atlanta, Dobbs had worked at Dr. James McDougal's Drugstore at the corner of Piedmont and Houston Streets while attending Atlanta Baptist College (Morehouse College). After passing the U.S. postal exam in 1903, he left school to become a postal clerk, a highly respected position for a turn-of-the century black man. Three years later he married Irene Ophelia Thompson, and together they would have six daughters, all of whom graduated from Spelman College.

B: Books and the Ballot

Despite their wealth and position, most black businessmen could not vote and chafed under the oppressive, demeaning Jim Crow laws that impacted every aspect of their daily lives. The most onerous burden was that their children were trapped in substandard public schools and were taught from outdated textbooks cast off from white schools. It was their quest for useful books for their children that pushed African Americans to fight for the ballot as a means of effecting change.

On February 12, 1936, John Wesley Dobbs gave a two-hour speech at Big Bethel Church to awaken the political conscience of 90,000 black Atlantans. Immediately following that speech he organized the Atlanta Civic and Political League to register 10,000 voters. It would become the first political action organization for black voters. He single-handedly trained black voters to successfully complete the racially biased registration process and escorted them to the polls, often paying the poll tax—created by white legislators to deter the black vote—himself. These efforts dramatically elevated the number of black voters from a few hundred to thousands. The ballot was the key to improving the living conditions of black Atlantans, and especially black public schools.

On the frontlines of this expanded battle for the ballot was the dynastic King family, three generations of Morehouse men who gave Atlanta three generations of church and civil rights leaders.

The King Family: Martin is third from left.
(Courtesy Morehouse College Archives)

THE REVEREND ALFRED DANIEL WILLIAMS

The King family's legacy as a religious and political powerhouse began with the Reverend Alfred Daniel Williams, the maternal grandfather of Martin Luther King, Jr. The second pastor of Ebenezer Baptist Church, he was an early pioneer of "social gospel," effectively combining the strategy for social advancement of Booker T. Washington, which emphasized black business development, with that of W.E.B. Du Bois, which called for immediate equal civil rights, a message well received by Atlanta's burgeoning middle and upper middle classes.

Early in 1917, A. D. Williams joined Atlanta University graduate Walter White in an initiative to organize a local branch of the National Association for the Advancement of Colored People (NAACP).

Upon chartering the branch, a successful campaign was initiated to impede the Board of Education's plan to close seventh grade classes in black schools in order to pay for a new junior high school for white students. However, subsequent petitions to improve the conditions of existing black schools were unheeded by the school board.

In a strongly worded petition, a NAACP committee led by John Hope, the first black president of Morehouse College and his wife, Lugenia Burns, it was argued, "You, with fifty schools, most of them ample, efficient and comfortable, for the education of your children, can square neither your conscience with your God nor your conduct with your oaths, and behold Negro children in fourteen unsanitary, dilapidated, unventilated school rooms, with double sessions in half of the grades, no industrial facilities, no preparation for high school and no high schools for the blacks."

A year later Williams was elected president of the NAACP and set about recruiting new members. Within five months the branch grew by 1400 members and immediately began registering black voters to challenge a local referendum on school taxes and bond issues for public works, which would allocate a disproportionate share of raised funds to black schools. The 2,500 black Atlantans who paid the poll tax and overcame other voter registration obstacles ably defeated the education measures twice. In March 1920, women were granted the vote and black voter registration more than doubled in two years. This larger, united black voting block convinced white community leaders to make a firm commitment to the black community. A new type of power sharing was born, one which would benefit all Atlantans. A new bond issue—with several million dollars earmarked to build eighteen new schools, including four black elementary schools and Atlanta's first public high school for black students—was overwhelmingly passed with a record turnout. Williams's grandson, Dr. Martin Luther King, Jr., would receive most of his public education in two of the new schools, David T. Howard Elementary School and Booker T. Washington High School.

The Atlanta Independent later reported that "[it] was the ballot that gave Atlanta Negroes modern . . . schoolhouses and facilities; and it was the inspiration that the race received from the local branch under the leadership of Dr. A. D. Williams that put the fight in their bones."

MARTIN LUTHER KING, SR.

In the year prior to successful passage of the bond issue a young, itinerant, barely literate preacher, Martin (then Michael) Luther King, Sr., moved from rural Georgia to Atlanta, where his life soon became inextricably linked with that of the city's most prominent Baptist preacher. Michael King met the only child of A. D. Williams while visiting his sister "Woodie," who boarded with the family on Auburn Avenue. When they met, sixteen-year-old Alberta Williams, a member of Atlanta's black aristocracy, was enrolled in Spelman Seminary's four-year high school program. Despite their age difference, the twenty-three-year-old King was soon attracted by Alberta's "gracious manners, captivating smile and scholarly manner." The mutual attraction resulted in a courtship, which persisted despite her father's insistence that she enroll in the Hampton Normal and Industrial Institute teaching program in Virginia.

Following graduation, Alberta returned to Atlanta. In 1924, the couple's engagement was announced at Ebenezer Baptist Church during Sunday services. On Thanksgiving Day 1926, the Reverend Michael (later known as "Martin Luther" King, Senior) and Alberta Christine Williams were married at Ebenezer in a service conducted by three of Atlanta's most prominent black Baptist ministers: Reverend Peter Bryant of Wheat Street, E. R. Carter of Friendship, and James M. Nabrit of Mt. Olive.

The couple took up residence in the Williamses' fifteen-room Victorian family home and had three children, Willie Christine, (Michael) Martin Luther, Jr., and Alfred Daniel, within their first four years of marriage. Following A. D. Williams's death, King Sr. took over his father-in-law's ministry and rescued Ebenezer Baptist from financial disaster precipitated by the Great Depression.

In 1934, King, who like his father-in-law was now a graduate of the Morehouse School of Religion and a recognized and respected pastor in his own right, traveled to the World Baptist Alliance in Berlin and changed his name and that of his son to Martin Luther King. As pastor of one of the largest and most influential churches in Atlanta, he, like his father-in-law before him, led the fight for racial equality—heading both the Atlanta Civic and Political League and the city's NAACP branch. His greatest impact, however, was probably made at the King's family home where King Sr. and his robust family continued to reside until shortly after his mother-in-law's death.

Whether in or out of the pulpit, the elder King's life was a civil rights sermon in which he actively resisted racial segregation and discrimination. In the community, he did not permit his children to attend segregated theatres and endure the humiliation of being treated as second-class citizens. At home, King Sr. expressed disdain for "the ridiculous nature of segregation in the South" during dinnertime discussions. And after dinner, King Sr. met with the most respected civil rights leaders of his day, raised socially conscious children and stressed the need for an educated, politically active ministry, often calling for "God to hasten the time when every minister will become a registered voter and a part of every movement for the betterment of our people."

MARTIN LUTHER KING, JR.

King Jr., known as "M.L." or "Mike" to his friends, answered his father's call, enduring beatings and arrests to march into history as perhaps the most compelling civil rights leader ever. While "I Have a Dream" is perhaps his best remembered speech, "Give Us the Ballot"—the leitmotif of a 1957 speech at the Lincoln Memorial before 20,000 people—became the battle cry of African Americans responding to the failure of cities and states to implement the decision in *Brown v. Board of Education* "with all deliberate speed" as mandated by the U.S. Supreme Court.

On May 17, 1957, in an effort to prod the federal government into enforcing the Supreme Court's three-year-old *Brown* decision, 28-year-old Morehouse College graduate Martin Luther King, Jr., and national civil rights leaders such as Bayard Rustin, Ella Baker, A. Philip Randolph, Stanley Levison, and Adam Clayton Powell, among others, had answered the pilgrimage call.

Speaking last and perhaps remembering his father's dinner conversations, King urged the president and every member of Congress to give African Americans the right to vote so that we would not have to bother "the federal government about our basic rights." Pressing on he implored them to "give us the ballot and we will fill the legislative halls of Congress with men who will not sign a 'Southern Manifesto' because of their devotion to the manifesto of justice. Give us the ballot and we will put judges on the benches of the South who will do justice and love mercy."

"Throughout the afternoon of May 17, 1957, the air was filled with shouts of
'amen' and 'hallelujah' as the speakers sounded their voices in defense of civil rights.
Handkerchiefs flew above the heads of the crowd as it listened to the fiery
orators. . . . There were jubilant sounds . . . sounds of disillusioned souls
discovering their country."

—Harold Sims, correspondent for the U.S. National Student Association

Eventually the ballot was won, but only at great personal sacrifice. In true Pauline tradition, patriots such as Dr. Martin Luther King, Jr., were "hard pressed on every side, but not crushed; perplexed, but not in despair; persecuted but not abandoned. Struck down, but not destroyed." (The Apostle Paul, 2 Corinthians 4:8–10) When beaten down with batons of injustice, they got up again.

The determination and resilience of these foot soldiers was most clearly demonstrated in Selma, Alabama, on March 7, 1965, "Bloody Sunday." Civil rights activists attempting to march to the state capitol in Montgomery were beaten back by troopers with billy clubs and tear gas before they could cross Selma's Edmund Pettus Bridge.

The police brutality against these peaceful protestors took place in full view of the national media, turning the tide of public opinion in favor of the activists, and President Lyndon Johnson signed the Voting Rights Act of 1965 in August of that year. The act suspended (and amendments to the act later banned) the use of literacy tests and other qualification tests to prevent blacks from registering to vote. The ballot ardently sought and fought for by three generations of the King dynasty, among others, was finally won!

C: Churches

According to King Jr., "the church has always been a second home for me." Likewise, for thousands of black Atlantans, the local black churches provided a second home in the years immediately following emancipation and beyond.

Following the Civil War the American Missionary Association (AMA) sent waves of teachers to the war-ravaged South to Christianize and educate former slaves, ill-equipped to face the future. By 1900, Atlanta boasted nearly a dozen black Baptist churches. In serving the spiritual and secular needs of the evolving black community, many of these churches became directly involved in the struggle for racial justice. When blacks were denied burial in Atlanta's Oakland Cemetery, several church leaders organized the South View Cemetery for blacks. In 1904 Reverend Peter J. Bryant of Wheat Street Baptist Church organized the Atlanta Benevolent and Protective Association, a small insurance society for blacks who were sick or in need of "a decent burial." This modest beginning was the forerunner to Alonzo Herndon's highly successful Atlanta Life Insurance Company.

As black churches became increasingly concerned with the secular needs of their growing congregations their relationship with black educational institutions continued to expand.

FRIENDSHIP BAPTIST CHURCH

Friendship Baptist Church, Atlanta's first black Baptist independent congregation, has enjoyed a unique role in educating black Atlanta, extending its hand and facilities to three of the six educational institutions comprising the Atlanta University Center. Unable to purchase property, the congregation began worshipping in a boxcar, sharing these facilities with a school for former slaves that later became Atlanta University. At the invitation of the Rev. Frank Quarles, both the Augusta Institute—originally founded in the basement of Augusta's Springfield Baptist Church—and Spelman College found a home in the basement of the Atlanta church. Augusta Institute changed its name to Atlanta Baptist Seminary and today is Morehouse College, located on a 66-acre campus near historic West End in Atlanta. Both Morehouse and Spelman enjoy an international reputation for producing leaders who have influenced national and world history, among them prominent civil rights leaders.

BIG BETHEL A.M.E. CHURCH

Like Morehouse, Spelman, and Atlanta University, Morris Brown College in Atlanta also had its beginnings in a black church, Big Bethel A.M.E. Church. Founded in 1847, the church later played a major role in the civil rights movement and boasts the oldest African-American congregation in the metropolitan Atlanta area.

WHEAT STREET BAPTIST CHURCH

Wheat Street Baptist Church, founded in 1869, was named for the street where it stands (later named Auburn Avenue). Once known as one of the largest black congregations in the South, Wheat Street was a pioneer in the black church movement for economic development. In the early days of the civil rights movement, strategists met at Wheat Street Baptist.

BUTLER STREET C.M.E. CHURCH

Butler Street C.M.E. Church dates from 1882 and is Atlanta's oldest Christian Methodist Episcopal church. Organized by the late Reverend S. E. Poe in 1882, it grew out of a Sunday school that operated on Gilmer Street. Today, the Butler Street C.M.E. Church is listed on the register of national historic sites.

Acknowledgments

As always thanks to my husband, J.R., and daughter, Ashley. This has been one of the more challenging books in the series. The hard work, however, has been worthwhile. Thanks for your love and support while enduring missed meals as I finished the cookbook. It's finally finished and instead of taking you out to dinner to celebrate, I will treat you to a really good home-cooked meal!

The author gratefully acknowledges the kind cooperation of the Robert W. Woodruff Library Staff at the Atlanta University Center. Special thanks to department head Ms. Karen James and library technical assistant Ms. Antoine James. Thanks also to Spelman College archivist Ms. Tarondra Spencer and Morehouse College archivist Rev. Herman "Skip" Mason, Jr., a noted historian and gifted author.

While only the author's name appears on this series of historic cookbooks, there is a dedicated army of skilled professionals lending their time and talent to each project that must be gratefully acknowledged. Working silently behind the scenes, they revise, edit, and re-edit to bring out each book's unique qualities. For their untiring efforts I am most humbly grateful. I could not do it without them. Thanks to Richard Ember, my tremendous new Citadel editor, and Margaret Wolf, who co-edited this book, and Jessica McLean, one of the finest promoters in the business.

INTRODUCTION

Southern Homecoming Traditions is a cookbook incorporating the history of the five historic black colleges and one university that constitute the Atlanta University Center (AUC). In the South a homecoming is a celebration of family. Most often it is a celebration of kinship involving only our families of birth. However, it can also reunite our families of choice—church, friends, and college classmates with whom we share a kindred spirit. When we come home we jubilantly celebrate our common root of kinship with wonderful food that reminds us of what we missed while away, each one bringing a special dish to the table. We also share the stories that unite and inspire us. In this way we honor those who have gone before us and guide the generations that follow as together we celebrate our "roots and wings." The collection of recipes found here is not uniquely southern but also celebrates the culinary diversity of the "new Atlanta." Each new family member has brought a unique dish to the table, as evidenced by the ubiquitous ethnic restaurants that are infusing so-called traditional southern food with a distinct and irresistible flavor. *Southern Homecoming Traditions* further celebrates the manner in which the AUC embraced these differences and its active role in unifying a once divided city, state, and nation. This unique partnership played a significant and historic role in the rebuilding of Atlanta as an economic and social leader of the new South.

The AUC began in 1929 when three schools—Atlanta University (chartered 1867), Morehouse College, a liberal arts college for men (1867), and Spelman College, a liberal arts school for women (1881)—agreed to become affiliated in a university plan. In accordance with this agreement, Atlanta University became exclusively dedicated to graduate education, while Morehouse and Spelman continued to provide undergraduate programs for AUC students. Later Clark College (chartered 1877); Morris Brown College, a coeducational college (1885); Interdenominational Theological Center, a federation of six seminaries (1958); and Morehouse School of Medicine (1983), the newest member, became affiliated with the Atlanta University Center. In 1988 Clark College and Atlanta University merged to form Clark Atlanta University and retained its affiliation with the AUC. Together, this consortium of six independent institutions constitutes the largest historically black educational complex in the world and is a tribute to the sense of unity of its founding members.

The AUC constituents enjoy an impeccable academic reputation. When *Black Enterprise Magazine* announced its pick of the "50 best colleges and universities for African Americans in 2003," three AUC institutions were in the top ten. Morehouse was ranked number 1; its sister school Spelman was ranked number 3, and Clark Atlanta came in at number 10. The AUC is rivaled only by Washington D.C.'s Howard University as the producer of the most black postgraduates.

Taught by civil rights leaders such as W.E.B. Du Bois, Whitney Young, and Dr. Benjamin E. Mays, Morehouse and Spelman alumni include movement leaders such as Dr. Martin Luther King, Jr., Lonnie King, Julian Bond, Ruby Doris Smith Robinson, and Marian Wright Edelman, among others. Morehouse men and Spelman women, joined by other AUC students, were in the forefront of a national movement that forever changed the face of a nation, while repeatedly resurrecting Atlanta from the ashes of a divisive and destructive conflict and returning her to a preeminent position as a major commercial and cultural center. In doing so, they created a "New South," one in which power sharing among blacks and whites produced economic opportunities for everyone. This economic growth and power sharing is in large part due to the AUC producing more African-American graduates than any other city in the world. And for the most part this educated populace has remained in Atlanta, creating opportunities for themselves and their communities while helping to rebuild a city once hopelessly divided over the issues of slavery and equal rights.

Southern Homecoming Traditions celebrates the success of this unique partnership and tells the story of courageous AUC students, already united in an academic consortium, now united in a civil rights movement to ensure equal rights for all Atlantans and Americans. The capstone of that united effort is found in their ability to remain united while sharing power to create a better Atlanta.

In the tradition of *The African-American Heritage Cookbook, A Taste of Freedom,* and *Celebrating Our Equality, Southern Homecoming Traditions* is more than a cookbook. It is a unique collection of recipes, vintage photographs, and historic narrative that shares the story of a once oppressed people's academic and economic triumph as they forged the iron bars of segregation into a strong black economic foundation and then expanded it to provide increased economic opportunities for all Atlantans. The schools on the cutting edge of Atlanta's socioeconomic transformation remain as relevant today as the day they were founded. Committed to their mission, they are strongly rooted in a historically rich and relevant heritage. Their growth is synonymous with that of the new Atlanta, whose skyline is one of the most recognizable in the country. Their union, formed to overcome the divisions caused by slavery, war, and segregation, has bound them together as a family of choice. This unity and commitment to a better Atlanta for all Atlantans has brought the city full circle, reuniting its population in such a way as to give cause for a Southern homecoming celebration!

Morehouse College

To engage in conflict, one does not bring a knife that cuts—but a needle that sews.

—African proverb

Appetizers

Atlanta Baptist College—the beginning of Morehouse!
(Courtesy Morehouse College Archives)

MOREHOUSE COLLEGE SONG

Morehouse College, Morehouse College,
Morehouse College, bless her name,
Whether in defeat or victory
We are loyal just the same;
And we'll cheer for Morehouse College,
Tis for her we'll fight for fame,
And we'll sing her praises loud in every land,
Morehouse College, bless her name!

The "Morehouse School Song" was written in large part by Dr. Mordecai Johnson while he was a student at Baptist College (later Morehouse). According to Johnson, the music was brought to Morehouse by faculty member Matthew W. Bullock. Johnson went on to become president of Howard University in Washington, D.C. When Atlanta Baptist College became Morehouse, the appropriate name changes were again made.

Dr. Mordecai Johnson, class of 1911, son of a former slave, graduate of Harvard University Divinity School and class commencement speaker in 1922, and first black president of Howard University in 1926.
(Courtesy Morehouse College Archives)

MOREHOUSE HYMN: DEAR OLD MOREHOUSE
J. O. B. Moseley

Dear old Morehouse, dear old Morehouse,
We have pledged our lives to thee;
And we'll ever, yea forever
Give ourselves in loyalty.

True forever, true forever,
To old Morehouse may we be;

So to bind each son the other
Into ties more brotherly.

Holy Spirit, Holy Spirit,
Make us steadfast, honest, true,
To old Morehouse, and her ideals,
And in all things that we do.

Early photograph of Graves Hall, built in 1889 and named in honor of Samuel T. Graves, the second president of Morehouse College.
(Courtesy Morehouse College Archives)

"We make our living by what we get. We make our life by what we give. Whatever you do, strive to do it so well that no man living and no man dead, and no man yet to be born can do it any better. As we face the unpredictable future, have faith that man and God will assist us all the way."

—Dr. Benjamin E. Mays, president, Morehouse College, 1940–67

"1867, set like a jewel between the years of the Civil Rights Act and the Fourteenth Amendment to the United States Constitution . . . saw the beginning of Augusta Institute, later Atlanta Baptist College, now Morehouse College."

—"Educational Cross Roads in the South," a radio address delivered by Reverend Maynard H. Jackson, Morehouse, 1914.

Morehouse: The Early Years

Like a child's toys, carelessly broken and discarded, the vestiges of war were haphazardly strewn over a southern landscape. Great guns that once boomed in defiance now stood mournfully silent, standing watch over an uneasy peace. Nearly four years had passed since the ground was consecrated at Gettysburg and only three since the Great Emancipator was laid to a hero's rest.

The year 1867 saw the struggle of rebuilding the South's cities and economy without slave labor. In many ways the country was still bitterly engaged in a new political war over the civil rights and equal protection of former slaves.

The Thirteenth Amendment abolishing slavery had been ratified at the end of 1865. Much of the impetus for Reconstruction involved the enforcement of civil rights for freed slaves in the

MOREHOUSE COLLEGE PRESIDENTS — Though separated by space and time, their leadership affects destiny and no one can tell where their i stops. For faith, hope, inspiration, enthusiasm, and vision our college forefathers penned the brightest pages in the history of our institution's 81 years e ence; their indomitable "spirit" keeps Morehouse men bound with "hoops of steel" to their Alma Mater. During the 81st anniversary celebration tribute w to the founder and presidents of the college. Pictured, left to right, are Dr. William J. White, founder; Dr. Henry L. Morehouse, for whom the college was nar Joseph T. Robert, first president; Dr. Samuel Graves, second president; Dr. George Sale, third president; Dr. John Hope, fourth president; Dr. Samuel A. Arch president; Dr. Charles H. Hubert, former acting president; and Dr. Benjamin E. Mays, sixth president, who now heads the college administration.

Morehouse College Presidents
(Courtesy Morehouse College Archives)

Southern states. The Fourteenth Amendment offered former slaves citizenship and equal protection under the law and was drafted to guarantee their rights and safety against retaliatory acts of disgruntled southerners. Congress passed the Fourteenth Amendment in 1866 but President Johnson advised Southern states to reject it, and except for Tennessee, they did.

It was against this social and political backdrop in 1867 that Augusta Institute, the beginning of present-day Morehouse College, was founded in Augusta, Georgia, by the Reverend William Jefferson White, a Baptist minister and cabinetmaker. Supporting him in this endeavor were the Reverend Richard C. Coulter, a former slave from Augusta, and the Reverend Edmund Turney, organizer of the National Theological Institute for Educating Freedmen in Washington, D.C.

However, the strong roots of Morehouse College reach further back in time to a place of childhood innocence when in the early 1830s a young boy named Billy gathered a large pile of prickly chestnuts in the forest and brought them to his mother as a surprise. His mother in turn had a gift for her son in mind. She instructed him to take a pail filled with some of the recently garnered chestnuts and to find a purchaser in town. When Billy returned home, triumphantly displaying the seven pence earned from the sale, his mother sent him back to town, this time to purchase a Webster's Blue Black Speller. Thus began Billy's lifelong love of learning. Book after book followed as he taught himself geography, arithmetic, grammar, algebra, and even music.

Billy White, the son of an American Indian woman married to a free black, always identified himself as a black

Reverend William Jefferson White
(Private collection)

man, although his natural father was a white man. At age nineteen White set out for Augusta, Georgia, where he apprenticed himself to a carpenter and learned the trade of cabinetmaking. Later he worked for an undertaker, where he almost certainly used his woodworking skills to make coffins.

During his apprenticeship, he continued with his academic pursuits at night, acquiring a significant library. He also began conducting clandestine literacy classes in the 1850s. When racial unrest forced one school to close, he would quickly open another. In 1853 he married Josephine Elizabeth Thomas, a slave trained as a seamstress, with whom he had eleven children.

During 1865, the Reverend Edmund Turney chartered the National Theological Institute in Washington, D.C., as a national school to train ministers at the branch level and one of the first institutions established for the training of freedmen. Among its students was thirty-year-old Richard C. Coulter, a former slave who began attending the Institute while working to raise money for his return to his native Augusta, presumably to teach.

In 1866, Coulter returned to Augusta and brought with him a letter from Dr. Turney authorizing the formation of a branch school in Augusta or any place of his choosing in the South. Coulter sought the aid of William Jefferson White, employed at the time at Platt Brothers' Furniture Store. History was made as the lives of these three men, White, Coulter, and Turney, converged to create what would become Morehouse College. The men agreed that as

Springfield Baptist Church
(Private collection)

soon as enough students warranted opening a school, a teacher would be sent to Augusta. The first order of business, however, was to secure a building to house the school.

White discussed the matter with his pastor, the Reverend Henry Watts of Springfield Baptist Church, who enthusiastically embraced the idea. Recruiting for the new school began almost immediately. On February 14, 1867, the school was organized with 37 students in attendance. Turney had no teacher immediately available, so rather than disappoint the students, White became the school's first teacher while remaining employed at Platt Brothers. Despite family obligations, he refused to accept pay for his work.

The school was established in the basement of Springfield Baptist Church (founded in Augusta in 1787, the oldest independent African-American church in America). Four difficult years followed, with threats from the Ku Klux Klan, who viewed the school's work as "infamous" and "diabolical," loss of faculty and leadership, poor facilities, and other problems. For a time the school moved to Harmony Baptist Church, pastored by Reverend White, who also taught one of the night classes. His " . . . sympathetic wife gave many a meal to hungry students and shared her meager supply of house furnishings, bed covering, and even the family clothing with those that came with scarcely more than a desire to know and the determination to satisfy that desire." —Morehouse alumnus, December 1932

William Jefferson White appointed the Rev. Dr. Joseph T. Roberts as the Institute's first president on August 1, 1871, and mandated him to prepare newly freed black men for the ministry and teaching. Upon accepting this mandate Roberts had very little with which to work. The physical plant and buildings were dilapidated and sorely in need of repair. And buildings, which were usable, lacked furniture. According to Morehouse archivist, Benjamin Brawley, there was only "a few nails in the walls and a few books on a bench."

Twelve years after its founding, the Augusta Institute, accepting the invitation of Rev. Frank Quarles, moved to the basement of Friendship Baptist Church in Atlanta and changed its name to Atlanta Baptist Seminary. Eventually, the Seminary acquired a sister school for women that ultimately became Spelman College, and after several changes of location, laid the cornerstone for its present site in Atlanta's West End community in 1889 under the administration of its second president, Dr. Samuel T. Graves.

At the time of its purchase in 1888 (through a gift

Reverend Frank Quarles
(Private collection)

Dr. Samuel Graves, the second president of Morehouse College, for whom Graves Hall was named.
(Courtesy Morehouse College Archives)

from John D. Rockefeller), the land was still marked by earthworks constructed by Confederate forces to resist the Union siege of Atlanta. The new building was " . . . dedicated to the improvement of humanity, the instruction and enlightenment of a neglected people, and the acquisition of the moral and intellectual qualities which fit men for usefulness and entitle them to the respect and confidence of mankind . . . " so that the men "who go forth from these walls prepared for high work publish the fame of this institution by their varied knowledge and enlarged views, by their fixedness of purpose and their earnest desire to bless fallen humanity. . . . " —C.T. Walker, from his address at the laying of the cornerstone for Graves Hall.

During the administration of Dr. George Sale, the Seminary was renamed Atlanta Baptist College. Sale, the institute's youngest president, continued developing the "whole man concept" approach to education. Upon accepting the position of superintendent of education for the schools of the American Baptist Home Mission Society, Dr. Sale left his students with this charge at the 1906 com-

President George Sale
(Private collection)

Graves Hall
(Archives and Special Collections: Robert Woodruff Library at the Atlanta University Center)

mencement: "Boys be men." The charge was so ably carried out by each succeeding class that they became impervious to its demeaning use by segregationists, in reference to black men.

A new era in Morehouse history dawned when faculty member Dr. John Hope was appointed the fourth president in 1906, the first black man to lead Morehouse College.

JOHN HOPE

John Hope was born in 1868 in Augusta. His mother was the daughter of an emancipated slave, and his father was a native Scotsman who had amassed a fortune as the owner of a dry goods business and a food establishment. The family was left penniless, however, when Hope's father died when the boy was ten and his business partners reneged on their agreement to administer his estate. Ten-year-old John began working to support his family, first for a lawyer and then for a black restaurant owner in Augusta. Reverend John Dart, a local pastor, encouraged Hope to

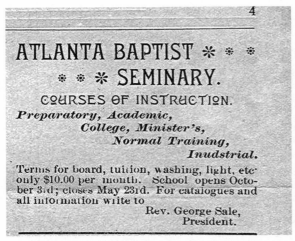

Atlanta Baptist Seminary advertisement.
(Courtesy Morehouse College Archives)

return to school. In 1886, he entered Worcester Academy in Massachusetts, graduating with honors in 1890, and studied philosophy at Brown University where he was elected to Phi Beta Kappa and was the class orator. After teaching at Roger Williams University in Nashville, Hope, now married, moved to Atlanta in 1898 to teach at Atlanta Baptist College. It was an exciting time to be in Atlanta, and Hope and W.E.B. Du Bois, who taught at Atlanta University, became close friends during this period. After Booker T. Washington gave his "Atlanta Compromise" address in 1895, calling for blacks to concentrate on achieving technical proficiency and to abandon, at least for the time being, the struggle for political and social equality, both Hope and Du Bois publicly disagreed with him, arguing that without full social and political equality, technical skill would prove worthless. The two of them worked together in support of the rights of

Dr. John Hope *(center)*, **fourth president and the first African American president of Morehouse College, pictured with the graduating class of 1912.**
(Courtesy Morehouse College Archives)

blacks to receive a liberal education instead of the traditional vocational education provided by most schools for blacks at the time.

Hope would be the only black college president to participate in the 1906 Niagara Movement meeting, the forerunner to the modern day NAACP. The first meeting was held on the Canadian side of the Falls when the group was denied permission to meet on the American side. In August of 1906 the group, considered the militants of their time, met for three days near the site of abolitionist John Brown's famous raid. They marched barefoot to a nearby Civil War battlefield, as a sign of reverence for the sacrifices made on it, while singing "The Battle Hymn of the Republic." These meetings culminated in a bold call for enforcement of the Constitutional amendments designed to protect freedmen, full voting rights, eradication of Jim Crow, equal education and more. In his address Du Bois, who headed the organization, would exclaim "We want our children educated . . . and when we call for education, we mean real education. Education is the development of power and ideal. They have a right to know, to think, to aspire."

Shortly afterward Hope assumed his duties at Morehouse. However, his first few days in office at Morehouse coincided with the Atlanta Race Riot of 1906, which was ignited following vague reports of African Americans harassing white women. Atlanta's police confiscated the guns of Atlanta's black citizens while allowing whites to remain armed. When the four days of rioting ended, it was officially reported that ten blacks and two whites were dead, hundreds were injured, and over a thousand had fled the city. Unofficial reports cited a much higher number of black casualties.

Following the riot, Hope became even more convinced of the ineffectiveness of social compromise and that a classical education was the best means of preparing African-American men to lead the fight for social and racial equality. As a result, he became an educational pioneer with an expansionist approach to educating African-American men as American leaders. Even the most liberal northerners seldom supported the idea of a liberal education, which was considered impractical by many, and as a result, securing financial support for the school was difficult. Hope turned to members of his own staff for friendship and support—among them Benjamin Griffith Brawley and Samuel Howard Archer. These three men would become a triumvirate, celebrated as the chief architects of the modern Morehouse College.

The new educational era was reflected in yet another change in name. Upon the death of William White in 1913, Atlanta Baptist College was named Morehouse College in honor of Henry L. Morehouse, the corresponding secretary of the Northern Baptist Home Mission Society.

After World War I, racial tensions grew. Returning black veterans, who had experienced very little racial prejudice while fighting for freedom abroad, grew even more resentful of the segregation and inequality in their own nation—a nation for which they had risked their lives.

Reverend Henry L. Morehouse
(Private collection)

Some Southern whites responded by increasing acts of violence, including lynchings, against "uppity" blacks who had forgotten "their place." Atlanta, and indeed the whole South, found itself once again divided, evidenced this time by signs that read "White" and "Colored"—at railway stations, above water fountains, at almost every turn outside the insular segregated neighborhoods. The term "boy" was frequently used when addressing black males, regardless of their age.

Aggravating the racial tension was the Great Depression, which brought the country to its financial knees. The black college enrollments in Atlanta dwindled. Endowment income decreased, as did faculty salaries. Sometimes faculty worked without pay. Out of this financial crisis was created the Atlanta University Affiliation. Hope was one of the major drafters of this creative plan that ensured the cooperative but independent existence of the six educational institutions entering into the agreement.

On April 1, 1929, the agreement of the affiliation uniting Morehouse College, Spelman College, and Atlanta University was signed. These institutions would share resources while remaining autonomous. Each would retain individual control of its own finances, board of trustees, president, and administrative officers. With the exception of Atlanta University, each institution would nominate three members to its board, and those nominated members would then select the remaining board members. The agreement secured the future of the participating schools and eventually included three additional educational institutions to make up what is now the Atlanta University Center. Morehouse would continue providing undergraduate education to men, while Spelman continued to provide undergraduate education to women. Only Atlanta University would offer postgraduate degrees.

Dr. Samuel H. Archer, the college's fifth president, guided Morehouse through the travails of the Great Depression. As an athlete and former Morehouse football coach, he once reprimanded a student who defended a questionable play by claiming to "only be trying to win" by snapping, "Aw son, I'd rather lose the game through fair playing than win it through dirty playing." The attitude of honesty and fair play that permeated his leadership was a major factor in developing the Morehouse man. Archer gave the school the colors of maroon and white, those of his alma mater, Colgate University.

"The charges for board include fuel, light, and laundry. Students are required to bring with them towels, table napkins, four sheets, three pillow-cases, two blankets, or quilts and a cretonne or gingham spread."

—*Morehouse College Bulletin,* April 1938

BENJAMIN MAYS

In 1940, Dr. Benjamin Elijah Mays, a Phi Beta Kappa graduate of Bates College and the University of Chicago, was appointed the sixth president of Morehouse College. During his 27-year tenure he elevated Morehouse to the next level in its growth by building its international reputation for excellence in scholarship, leadership, and service. The son of former slaves, Mays led a 15-million-dollar increase in donations and oversaw the construction of eighteen new buildings. Morehouse was increasing in strength and attracting some of the best and brightest young minds in the country.

Mays successfully integrated his Christian love of humankind with his duty to reject the hatred of racism by demanding God's justice for all people. He encouraged Morehouse men to

Dr. Benjamin E. Mays, son of former slaves,
dean of the Howard University School of Religion,
prolific author, nationally noted educator,
mentor to Dr. Martin Luther King, Jr.,
and sixth president of Morehouse College (1940–67).
(Courtesy Morehouse College Archives)

stand strong in accepting nothing less than full equality. During his tenure the term "Morehouse man" came to define young black men as confident, intelligent, and honest leaders. Mays once said, "There is an air of expectancy at Morehouse College. It is expected that the student who enters here will do well. It is also expected that once a man bears the insignia of a Morehouse graduate he will do exceptionally well. We expect nothing less." —Benjamin Mays, charge to the graduating class of 1961.

Among the students Mays inspired "to do exceptionally well" was Martin Luther King, Jr. In 1948, during one of Mays' Tuesday morning chapel addresses, he introduced King Jr. to Gandhi's philosophy of nonviolence—a philosophy King would courageously use in the struggle to free his race from the bondage of Jim Crow segregation. With a shared commitment to non-violent social change, a friendship soon blossomed between Mays and King. When King won the Nobel Peace Prize in 1964, it was Mays who organized a successful citywide celebration in Atlanta for his protégé and friend. When King was assassinated just four years later, Mays gave the eulogy. Dr. King once remembered Dr. Mays as his "spiritual mentor" and "intellectual father," and King's legacy has resulted in Dr. Benjamin Elijah Mays being remembered as one of the most influential educators of twentieth-century America.

Alumni Presidents

In the second half of the twentieth century, Dr. Hugh M. Gloster, class of 1931, became the first alumnus to become president of Morehouse College. Gloster doubled student enrollment and established several new majors, including eight in the department of business and a dual-degree engineering program with the Georgia Institute of Technology and Boston University. Gloster was followed in office by Dr. Leroy Keith, '61, who increased the Morehouse endowment to more than $60 million, and Dr. Wiley A. Perdue, '57, who upgraded the computer information systems and undertook construction of a 5,700-seat gymnasium.

Under its ninth president, Dr. Walter E. Massey, class of 1958, Morehouse expanded its dual-degree master's program in natural sciences with the Georgia Institute of Technology to include other institutions and social science majors; launched the Center for Excellence in Science, Engineering and Mathematics with a 6.7-million-dollar U.S. Department of Defense grant; and established a new African-American Studies program. Morehouse also recently established a new Center for International Studies, named for former U.N. Ambassador Andrew Young, and a new Leadership Development Center, which includes diverse programs that foster leadership skills and encourage community involvement.

Hugh M. Gloster
(Archives and Special Collections:
Robert Woodruff Library at the Atlanta University Center)

Changing of the Guard: Dr. Hugh Gloster *(far right)*,
pictured with his wife, Mrs. Yvonne King Gloster, Esq.,
eventually followed Dr. Benjamin Mays *(far left)*,
pictured with his wife, Mrs. Sadie Mays,
to become the first alumni president of Morehouse College.
(Courtesy Morehouse College Archives)

Early Atlanta Baptist College baseball team.
(Courtesy Morehouse College Archives)

Today, as Morehouse celebrates 139 years of challenge and change, the college continues to deliver an exceptional educational experience that meets the intellectual, moral, and social needs of students representing more than 40 states and 18 countries—a unique institution dedicated, as always, to producing outstanding men and extraordinary leaders to serve humanity with a spiritual consciousness.

Morehouse is perhaps best known for the achievements of its distinguished alumni, including Martin Luther King, Jr., Olympian Edwin Moses, filmmaker Spike Lee, former mayor of Atlanta Maynard Jackson, activist Julian Bond, and several United States congressmen. Morehouse men were often the college's best recruiters.

Morehouse men at chapel service.
(Courtesy Morehouse College Archives)

APPETIZERS

SWEET AUBURN AVENUE WINGS

Once known as the hub of black Atlanta, in its heyday Auburn Avenue was recognized by *Forbes* magazine as the "richest Negro street in America." It is also the birthplace of Dr. Martin Luther King, Jr.

Served piping hot or at room temperature, these succulent wings will be the hit of your party. The unusual blend of aromatic flavors will have you playing Twenty Questions with your guests as they try to guess the ingredients. Start preparing this dish one day in advance to allow your wings to marinate 24 hours before baking them.

5 pounds chicken wings	1½ cups pineapple juice
1½ cups freshly squeezed orange juice	1½ cups honey
¼ cup freshly squeezed lime juice	¾ cup soy sauce
3 tablespoons freshly grated orange zest	7 garlic cloves, minced
1 teaspoon grated lime zest	1 teaspoon cayenne pepper (or to taste)
	Salt
	Freshly ground black pepper

Rinse the chicken wings, pat dry, and set aside. In a large bowl, combine the remaining ingredients and mix to blend. Add the chicken wings to the marinade and turn well to coat. Cover tightly and refrigerate for at least 24 hours and up to 2 days, turning occasionally to coat with the marinade. Preheat the oven to 400°F. Line two large baking sheets with aluminum foil. Arrange the wings on the baking sheets in a single layer. Bake for 15 minutes, baste with any leftover marinade, and turn basted wings over. Bake the wings for 15 to 20 minutes or until they are cooked through and golden brown. Serve hot or at room temperature.

Makes 6 servings.

PEACH STREET WINGS WITH PEACH MUSTARD SAUCE

Peach Street is one of Atlanta's main thoroughfares; however, you needn't travel that far to enjoy these soul-satisfying wings!

3	pounds chicken wings		$1^1/_4$	teaspoons cayenne pepper
2	teaspoons dry mustard		$^3/_4$	teaspoon salt
$1^1/_4$	teaspoons dried thyme		$^1/_4$	teaspoon black pepper
1	teaspoon brown sugar		$^1/_4$	cup lemon juice

Cut tips off wings; reserve for stock. Wash under cold running water and set aside to drain. In small bowl, combine the remaining ingredients to make a paste. Use a pastry brush to brush the paste over the wings. Arrange the wings, meaty side down, on lightly greased foil-lined baking sheets and allow to stand for 30 minutes at room temperature. Preheat the oven to 475°F. Place wings in oven and bake for 15 minutes; turn wings over and bake for an additional 15 to 20 minutes or until brown, crisp, and no longer pink inside.

Makes 12 servings.

PEACH MUSTARD SAUCE

The secret's in the sauce.

¹/₂	cup peach jam	1 teaspoon cider vinegar
1	tablespoon Dijon-style mustard	4 cloves garlic, minced
		2 teaspoons paprika

Place jam in a saucepan; cook and stir over low heat. Add remaining ingredients and stir until melted and well-blended, approximately 3 to 4 minutes. Serve separately as a dipping sauce for the wings.

Makes about ¹/₂ cup of sauce.

Dr. Benjamin Griffith Brawley, Morehouse '01

"In the old days, Dr, Brawley was dean and registrar of each student in the academy and college, in many instances giving oral and qualifying examinations to new students. In addition to this he taught a full schedule, coached dramatics and debating and trained speakers for the weekly rhetoricals."—Bulletin of Morehouse College, 1939. His many contributions to the school resulted in his recognition along with John Hope and S. H. Archer as a member of the triumvirate credited with building the modern Morehouse College.

Atlanta Baptist College, graduating class of Dr. Benjamin Brawley.
(Courtesy Morehouse College Archives)

HONEY & SPICE WINGS

Mmmmm. These spicy morsels will keep your guests guessing about the identities of the exotic ingredients that suffuse these tantalizing wings with unique flavor.

3	pounds chicken drummettes	1	teaspoon ground ginger
	Salt and pepper	$1/8$	teaspoon ground cumin
1	cup honey	$1/2$	teaspoon cayenne pepper, or to
2	tablespoons curry powder		taste

Preheat oven to 400°F. Rinse drummettes under cold running water, pat dry, salt and pepper to taste, and arrange in single layer on a baking sheet. Place drummettes in the preheated oven and bake for 10 minutes. While the drummettes are baking, combine the remaining ingredients in a small bowl and mix until well blended. Remove drummettes from the oven and brush them with half of the honey mixture; bake an additional 10 minutes. Use tongs to turn the drummettes over, brush them with the remaining honey mixture, and bake an additional 10 minutes. Cool slightly at room temperature before serving.

Makes 6 to 8 servings.

JAMAICAN JERK HOT WINGS

"Yah-mahn." Jerk, a method of cooking attributed to the Carib-Arawak Indians, imparts a sweet and spicy smoke flavor to meat. After thoroughly cleaning captured game, the Indians "jerked" the animal's flesh with sharp objects and filled the openings created by jerking the meat with a variety of aromatic spices. It was then placed in a deep, stone-lined pit and covered with green wood which, when burned, smoked heavily, adding to the rich flavor of the superb results: a spicy, moist, and tender meat dish.

5   pounds fresh chicken wings
    or drumettes (do not use
    frozen)
1   tablespoon ground allspice
1¼ teaspoons salt
1½ tablespoons dried thyme
1¾ teaspoons cayenne pepper
1   teaspoon freshly ground black
    pepper
1½ teaspoons ground sage
¾   teaspoon ground nutmeg
¾   teaspoon ground cinnamon
2   tablespoons finely grated
    fresh garlic

1   tablespoon brown sugar
¼   cup olive oil
¼   cup soy sauce
½   cup white vinegar
¼   cup pineapple juice
½   cup orange juice
½   cup lime juice
2   tablespoons grated ginger
2   habañero (or Scotch bonnet)
    peppers, seeded and
    chopped
4   green onions, finely chopped

Wash drummettes under cold running water and set aside to drain. In a large bowl, combine the allspice, thyme, cayenne pepper, black pepper, sage, nutmeg, cinnamon, salt, garlic, and brown sugar. With a wire whisk, slowly add the olive oil, soy sauce, vinegar, pineapple juice, orange juice, lime juice, and grated ginger. Add the Scotch bonnet pepper and onions, and mix well. Add the chicken wings, cover, and marinate for at least 3 to 4 hours, or longer if possible.

Preheat an outdoor grill.

Remove the wings from the marinade and grill for 3 to 4 minutes on each side or until fully cooked. While grilling, baste with the marinade. Bring the leftover marinade to a rapid boil. Boil 5 to 6 minutes, remove from heat, and serve on the side for dipping.

Note: The Scotch bonnet pepper or habañero is the hottest of the capsicum peppers. It is truly incendiary, and therefore should be approached with extreme caution. Wear gloves when handling it and wash hands thoroughly after use. Whatever you do, do not put unwashed hands anywhere near your face. If habañeros are unavailable, or if my warnings have left you quaking in your culinary boots, substitute serrano, Thai bird chiles, or jalapeño peppers. Serve the finished dish immediately with lots of very cold beer.

Makes 10 to 12 servings.

Mordecai Johnson, Morehouse '11

Wyatt Mordecai Johnson was born in 1890 to Reverend Wyatt and Carolyn Freeman Johnson.

From the day of his birth, Johnson's mother believed that he was destined for greatness. Inspired by the biblical role of Mordecai in rescuing his people from oppression and death, she provided him with the middle name Mordecai because she believed that her son was also destined to ensure the welfare of his people while promoting peace amongst all people. She was right. Johnson was the first African-American president of prestigious Howard University. Under his administration faculty tripled, salaries doubled, congressional appropriations increased to $6,000,000 annually, and Howard University's Freedmen's Hospital was producing half of the African-American physicians in the country. Perhaps Dr. Johnson's greatest contribution, however, was the development of the university's law school into the preeminent source of civil rights attorneys and law professors. Nine of the ten attorneys who argued *Brown v. Board of Education*, the landmark public school desegregation case, were either Howard University law professors or graduates of the law school. Brown helped launch the modern civil rights movement, and led to other court decisions that struck down all forms of legalized racial discrimination.

Football, Sat., Nov. 6, at 2:30

A. U. versus MOREHOUSE

Morehouse College and Atlanta College engaged on the field of competition.

(Courtesy Morehouse College Archives)

JAMAICAN SHRIMP

2½   pounds large fresh shrimp in shells
¼   cup salad oil
3   tablespoons white wine vinegar
3   tablespoons lime juice
2   jalapeño peppers, seeded and finely chopped
1   tablespoon honey

2½   teaspoons Quick Jamaican Jerk Seasoning (see recipe below)
1   medium mango, pitted, peeled, sliced, and halved crosswise
1   small lime, halved crosswise and sliced
1   small red onion, quartered and thinly sliced

Place shrimp in lightly salted boiling water for 1 to 3 minutes or until shrimp turn pink and the tails begin to turn. Drain immediately and cool under cold running water. Peel shrimp, leaving tails intact, and devein. Place shrimp in a heavy plastic bag. At this point, you can seal the bag and chill for up to 24 hours.

Next, prepare the marinade by combining the salad oil, white wine vinegar, lime juice, jalapeño pepper, honey, and the Jamaican Jerk Seasoning in a screw-top-covered jar. Cover and shake well to mix. Pour over shrimp in plastic bag, reseal the bag, and chill for 1½ to 2 hours, turning bag occasionally.

To serve, pour shrimp and marinade into a large serving bowl and garnish the sides with alternating slices of sliced mango, limes, and onions.

Makes 10 to 12 appetizer servings.

Morehouse College track team.
(Courtesy Morehouse College Archives)

QUICK JAMAICAN JERK SEASONING

2	teaspoons onion powder	$^1/_4$	teaspoon ground cinnamon
1	teaspoon sugar	$^1/_4$	teaspoon ground nutmeg
1	teaspoon ground thyme	$^1/_4$	teaspoon cayenne pepper
1	teaspoon salt	$^1/_4$	teaspoon ground cumin
$^1/_2$	teaspoon ground allspice		

Combine the above ingredients and mix well.

Morehouse College basketball team.
(Courtesy Morehouse College Archives)

RUM-GLAZED TIGER PRAWNS

A mouth-watering treat, these delectable prawns will have your guests circling the grill for more.

3	pounds fresh tiger prawns	$^1/_2$	teaspoon crushed red pepper
$^3/_4$	cup light rum, divided	$^1/_2$	teaspoon salt
$^1/_4$	cup + 2 tablespoons fresh lime juice	$^1/_4$	cup white cider vinegar
$^1/_4$	cup vegetable oil	$^1/_2$	cup firmly packed dark brown sugar
4	large garlic cloves, minced		

Peel and devein prawns, leaving tails intact. Place them in bowl with ¼ cup of the rum, lime juice, oil, garlic, crushed red pepper, and salt; toss to coat thoroughly. Cover; refrigerate, and allow to marinate for 1 hour.

Preheat grill according to manufacturer's instructions. In small bowl, combine brown sugar, vinegar, and remaining 2 tablespoons of the rum. Thread shrimp on skewers; lightly brush with brown sugar glaze.

Grill over a medium-hot fire about 3 minutes per side, brushing with additional glaze, until shrimp are opaque.

Note: If using bamboo skewers, soak them in water for 30 minutes before grilling.

Makes 6 to 8 servings.

James M. Nabrit, Sr., Morehouse 1898

James M. Nabrit, Sr., a distinguished alum and trustee of Morehouse College, and well known Baptist minister pastored some of the country's major African-American churches, including Mount Olive Baptist Church in Atlanta. Perhaps his most significant accomplishment, however, was the success of his eight children. Civil rights attorney James M. Nabrit, Jr., Dr. Samuel Nabrit, and another brother graduated from Morehouse College; all five of his daughters graduated from college as well, with two receiving their undergraduate degrees from Spelman College.

James Nabrit, Jr., Morehouse '23

"My father was always busy and had great intellectual abilities, but he was a kind and devoted parent who came home to dinner regularly and played ball with my friends and me."

—James M. Nabrit III, civil rights attorney

James M. Nabrit, Jr., a pioneer in civil rights law, argued *Bolling v. Sharpe,* one of the five cases that were eventually to be consolidated and tried as *Brown v. Board of Education.* Rather than merely arguing for equalization of black schools, Nabrit successfully argued that school segregation was entirely unconstitutional. The Supreme Court agreed, ruling in favor of Bolling and ultimately deciding in *Brown* that "in the field of education the doctrine of separate but equal has no place." In recognition of his achievement in the field of civil rights, most specifically his work with the overall *Brown* case, Morehouse conferred on Nabrit the honorary degree of Doctor of Laws in 1955. Howard University honored him as well; from 1958 to 1960 he served as dean of the Howard University School of Law. He was then selected as the second black man and second Morehouse graduate to head prestigious Howard University. He served in that position from 1960 to 1965, represented the United States as deputy ambassador to the United Nations in 1966, and then returned to preside over the university from 1968 until 1969.

His son James Nabrit III did not attend Morehouse; however he followed in his father's footsteps by becoming a leading civil rights lawyer in his own right, filing the lawsuit seeking the right for Hosea Williams, John Lewis, Amelia Boynton, Martin Luther King and others to march across Selma's Edmund Pettus Bridge and into history following the events that would become known as "Bloody Sunday."

SHRIMP IN ALE

3	pounds large shrimp (20–24 count per pound)		3	bay leaves
36	ounces beer		4	teaspoons Tabasco
8	large garlic cloves, peeled and crushed		1 1/2	teaspoons celery seed
1/4	cup Seafood Seasoning (see recipe below)		2	teaspoons cayenne pepper
2	tablespoons salt			Juice of 2 lemons
				Melted butter seasoned to taste with additional Seafood Seasoning

Wash shrimp, but do not remove the shells. Combine the remaining ingredients except the lemon juice and butter in a saucepan and bring to a rapid boil. Add shrimp and bring to a second boil. Reduce heat to low and simmer uncovered until shrimp are pink and tender, approximately 2 to 3 minutes. Drain. Combine lemon juice and butter and serve shrimp hot with melted lemon butter. Yields 60 to 72 shrimp.

SEAFOOD SEASONING

2 tablespoons celery salt	1 teaspoon cayenne pepper
1 tablespoon ground bay leaves	1 teaspoon ground nutmeg
1 tablespoon salt	1 teaspoon dried oregano
1$^1/_2$ teaspoons paprika	1 teaspoon ground thyme
1 teaspoon onion powder	$^3/_4$ teaspoon ground cloves
1 teaspoon dry mustard	$^1/_4$ teaspoon ground allspice
1$^1/_2$ teaspoons garlic powder	

Combine the above ingredients, mix well, and store in an airtight container until ready for use.

Makes approximately $^1/_2$ cup.

Samuel M. Nabrit, Morehouse '25

Samuel M. Nabrit, scientist, scholar, and second president of Texas Southern University, was the first Morehouse student to receive a Ph.D. A series of "firsts" followed in his highly successful career, including becoming Brown University's first black trustee. However, in 1955, shortly after the decision in *Brown v. Board of Education* and just when the South was becoming a hotbed of student protest activity, Nabrit had just begun an 11-year term as the president of Texas Southern University.

    While president of Texas Southern University, he supported student protesters in their successful effort to end segregated public accommodations in Houston. He stood staunchly behind the student protesters resisting the pressure of white politicians and businessmen who tried to convince him otherwise. Although he removed the protesters' headquarters from the TSU campus, he promised that no student would ever be expelled for civil rights activities as long as he was president of the university. And he publicly supported the students' right to protest.

GARLIC HERB MUSSELS

This is a wonderful appetizer. Mussels may come already cleaned, but cleaning fresh mussels is not as intimidating as it appears to be. In fact, it's really simple. Place the mussels in a pot, cover them with water, and stir a cup or two of cornmeal into the water. Let sit for a couple of hours. During this time, the shellfish will eliminate any sand (the technique works equally well for clams). Every fifteen minutes or so, jostle the bowl to create a wave. This stimulates them to ingest cornmeal and expel sand. To debeard a mussel, simply grab hold of the black stringy "beard" sticking out of the shell (not all mussels will have these) and yank! That's all there is to it.

This very traditional and simple recipe is a wonderful way to prepare mussels. The best part is that the mussels can be prepared well in advance and quickly reheated just before serving, making them perfect for parties and busy holiday dinners.

2	pounds mussels in the shell		$^1/_4$	cup chopped fresh parsley
$^1/_2$	cup butter, softened		$^1/_4$	cup chopped fresh chives
4	garlic cloves, minced		2	tablespoons chopped fresh dill

If not already cleaned, scrub and clean mussels. When using cornmeal soak to clean mussels, carefully remove the mussels from the soaking water to cook pot in batches without disturbing sand on the bottom of the bowl. Boil the mussels in batches in a large saucepan until the shells open, approximately 3 to 5 minutes. Remove each batch and boil the next until they are all cooked. Lift off the top shell of each mussel. Discard any mussel that does not open. Place the mussels in an ovenproof dish. Mix the butter, garlic, and herbs together. Spread the butter mixture evenly over the mussels and refrigerate until ready to serve. Right before serving, broil until the tops are lightly browned and aromatic.

Makes 6 servings.

A Morehouse Moment

Olawabusayo "Topé" Folarin, a political science major from Grand Prairie, Texas, was named Morehouse College's third Rhodes scholar in 2004. Morehouse produced two other Rhodes scholars, Christopher Elders (2002) and Nima Warfield (1993).

HOPPING JOHN DIP

8	slices bacon	2	cups chicken broth
1	cup chopped onion	$^1/_2$	teaspoon salt
$^1/_4$	cup chopped green pepper	$^1/_4$	cup uncooked rice
1	teaspoon fresh jalapeño pepper, chopped	1	teaspoon fresh lemon juice
1	clove garlic, peeled and minced	$^1/_2$	cup ham, finely chopped Cayenne pepper to taste
1	10-ounce package frozen black-eyed peas		

Fry bacon until crisp and remove to a paper towel–lined plate to drain. Reserve the bacon drippings in the frying pan, and sauté onions, green pepper, jalapeño, and garlic, stirring constantly. Cook until the onion is transparent. Add black-eyed peas, chicken broth, and salt. Cover and cook over medium heat for 15 minutes, stir in the rice, and re-cover. Reduce heat to low and cook for 25 to 30 minutes or until the rice is cooked through. Allow mixture to cool before placing it in a food processor or blender to puree. Add lemon juice. If mixture is too thick, add additional chicken broth. Garnish with bacon, chopped ham, and cayenne pepper.

Makes 12 servings.

CORN & FIELD PEA DIP

2 15.8-ounce cans field peas with snaps, rinsed and drained	$^1/_3$ cup finely chopped onion
2 11-ounce cans white shoepeg corn, drained	3 garlic cloves, minced
$1^1/_4$ cups peeled and seeded diced tomatoes	2 tablespoons finely chopped fresh parsley
2 jalapeño peppers, seeded and finely minced	$^1/_2$ cup vegetable oil
	$^1/_2$ cup red wine vinegar
	$^1/_4$ cup fresh lemon juice
	$^1/_2$ teaspoon salt

Combine the first 7 ingredients; cover and chill at least 8 hours. Whisk oil together with remaining ingredients. Drizzle over bean mixture, and toss. Chill at least 8 hours and drain immediately before serving with corn chips.

Makes 8 cups.

A Morehouse Moment

Morehouse College, the nation's largest liberal arts college for men, graduates approximately 500 students each year. As a result, it confers bachelor's degrees on more black men than any other college or university in the United States.

Commencement exercises at Morehouse College.
(Courtesy Morehouse College Archives)

PICKLED BLACK-EYED PEA DIP

2	16-ounce cans black-eyed peas, rinsed and drained		1	jalapeño pepper, seeded and minced fine
$^2/_3$	cup vegetable oil		2	garlic cloves, minced
$^1/_3$	cup white wine vinegar		$^1/_2$	teaspoon salt
1	small onion, diced		$^1/_8$	teaspoon cayenne pepper
$^1/_2$	red pepper, seeded and diced			

Combine the above ingredients; cover and chill the mixture for at least 2 hours before serving with tortilla chips.

Makes 5 cups.

SMOKED BACON & BLACK BEAN DIP

As a general rule allow $\frac{1}{4}$ to $\frac{1}{3}$ cup dip per person.

5	slices smoked bacon, fried crisp and coarsely chopped (reserve drippings)	1	clove garlic, minced
1	medium onion, chopped	$\frac{1}{2}$	teaspoon ground cumin
1	small red bell pepper, chopped	$\frac{1}{2}$	teaspoon oregano
1	jalapeño pepper, stemmed, seeded, and chopped	1	16-ounce can black beans, rinsed and drained
			Salt
			Pepper
		$\frac{1}{2}$	cup sour cream

Pour off all but $1\frac{1}{2}$ tablespoons of the bacon drippings. Add onion, red pepper, jalapeño pepper, and garlic; sauté until the onion is soft, approximately 5 to 6 minutes. Add cumin and oregano and sauté for an additional minute. Add beans with their liquid and simmer over medium-low heat until slightly thickened, about 5 minutes. Stir occasionally to prevent burning.

Remove bean mixture from heat and allow to cool for 10 minutes. Transfer 1 cup of the mixture to a blender or food processor and process until smooth. Return blended beans to bean mixture, and stir to blend. Season the dip to taste with salt and pepper. Transfer to a serving bowl and refrigerate at least 2 hours before serving. Immediately before serving, gently stir in $\frac{1}{2}$ the bacon. Top with the sour cream and garnish with remaining bacon.

Makes 3 cups.

"The class of '27 held its tenth anniversary reunion during the commencement season. Eleven of the thirty-two members of the class met at Mr. and Mrs. S.H. Archer's home at eight o'clock June 6, for their reunion banquet.... Mrs. Archer ... said she was glad to welcome the men of '27 again.... [And] Mrs. Lula Eichelberger prepared the food just as she did ten years ago."

—*Bulletin of Morehouse College,* June 1937

BACON, TOMATO & CHEESE DIP

1   cup sour cream
2   4-ounce packages blue
     cheese, crumbled
2   3-ounce packages cream
     cheese, softened
$^1/_4$ teaspoon hot sauce

$^1/_4$ cup + 1 tablespoon white
     onion, diced
9   slices cooked bacon, crumbled
$^1/_3$ cup seeded and peeled chopped
     tomato

Process the first 5 ingredients in a blender or food processor until the mixture is smooth. Stop occasionally to scrape down the sides. Stir in half of bacon and chopped tomatoes. Cover and chill 2 hours. Sprinkle with remaining bacon. Delicious served with vegetable crudités or crackers.

Makes 1$^1/_2$ cups.

**Professor William E. Holmes, was an alum and
an early instructor at Morehouse College.**
(Courtesy Morehouse College Archives)

THREE-ONION DIP

3 tablespoons butter

1¹/₂ cups chopped Vidalia onion

2 tablespoons finely chopped red onion

2 tablespoons thinly sliced green onion

1 8-ounce carton dairy sour cream

¹/₄ teaspoon salt

¹/₄ teaspoon coarsely ground black pepper

¹/₈ teaspoon cayenne pepper

Heavy cream, chilled (optional)

1 tablespoon fresh chives, snipped

Assorted chips and vegetables for dipping, such as sliced fennel, baby carrots, sliced cucumbers, and sliced zucchini

In a medium skillet melt butter over medium-high heat, and cook the onions in the butter for approximately 5 minutes or until tender. Allow onions to cool before combining them in a blender or food processor with sour cream, salt, black pepper, and cayenne pepper. Cover and blend or process until smooth. Spoon mixture into a smaller bowl; cover and chill for 1 to 24 hours. Immediately before serving, stir in cream 1 teaspoon at a time, if necessary, to adjust dipping consistency. Garnish with chives and serve with a variety of dippers, such as chips and sliced raw vegetables.

Makes 1¹/₂ cups.

Dr. William H. Borders, Morehouse '29

William Holmes Borders, the son of a former slave, taught at Morehouse College and accepted a pastorate at historic Wheat Street Baptist Church, where he began a brilliant ministry and was internationally recognized for his rich oratorical skills used in support of the civil rights struggle. In 1969 Morehouse College would confer the honorary degree of Doctor of Divinity upon him with these words: "William Holmes Borders, you are one of the great preachers of our time. You have a comprehensive knowledge of your chosen field of theology. You are also a master of the spoken word, and you exploit the resources of the English language in your sermons. . . . But you are more than a preacher who delivers eloquent sermons on Sunday mornings and points the way to bliss and heaven: you are also a minister who builds the church triumphant and implements the teachings of Jesus Christ in this world.

"When you became pastor of Wheat Street Baptist Church 32 years ago, it was laden with debt and consisted only of a basement level. Today it is one of the country's most impressive and influential churches. Under your leadership Wheat Street has 5,000 members, uses four choirs and conducts special services for [the] deaf and prison inmates. . . . This powerful church also sponsors a job placement office, a shopping center, a federal credit union with assets over 350,000 dollars, and a 5,000,000-dollar housing project with more than 500 housing units.

"Besides developing Wheat Street Baptist Church into a center of religious and social service, you have played a prominent role as a champion of your people in the broader arena of civil rights. In Atlanta you have been a leader in successful campaigns to register voters, to provide better medical care for the poor, to equalize teachers' salaries, to desegregate city buses, and to increase the number and proportion of Negro firemen and policemen. You have tried to improve Atlanta because you love her and want her to become a model for other American cities to emulate. . . . William Holmes Borders, because of your talents and contributions as a 'Handyman of the Lord,' to use the words of your biographer, James W. English, I am pleased to honor you today."

As we here at Morehouse celebrate our eightieth anniversary, we dedicate ourselves anew to the proposition that the end of all education is to improve life and to make men better.

VIDALIA ONION DIP

1 large Vidalia onion, finely chopped	$^1/_4$ teaspoon fresh lemon juice
1 cup real mayonnaise	$1^1/_4$ cups grated Parmesan cheese
	Paprika

Preheat oven to 350°F. Lightly oil a 3-cup, oven-proof serving dish and set aside. Combine the onion, mayonnaise, lemon juice, and Parmesan cheese; mix well. Evenly spread the mixture into the prepared dish and garnish with a sprinkle of paprika. Bake in the preheated oven for 25 minutes, cool, and serve with baked pita chips.

Makes approximately 2$^1/_2$ cups.

BLOOMING VIDALIA ONION & DIPPING SAUCE

1	egg		$^1/_2$	teaspoon paprika
1	cup milk		$^1/_4$	teaspoon oregano
1	very large Vidalia onion		$^1/_8$	teaspoon ground nutmeg
1	cup flour		$^1/_8$	teaspoon thyme
1$^1/_2$	teaspoons salt		$^1/_8$	teaspoon cumin
$^1/_2$	teaspoon black pepper			Oil for deep frying
1	teaspoon cayenne pepper			

In a medium-size bowl, combine the egg and milk, and beat well to blend. In a separate bowl, combine the next 9 dry ingredients. Slice off $^1/_2$ to $^3/_4$ of the top and bottom of the onion and remove skin. Cut out a 1-inch core and make slices about $^3/_4$ of an inch down all the way around the onion to form the petals. Submerge the onion in boiling water for a minute or two to separate the petals. Remove the onion from the boiling water and set aside to cool. Next, dip the onion in the milk mixture to coat and then dip the onion in the flour mixture to coat. Repeat the dipping process and refrigerate the onion for approximately fifteen minutes to allow the coating to set. While the onion is setting, prepare the Dipping Sauce (see recipe below). Heat oil in a deep fryer according to manufacturer's directions and fry onion right side up for 10 minutes. When the onion is tender and golden brown, remove it from the deep fryer and drain on a paper towel. Serve with dipping sauce. (See recipe below.)

Makes 2 to 4 servings, depending on the size of the onion and your guests' appetites.

DIPPING SAUCE

$^1/_2$ cup mayonnaise

1   tablespoon ketchup

2   tablespoons cream-style
     horseradish

$^1/_8$ teaspoon cayenne pepper

$^1/_4$ teaspoon paprika

$^1/_4$ teaspoon salt

$^1/_8$ teaspoon dried oregano

Combine the above ingredients, mix well, and refrigerate until ready to serve.

Makes approximately $^3/_4$ cup.

God give us men! A time like this demands
Strong minds, great hearts, true faith and ready hands
Men whom the lust of office does not kill
Men whom the spoils of office cannot buy
Men who possess opinions and a will . . .

—Benjamin E. Mays, February 15, 1947

Martin Luther King, Jr.,
graduation photo.
(Courtesy Morehouse College Archives)

Martin Luther King, Jr., Morehouse '48

In September 1944, 15-year-old Martin Luther King, Jr., a future Nobel Peace Prize laureate and civil rights leader, began studies at Morehouse College in Atlanta, following in the footsteps of his father, Martin Luther King, Sr., and his grandfather, A. D. Williams. While at Morehouse he met Walter McCall, a dirt-poor student who supported himself by cutting hair for a dime in the basement of Graves Hall. King, a son of privilege, was handsomely sartorial in his dress. The two became inseparable friends. Both were quick wits and enjoyed the polysyllabic word games of Professor Gladstone Chandler, who smoked a pipe and appeared quite urbane in his tweed jackets. He encouraged flamboyant rejoinders to simple questions as a means of improving vocabulary. For instance, if Professor Chandler asked "How are you?" King, using his vast vocabulary, would fire off, "I surmise that my physical equilibrium is organically quiescent."

   Word games were just one aspect of the sophomoric humor and fun shared by the "Mac and Mike" clique. (Despite the earlier name change to Martin following King Sr.'s visit to Germany, most of King's friends continued referring to him as "Mike.") Neither McCall nor King felt a specific calling to the ministry at the time, so they freely engaged in activities frowned upon by the Baptist Church such as dancing and card playing.

GEORGIA PEACH SALSA &
JICAMA WEDGES

Georgia peaches should have a creamy gold to yellow under-color. The red "blush" of a peach indicates ripeness. And as a member of the rose family it should have a sweet fragrance. Finally, it should be soft to the touch but not mushy. However, don't squeeze it because it bruises very easily!

2¹/₄   cups peeled, pitted, and
       coarsely chopped peaches
¹/₃   cup peeled, seeded, and
      chopped cucumber
¹/₃   cup chopped Bermuda onion
1   jalapeño pepper, stemmed,
     seeded, and chopped
2   tablespoons honey

3   tablespoons lime juice
2   tablespoons finely chopped
     cilantro
1   large tomato, seeded and finely
     chopped
     Jicama wedges, ¹/₄-inch thick
     Fresh lime juice
     Fresh lime wedges

Combine the first 8 ingredients and refrigerate to chill. Peel and slice jicama; place in a shallow dish; squeeze lime juice over the slices to prevent discoloration, and refrigerate. Serve with chilled wedges of jicama and fresh limes. Jicama, a white fleshed root vegetable, is readily available in the fresh vegetable section of your local grocery store. A good source of vitamin C, when eaten raw, it has the cool, crisp and refreshing texture of an apple. When paired with flavorful Georgia Peach Salsa, it provides a healthful alternative to chips. When shopping look for a jicama with a hard and unblemished skin. The salsa is a great accompaniment to pork and poultry dishes.

WATERMELON SALSA

Watermelon should be stored in a cool place and chilled just before serving. Once cut, it should be served within two days. Uncut, it can last as long as two weeks.

3   tablespoons thinly sliced
     fresh basil
¹/₄   cup fresh lime juice
1   teaspoon salt
¹/₄   cup pepper
1   4-pound seedless watermelon,
     diced (approximately
     6 cups)

³/₄   cup finely chopped Bermuda
      onion
1   jalapeño pepper, seeded and
     finely minced (or more to
     taste)
     Tortilla chips

Combine the first four ingredients, whisk to mix well, and set aside. Drain watermelon and place it in a serving bowl with onion and jalapeño peppers, gently mix to blend. Drizzle with lime juice dressing and refrigerate 1 to 2 hours before serving with corn chips.

Makes 6 to 8 servings.

Glimpses of Morehouse Men

Dr. E. R. Carter, '84, a trustee of the college and for 53 years pastor of Friendship Baptist Church, recently observed with Mrs. Carter their 60th anniversary.

Dr. J. M. Nabrit, Sr., '98, a trustee of the college, president of the Georgia Baptist Convention, secretary of the National Baptist Convention, and pastor of Mount Olive Church, Atlanta; has gone to Nashville, Tennessee, to direct the activities of the National Baptist Theological Seminary and Training School.

Maynard H. Jackson, '14, formerly alumni and endowment secretary of Morehouse College, now pastor of New Hope Baptist Church, Dallas, Texas; spoke to the students in chapel during opening week. Mrs. Jackson (Irene Dobbs, Spelman, '29) came with Reverend Jackson to the campus.

J. M. Nabrit, Jr., '23, was recently called from his law practice in Houston, Texas, to serve as assistant professor in the Howard University College of Law.

S. M. Nabrit, '25, chairman of the Department of Biology at Atlanta University and Morehouse, spent a large part of the summer carrying on research at the Marine Biological laboratory, Woods Hole, Massachusetts.

—*Morehouse Alumnus,* November 1936

A Morehouse Moment

One of the firm traditions of Morehouse is observed when members of each outgoing class meet at eight o'clock for a final class breakfast. The tradition was started by Howard Thurman and the class of '31!

Morehouse men dining at the home of
President Benjamin Mays *(far right, seated)* and his wife,
Mrs. Sadie Mays *(far left, standing).*
(Courtesy Morehouse College Archives)

ROSEMARY EGGPLANT DIP

This roasted eggplant dip will convert those most opposed to this vegetable. Its superb smoky flavor is delightful when paired with sliced vegetables, pita crisps, crackers, baguette slices, or breadsticks. The dip can be made up to two days in advance and stored tightly wrapped in the refrigerator.

1	large eggplant			Freshly ground black pepper
4	cloves garlic		$1/8$	teaspoon cumin
$1/2$	cup sour cream		1	tablespoon chopped fresh
$1/4$	cup softened cream cheese			rosemary
	Salt			

Puncture eggplant with a fork several times to allow steam to escape while baking. Bake the eggplant in a 425°F oven until the skin is charred and the flesh is tender, turning occasionally. The cooking time varies depending upon the size and ripeness of the eggplant. Upon completion of cooking time, remove the eggplant from the oven and allow it to cool until it can be safely handled. Next, cut it in half and scoop out the flesh. Place the flesh in a food processor with the remaining ingredients and process until smooth. Refrigerate at least 2 hours prior to serving.

Makes 4 servings.

HUMMUS BI TAHINI

2   15-ounce cans chickpeas
3   garlic cloves, peeled and
      mashed
1   teaspoon salt
1/2   teaspoon ground cumin
1/8   teaspoon sesame oil
1/3   cup olive oil
3   tablespoons sesame tahini
      (available in health food
      stores)

Juice of 3 to 4 lemons
Chopped parsley and cayenne
      pepper for garnish
Olive oil
Pita bread

Drain chickpeas and rinse. Place well-drained chickpeas in a mixing bowl. Add mashed garlic and salt to chickpeas and mix to blend. Puree mixture in a blender or processor. Add cumin, oils, and tahini; blend. Gradually add lemon juice to taste. Mix to a fine, smooth paste. If the hummus is too thick, thin by adding a little cold water. Serve in a shallow serving dish and garnish with chopped parsley and red pepper. Offer olive oil in a separate dish and pita bread for dipping.

Makes 12 to 18 servings.

Robert E. Johnson, Morehouse '48, former Executive Editor and Associate Publisher, *Jet* magazine

Graduating with Martin Luther King, Jr., that June was former *Morehouse Maroon Tiger* editor and classmate Robert E. Johnson. Johnson, who played a major role in publicizing King's civil rights crusade, was the first representative from a major national publication to report the beginning of the Montgomery bus boycott. After serving in the navy and on the staff of the *Atlanta Daily World,* the nation's first black newspaper, Johnson joined a new black national publication, *Jet* magazine, two years after its founding. This became the great love of his life. Of the man and his career, his lifelong friend the Reverend Jesse Jackson would say, "Bob was a nexus, a modern-day Griot. He was the web that connected music, culture, religion, history, and social developments. He was one of the great communicators of our times." Another friend and associate would add, "He helped change the color of American journalism."

Lerone Bennett, Jr., Morehouse '49, Executive Editor, *Ebony* magazine

"Most of the black men I saw who carried themselves like men or acted like men were Morehouse Men. . . . The great mission of Morehouse in 1945, when I came here, was to make young African American men believe in themselves, despite an unfavorable societal environment, and to let them know they could do anything they wanted to do."

—Lerone Bennett, Jr.

Morehouse man Lerone Bennett, Jr., executive editor of *Ebony* magazine for more than forty years, is one of America's most successful writers. A social historian, Bennett is also an early pioneer in the writing of popular black history. Often commended for his interesting and easy to read writing style, his books include *What Manner of Man: A Biography of Martin Luther King, Jr.; Confrontation: Black and White Black Power U.S.A.; The Human Side of Reconstruction, 1867–1877; Forced into Glory: Abraham Lincoln's White*

Dream; Before the Mayflower: A History of Black America, a comprehensive examination of African-American history in the United States; and *The Shaping of Black America.*

OLIVE SPREAD

This quick, flavorful Mediterranean olive spread is excellent served with pieces of good crusty bread.

3 cups whole, pitted kalamata olives	3 cloves garlic
	$1/3$ cup olive oil

Coarsely blend or process olives and garlic, then add olive oil in a stream while puréeing; process until mixture becomes a thick, but not too smooth, paste.

Makes 14 servings.

KALAMATA CAVIAR

A distinctive blend of magnificent flavors separates this spread from the rest. This olive, cheese, and nut mixture is delicious spread on slices of warm Cuban or French bread.

8 ounces whole, pitted kalamata olives	$1/2$ cup chopped pistachio nuts
1 4-ounce package feta cheese	4 cloves garlic, peeled
	Up to 2 tablespoons olive oil

Blend or process kalamata olives, feta cheese, pistachios, garlic, and olives. Add olive oil as needed to attain a pesto-like consistency. Serve with warm Cuban or French bread.

Makes 8 servings.

Maynard Holbrook Jackson, Morehouse '56

"Morehouse was written all over Maynard Jackson. The impressive, darn near regal bearing. The courage, conviction, and morality. Jackson graduated from Morehouse in 1956, but the college never left him. It showed in the way he represented its best ideals."

—Walter Filiker, director of the Morehouse College Leadership Center

Maynard H. Jackson, Jr., grandson of John Wesley Dobbs, the unofficial mayor of Auburn Avenue, and the proud great-grandson of slaves on both sides of his family tree, was swept into power by the new black majority in 1973, and would eventually serve three terms as mayor of Atlanta. He oversaw construction of what would become the nation's busiest international airport, battled a rising homeless rate, and helped attract the 1996 Olympic Games to Atlanta. In addition, he established affirmative-action programs for hiring city workers and contractors and provided black neighborhoods a voice in city planning.

As mayor his crowning achievement was, as he often boasted, bringing in the Atlanta Airport "ahead of time and under budget" with significant minority contractor participation. During his administration city contracts granted to minorities soared from less than

A youthful Maynard Jackson.
(Courtesy Morehouse College Archives)

A quintessential Morehouse man, Maynard Jackson served on
the Morehouse board of trustees for 18 years. His alma mater
bestowed an honorary Doctor of Laws degree upon him in 1974.
(Courtesy Morehouse College Archives)

1 percent in 1973 to nearly 39 percent within five years. As a result, Atlanta gained dozens
of new black millionaires as well as a new sense of economic power-sharing from the new
joint ventures arising between minority-owned companies and white-owned companies,
who suddenly saw the light and the writing on the wall.

According to Michael L. Lomax, also a graduate of Morehouse College and speech-
writer for Mr. Jackson in the 1970s, "When Maynard got elected . . . that's what gave
black people a piece of the pie and put that city on the map for every young black person
in America who had ambitions of doing something spectacular with his or her life. . . . In
many ways," according to Lomax, "Maynard's the architect of modern Atlanta."

Morehouse Moment

Donn Clendenon, '56, New York Mets outfielder, was the 1969 World Series MVP. A .274
career hitter, he hit 159 home runs. While at Morehouse, Clendenon, a classmate of Maynard Jackson, Jr., was a three-sport All-American. After graduating he worked a full-time
job while playing for Major-League Baseball, and after retiring from baseball, he earned
his law degree.

SPICY TOASTED PECANS

Try this great alternative to "party peanuts" at your next cocktail social!

1	cup pecans	$^1/_8$	teaspoon cayenne pepper
$^1/_4$	teaspoon kosher salt	$^1/_2$	teaspoon toasted and ground cumin
$^1/_2$	teaspoon paprika		
$^1/_4$	teaspoon onion powder	$^1/_2$	teaspoon extra virgin olive oil

Preheat oven to 350°F and toast pecans for 10 minutes. While pecans are toasting—watching them carefully to prevent burning—mix together the seasoning ingredients. Remove slightly browned and crispy pecans from the oven and allow them to cool slightly before tossing them in the seasoning mix. Delicious served with drinks or served alone as a snack.

Makes 1 cup.

BLUE CHEESE & TOASTED PECAN SPREAD

Simply elegant! This popular appetizer will be the toast of your next party.

8	ounces cream cheese, softened		Baguette bread, sliced thinly
2	ounces blue cheese, crumbled	2	unpeeled Granny Smith apples, cored and sliced into eighths
2	tablespoons toasted and coarsely chopped pecans	2	unpeeled Macintosh apples, cored and sliced into eighths
	Pinch of kosher salt		Lemon juice
	Minced parsley		

Combine the first 4 ingredients and mix well. Place the mixture in a serving bowl and garnish with minced parsley. Serve immediately as a spread for the baguettes and apples. Or refrigerate and serve later. Before serving, dip the apple slices in fresh lemon juice to prevent browning.

Makes 10 to 12 servings.

Morehouse Moment

Black Enterprise magazine twice ranked Morehouse College as the number one college in the nation for educating African-American students. Morehouse, the nation's largest private, liberal arts college for African-American men, enrolls approximately 1,800 students annually. With an undergraduate enrollment of approximately 3,000 students, it confers bachelor's degrees on more black men than any other institution in the world. Morehouse offers a number of programs and activities to enhance its challenging liberal arts curriculum through the Leadership Center at Morehouse College, Morehouse Research Institute, and Andrew Young Center for International Affairs. According to Morehouse, it is one of only two historically black colleges or universities to produce three Rhodes scholars.

BLUE CHEESE DIP

8 ounces cream cheese, softened	1 tablespoon sour cream
$^1/_4$ cup buttermilk	$^1/_8$ teaspoon garlic powder
	4 ounces blue cheese, crumbled

Process first 4 ingredients and half of the blue cheese until a smooth mixture forms. Stop occasionally to scrape down the sides. Stir in remaining blue cheese. Cover and chill 2 hours. Serve with vegetable crudités and apple or pear slices.

Makes 3 cups.

BLUE CHEESE, CRANBERRY, PINE NUT, & GOAT CHEESE SPREAD

Inspired by cheese balls sold in Paris delis, this unique combination of ingredients will have you asking, *"Pouvez-vous dire délicieux?"* ("Can you say delicious?") Serve with toasted baguette slices.

8 ounces goat cheese, softened	2 tablespoons dried cranberries
2 tablespoons Crème de Cassis liqueur	³/₄ cup chopped toasted pine nuts
	Baguette slices

Blend or process the goat cheese and liqueur until it forms a smooth, creamy mixture. Chill for an hour before rolling the mixture into a smooth ball. Spread the cranberries and pine nuts on a plate. Roll the goat cheese ball in the cranberries and pine nuts. Chill for a minimum of two hours before serving. Serve at room temperature or chilled.

Makes 6 servings.

"From 5 to 7 o'clock in the afternoon, June 1, President and Mrs. B.E. Mays were 'at home' to members of the Morehouse graduating class, their parents, relatives, and friends, and to the alumni and friends of the college in an outdoor reception held on the lawn of the President's residence on Morehouse Campus."

—Morehouse College Bulletin, 1952

Lt. Gen. James R. Hall, Morehouse '57

Born in Anniston, Alabama, Hall entered the United States Army after graduating from Morehouse College. Commissioned a second lieutenant in 1958, Hall served as a company commander in Vietnam and a battalion commander in Korea. From 1986 to 1988,

Hall was commanding general of the 4th Infantry Division (Mechanized) at Fort Carson, Colorado—only the second African American to command a United States Army Infantry division according to the U.S. Army Center of Military History.

Following retirement from the army in October 1991, General Hall served on the Atlanta Committee for the 1996 Centennial Olympic Games, and joined Morehouse College as Vice President for Campus Operations in December 1996. He also serves on the board of advisors of Vetjobs.com, owned and operated by United States military veterans and headquartered in the Atlanta suburb of Marietta, the largest résumé database and job-posting Internet firm for U.S. military veterans transitioning to jobs in the civilian sector.

HONEYED SWEET POTATO CHIPS

Nothing says Southern cooking like sweet potatoes and honey roasted peanuts.

1	cup honey roasted peanuts	10	tablespoons melted butter
	Pinch of nutmeg		Salt
2	large sweet potatoes, sliced thin		

Preheat the oven to 475°F. Line 2 baking sheets with aluminum foil and grease well. Process the peanuts to a fine powder. Place the powder on a plate, add nutmeg, and mix well. Dip each potato slice into the butter until it is well coated. Coat both sides of each buttered potato slice with the peanut powder and arrange in a single layer on the prepared pans. Bake the potatoes for 12 to 18 minutes, or until they are tender and lightly browned. Make sure not to overcook as they will burn easily. Drain on paper towels, sprinkle with salt if desired, and serve warm.

Makes 3 to 4 servings.

JUBILEE DIP

2   10-ounce bags frozen corn,
      thawed
2   14- to 16-ounce cans whole
      black beans, drained and
      rinsed
1   medium red onion, finely
      chopped
1   cup diced green bell pepper
1/2 cup diced red bell pepper

1   tablespoon parsley, finely
      chopped
1/4 cup sour cream
2   tablespoons red wine vinegar
1/2 cup mayonnaise
1   teaspoon ground cumin
1   teaspoon chili powder
    Salt and pepper

In a large bowl, combine corn, black beans, red onion, peppers, and parsley. In a small bowl, whisk together the sour cream, vinegar, mayonnaise, cumin, and chili powder until well combined. Toss dressing with corn and black bean mixture. Add salt and pepper to taste. Serve with corn chips.

Makes 12 to 14 servings.

Julian Bond

A student and social activist who faced jail for his convictions, and a U.S. legislator and black civil rights leader who fought to take his duly elected seat in the Georgia House of Representatives, Horace Julian Bond has remained on the cutting edge of social reform in America since his days as a student protest leader at Morehouse College.

Born in 1940 to prominent educators, Bond began his career as a social activist at Morehouse, first as a founder of the Committee on Appeal for Human Rights (COAHR), a student civil rights organization that fought to integrate Atlanta's movie theaters, lunch counters, and parks; and then as a member of the Student Non-Violent Coordinating Committee, a protest powerhouse that forced states to enforce *Brown v. Board of Education* and pushed the federal government to enact more sweeping civil rights legislation.

Bond entered the political arena in 1965 after winning a one-year term to the Georgia House of Representatives, whose members refused to admit him because he had

Julian Bond, '71, student activist, member of the
Georgia General Assembly for twenty years,
and chairman of the NAACP.
(Courtesy Morehouse College Archives)

endorsed a SNCC statement accusing the United States of violating international law in
Vietnam. He would be elected twice more before the Supreme Court unanimously ruled
his exclusion unconstitutional. He was finally seated on January 9, 1967, and would hold
his House seat for more than eight years. Bond also served as the first president of the
Southern Poverty Law Center and chaired the national board of directors of the National
Association for the Advancement of Colored People.

A Morehouse Moment

At the Democratic National Convention in 1968, Julian Bond led a delegation of insur-
gents that won half the Georgia seats. He seconded the nomination of Eugene McCarthy
and became the first black man to be nominated as the vice presidential candidate of a
major party. He withdrew his name, however, because he was too young to meet the minimum age required under the Constitution.

Dr. Martin Luther King, Jr.,
with student activists.
(Courtesy Morehouse College Archives)

The Second Battle of Atlanta

One day Julian Bond was sitting in a student café when an older student by the name of Lonnie King (no relation to Martin Luther King, Jr.) approached him with a newspaper that announced, "Greensboro Students Sit In for Third Day." "Hey, that's pretty good, that's great, that's fabulous. I'm so happy they're doing that," Bond responded. Not yet receiving the response he was looking for, King pressed the point. "Don't you think somebody ought to do that here in Atlanta where we are?" And Bond said, "Oh, somebody is going to do it, you know somebody is going to do that, somebody is going to do that." It was then that King issued the challenge that would make Atlanta the center of the student protest movement. "Why don't we do it?"

Well-organized student protest demonstrations began in Atlanta in March of 1960 with eighty well-dressed students. With no training in nonviolent tactics, Bond's group went to the Atlanta City Hall Cafeteria. The first in line, Bond approached the white cashier manager, who according to Bond politely said, "Oh, I'm awfully sorry, this is for city hall employees only."

After Bond directed her attention to a sign that read, "City Hall Cafeteria, the public is welcome," the woman demurred, saying, "We don't mean it." Bond then promised to "stand here until you do."

While Julian Bond's group staged a sit-in at City Hall's municipal cafeteria, Lonnie King and thirty-five protesters were joined by the Reverend Martin Luther King, Jr., in Rich's department store, where they launched what one journalist later called "the Second Battle of Atlanta." As a result, King spent his first night in an Atlanta jail, was released, and then was immediately rearrested for violating probation in an earlier DeKalb county traffic case. For driving without a license, the judge sentenced Dr. King to four months' hard labor.

This unusually harsh sentence appalled President John F. Kennedy, who called Coretta King promising to help free her husband. Robert Kennedy persuaded the judge to reverse his decision, and King was released on bond. King's arrest and the intervention of the Kennedy brothers literally took place on the eve of the November 1960 elections.

The following year witnessed the desegregation of Rich's department store as well as the previously segregated public schools. By 1962 all public transportation was desegregated. In 1963 a "New South" mayoral candidate, Ivan Allen, Jr., defeated old guard mayor Lester Maddox. Allen immediately rescinded ordinances supporting segregation, which gave rise to the claim by Atlantans that Atlanta was "the city too busy to hate."

CLASSIC CLAM DIP

Simply delicious and so easy that you will never purchase packaged clam dip again. Whip it up quickly when unexpected guests drop in, or up to two days in advance.

2 6^1/$_2$-ounce cans of minced clams	2 tablespoons minced fresh parsley
8 ounces cream cheese, softened	2 garlic cloves, minced
^{1}/$_4$ cup sour cream	Dash cayenne pepper
^{3}/$_4$ teaspoon Worcestershire sauce	Freshly ground black pepper

The Queen of Soul, Aretha Franklin, with student admirers in 1971.
(Courtesy Morehouse College Archives)

Drain the clams, reserving ¹/₄ cup of juice. Beat the juice with the cream cheese, sour cream, and Worcestershire sauce. Fold in the clams, parsley, garlic, cayenne, and black pepper. Serve immediately or chill.

Makes about 2 cups.

LAYERED CRAB DIP

2	8-ounce packages cream cheese, softened
2	tablespoons mayonnaise
1	tablespoon Old Bay seasoning
1¹/₂	cups fresh crab (claw meat), shredded
1	cup diced tomatoes
¹/₄	cup sliced green onions
¹/₄	cup (about 2 ounces) sliced black olives

Combine the cream cheese, mayonnaise, and Old Bay seasoning in a medium-size bowl and mix thoroughly. Spread the cream cheese mixture evenly on the bottom of a 9-inch pie pan. Sprinkle crab meat, tomatoes, green onions, and black olives in layers over cream cheese mixture. Serve with tortilla chips and assorted crackers.

Makes 16 servings.

Howard E. Jeter, Morehouse '70

Besides serving as U.S. ambassador to both Nigeria and Botswana, career diplomat Howard F. Jeter served as deputy assistant secretary of state for African affairs from 1999 to 2000, as director of West African affairs from 1997 to 1999, and as special presidential envoy for Liberia. He holds a B.A. degree in political science from Morehouse College in Atlanta, an M.A. in international relations and comparative politics from Columbia University, and an M.A. in African area studies from the University of California, Los Angeles. Ambassador Jeter is a former Ford Foundation doctoral fellow, international fellow at Columbia University, Merrill overseas study-travel scholar, legislative intern in the Georgia House of Representatives, and a participant in Operation Crossroads Africa. He is a member of Phi Beta Kappa, the American Foreign Service Association, and the Council on Foreign Relations.

Maceo K. Sloan, Morehouse '71

Attorney Maceo K. Sloan, a descendant of the founders of North Carolina Mutual Life Insurance Company, the oldest and largest African-American owned and operated insurance company in the United States (an investment management legacy dating back to 1898), is chairman, president, and CEO of Sloan Financial Group, Inc., and chairman, CEO, and CIO of NCM Capital Management Group, Inc. Mr. Sloan is a trustee of The Teachers' Insurance and Annuity Association–College Retirement Equities Fund (TIAA-CREF) Funds Boards, and a member of the board of directors for the SCANA Corporation and M&F Bancorp, Inc. He has also served as chairman of the Rainbow/PUSH Wall Street Project. Mr. Sloan earned his B.A. from Morehouse College, his M.B.A. from Georgia State University, and a J.D. from North Carolina Central University School of Law.

Samuel L. Jackson, Morehouse '72

One of the highest-grossing actors of all time, Samuel L. Jackson has appeared in more than fifty feature films, including *Jungle Fever* (1991), *Pulp Fiction* (1994), *Die Hard: With a Vengeance* (1995), *Losing Isaiah* (1995), *A Time to Kill* (1996), *Changing Lanes* (2002), *Basic* (2003), *Kill Bill, Vol. 2* (2004), and *Coach Carter* (2005), as well as in numerous stage productions. At Morehouse, he was encouraged to attend public speaking classes to help him control a terrible stammer that had afflicted him since childhood. It was there that he met his future wife, actress and Spelman graduate La Tanya Richardson. The rest, so to speak, is history.

Edwin C. Moses, Morehouse '78

Edwin C. Moses, 1978 Olympic champion and currently a sports administrator, sports diplomat, and businessman, is one of the most respected and recognized athletes of our time. He has served and promoted the Olympic movement, fostered the development of drug-free sports, and supported the rights of amateur athletes at all levels. His experience as a distinguished Olympic champion and world record holder has earned him the esteem of the international sports community.

Moses, a physicist from Morehouse College, is known for utilizing the applied sciences to perfect the technical aspects of his athletic performances in his event, the 400-meter hurdles. This knowledge also enabled him to create, implement, and administer the world's most stringent random and out-of-competition testing systems for performance-enhancing drugs in sports.

In 1979, Edwin took a leave of absence from his engineering position at General Dynamics to pursue athletics full-time. Determined to find a method through which U.S.

athletes could generate financial support to offset training expenses and earn some income, Moses helped to persuade The Athletics Congress to adopt an Athletes' Trust Fund Program. The Trust Fund would enable athletes to create accounts administered by their respective sport bodies, within which government or privately supplied stipends, direct payments, and moneys derived from commercial endorsements could be deposited and periodically drawn from by an athlete for training and other expenses without jeopardizing their Olympic eligibility. Following Moses's persuasive and innovative presentation to Juan Antonio Samaranch, president of the International Olympic Committee, the concept was ratified by Samaranch and the IOC commission in late 1981. The Trust Fund is currently the basis of many Olympic athlete subsistence, stipend, and corporate support programs, including the U.S. Olympic Committee's well-funded Direct Athlete Assistance Programs.

Moses was inducted into the U.S. Track and Field Hall of Fame on December 3, 1994. He currently works as a financial consultant in investment management consulting and managed money via the Consulting Group, a division of the New York–based investment bank Salomon Smith Barney.

Shelton "Spike" Lee, Morehouse '79

Atlanta-born writer-director, actor, producer, author, and entrepreneur Spike Lee revolutionized black filmmaking in America. His debut film, *She's Gotta Have It*, established him as a filmmaker on the cutting edge of black American cinema. His second feature, *School Daze*, launched the cinematic careers of several black actors. Audiences did not have to wait long for an encore performance from the talented director. *Do the Right Thing* earned him an Academy Award nomination for Best Original Screenplay and Best Film and Director awards from the Los Angeles Film Critics Association.

When he was making *Malcolm X* for Warner Brothers, Lee refused to cut the budget and the running time of the project. Taking a lesson from the life of Malcolm, who believed in self-reliance for African Americans, Lee contacted a list of prominent African Americans including Bill Cosby, Oprah Winfrey, Magic Johnson, Michael Jordan, Tracy Chapman, Prince, and Janet Jackson, who wrote him six-figure checks.

Lee has also produced and directed music videos for artists such as Miles Davis, Tracy

Old School!
(Courtesy Morehouse College Archives)

Chapman, Anita Baker, Public Enemy, and Bruce Hornsby. He founded 40 Acres and A Mule Film Works and Music Works; created two retail companies, Spike's Joint, based in the Fort Greene section of Brooklyn, and Spike's Joint West in Los Angeles; and collaborated with basketball legend Michael Jordan on several television commercials. He has also written six books on the making of his films.

"Morehouse is not in Atlanta, Georgia, alone but throughout the United States and the world wherever Morehouse men are found."

—Dr. Benjamin E. Mays

Founder's Day tribute.
(Courtesy Morehouse College Archives)

SPELMAN COLLEGE

Teach a woman and you teach a nation.

—African Proverb

BEVERAGES

SPELMAN SCHOOL SONG

Spelman, thy name we praise
Standards and honor raise
We'll ever faithful be
Throughout eternity
May peace with thee abide
And God forever guide
Thy heights supreme and true
Blessings to you.

Through years of toil and pain
May thy dear walls remain
Beacons of heavenly light,
Undaunted by the fight:
And when life's race is won,
Thy noble work is done
Oh, God forever bind
Our hearts to thine.

—Words and music by Eddye Mae Money, Spelman '34

Students in cooking class, ca. 1890.
(Courtesy Spelman College Archives)

Spelman Seminary faculty, 1890.
(Courtesy Spelman College Archives)

*"The rise of all the freemen's schools in the South . . . has seemed almost miraculous.
But perhaps Spelman Seminary is the most resplendent miracle. It was the first
considerable movement in the South to educate colored women."*

—*Spelman Messenger,* December 1887

"I am building for a hundred years hence, not only for today."

—Quote attributed to Sophia Packard by Carol Bell Finely
(High School '94, College '31) in *Spelman Messenger,* 1931

Harriet Giles (*left*) and Sophia Packard *(right)*
(Courtesy Spelman College Archives)

"And as we think of the early days we remember those consecrated Christian women of New England who worked so heroically and prayed with such faith for the establishment of a girl's school."

—Miss Lucy Hale Tapley, president emeritus of Spelman College,
Spelman Messenger, January 1931

On April 11, 1881, Spelman, one of the nation's most highly regarded colleges for women, was founded in the basement of Friendship Baptist Church in Atlanta, Georgia, by Sophia B. Packard and Harriet "Hattie" E. Giles. The two friends, who often dressed alike, "had made a compact to enter jointly upon the profession of teaching and as soon as practicable establish a school of their own." In 1879 Packard was commissioned by the Woman's American Baptist Home Mission Society (WABHMS), which she had helped to found, to study the living conditions "among the freedmen of the South." As an educator and administrator of several outstanding New England Academies, she was especially concerned with the lack of educational opportunities for black women. While in New Orleans, she became ill and sent for Giles to assist her. Giles was equally appalled by the circumstances of Southern blacks, especially women, and the pair returned to Boston convinced that they were called by God to establish a school for the education and elevation of black women in the South.

Others were not so certain. At 56 and 47, respectively, Packard and Giles were considered too old for the task. The WABHMS treasury was empty. And the organization was hesitant to take on a project as daunting as supporting a Negro school for women. Packard and Giles pointed out that while the Baptists had a school for blacks in almost every southern state, there was no provision for educating women and girls in Georgia, which had the largest population of black Baptists. Discouraged by the delay, the women opted to raise the money themselves. One diary entry read: "Sold my Piano—a hard thing for me to do, but thought it best." —Harriet E. Giles, March 11, 1881.

Miss Packard and Miss Giles reached Atlanta on April 1, 1881, and were met at the depot by Dr. Shaver, a teacher at the Atlanta Baptist Seminary. The next day, after locating accommodations, they were introduced to Reverend Frank Quarles. With a congregation of 1500, he was one of the most influential black preachers in the city. Upon explaining their mission to him, Reverend Quarles exclaimed, "When I was praying, the Lord heard and answered. I was on my

Giles Hall, named for Harriet E. Giles.
(Archives and Special Collections: Robert Woodruff Library at the Atlanta University Center)

knees pleading with God to send teachers for the Baptist women and girls of Georgia. We fully believe the Lord sent you."

Following a meeting of the local clergy in Reverend Quarles's study, which was called by Packard and Giles "to consider what steps should be taken to promote the education of the young ladies connected with your congregation," one week later, on April 11, 1881, the first class convened in the basement of Friendship Baptist Church. "On that momentous day . . . eleven women of varying ages and attainments constituted the student body, women earnest, ardent, and ambitious, but the most daring ambition of any of them did not reach a high school diploma." —Claudia White Harreld, Spelman '01.

The first 11 pupils, ten women and one girl, were mostly ex-slaves determined to learn to read the Bible and write to their children. The second day they had 25 scholars. The school that would one day become Spelman College began with 100 dollars provided by the congregation of the First Baptist Church of Medford, Massachusetts. Equipped with only a Bible, two notebooks and two pencils, Packard and Giles were totally dedicated to the enormous task before them. Many students arrived with their children and took in washing to support themselves. Others walked eight to ten miles to attend classes.

Claudia White
(Courtesy Spelman College Archives)

The church basement that provided them their first educational home was embraced by the women despite the fact that "it was dark and very damp, the floor laid right upon the bare earth . . . glass broken from the windows . . . in fact everything unfavorable for a school room." —S. B. Packard, April 12, 1881. In the absence of desks and chairs, benches, hard and straight, served as seats. Floor boards were decayed, loose, and in places, missing. "You certainly had to watch your steps, for the gaps between the boards were many, and the loose boards would fly up and trip you should you happen to step on the wrong end. . . . " —Clara A. Howard, Spelman 1887, *Spelman Messenger,* January 1931.

"When it rained, we had water about on the floor, in which our teachers must stand . . . we were very sorry to have those to whom our hearts were so closely tied stand on such, not damp, but wet floors. So some of the wise heads brought pieces of carpet and others corn sacks and made rugs for them to stand on." —Rosella B. Humphreys, Spelman '88. The light was so poor that during inclement weather it was often difficult to see. "On cloudy days the lamps were lighted in some of the corners—for all classes were heard in that one large room. . . . Often when too dark or cold to attend to studies, Miss Packard would say, 'We will spend the time in prayer.' During these waiting periods, many students gave their hearts to Jesus. Shortly afterward the

Basement of Friendship Baptist Church, 1881.
(Courtesy Spelman College Archives)

clouds passed and the sun shone. After the school had sung 'There Shall Be Showers of Bless-ings,' with Miss Giles at the organ, studies were resumed. . . . Every cloud has its silver lining." —Clara A. Howard, Spelman 1887 . . .

Not only was it dark, but often too cold to teach. "This is a very stormy cold day. We need a fire but have no coal. The sexton said he would see to it but none was brought. . . . Long to go to a lively prayer meeting tonight." —Sophia Packard, April 14, 1881. On April 15, Sophia wrote, "Have been obliged to send out for coal. We took cold yesterday trying to stay in this cold room. Two of our young ladies are quite sick. Paid two dollars for 5 bushels of coal."

When the stove did have coal, it "would lose a part of its pipe, and the smoke would pour forth, and our next job would be to mend that dear old companion." —Rosella B. Humphreys, 1888. "Sometimes the smoke was so thick you could scarcely see. . . . However, things moved on pretty well, all would go out to the sidewalk until the church janitor got the chimney in order." —Clara A. Howard, Spelman 1887.

Within three months enrollment increased to 80. "At the close of these first three months, Miss Packard and Miss Giles remained in the South, spending the summer visiting churches, conducting meetings for women, visiting homes, teaching in the Sunday Schools, organizing temperance bands, holding regularly children's and young people's meetings at different churches—to which all would go, no matter in what part of town they were held. In October the school reopened with a large number of students, great and small, old and young. . . ." —Clara A. Howard, 1887.

Within a year enrollment increased to 200 women, ranging in age from 15 to 52. Of her experience one mother who arrived at the school with her four daughters would excitedly recall, "I reckon I am the happiest woman in town. One year ago, I did not know a letter; today I can read my Bible and I am going on fifty-two years old."

In later years Clara Howard would recall, "How well I remember that October morning when I edged my way through the crowded room, missing the gaps, to the front to be inter-viewed by Miss Packard for entrance. . . ."

As demand continued to increase two new teachers were recruited to the school. However, with the arrival of Sarah Champney in April of 1882 and Caroline Grover later the same year, the question of a more spacious and functional facility became even more pressing. Upon Miss Champney's arrival the main room was full and only one room remained—the coal bin! "So the coal bin with one small window for shoveling coal was her recitation room. It was hastily put in order and soon overflowed with students."

According to remarks made by Miss Grover during the school's tenth anniversary celebra-tion, the classroom space was divided in this manner: "At the desk was Miss Packard with her advanced classes of Fourth Reader, Fractions, and Green's Grammar. . . . At her right, near the window, Miss Giles's class was seated on three sides of a hollow square formed of the movable benches. The water from the movable street oozing through the wall glistened in the uncertain light. . . . In the opposite corner was another class arranged in the same hollow square [Miss Grover's class]. Here the words 'Loud! *Louder!'* were spoken since the only hope at times of hearing a recitation was by excelling in tone the other classes. In the coal-room Miss Champney held gentle sway with her open door to let in light and heat until the noise of the other classes led to the closing of it." —Miss Caroline Grover, 1891.

Yet somehow the crowded, noisy, and often inhospitable space was ably used for teaching. In later years, the "basement students" would recall, Miss Giles would break up a lot of little sticks and lay them across the seams of the planks, where there were planks, and make us count them, and take up one, and so they learned to add and subtract.

During this period Miss Packard and Miss Giles each taught ten or eleven classes per day, five and a half days per week. In addition, they each led four prayer meetings and four Bible readings, taught two Bible classes a week, made thirty-five to forty-five religious visits, and distributed in October about two hundred Bibles and tracts. "Tired, tired, tired, tired, tired, tired." —Packard diary entry, 1881.

Packard and Giles carried the banner for more room and better facilities north. In Cleveland they met John D. Rockefeller, who pledged 250 dollars toward the building fund. He told them, "You know, there are so many who come here and get us to give money. Then they're gone, and we don't know where they are—where their work is. Do you mean to stick? If you do, you'll hear from me again."

So began what was later described as the year of miracles. In June 1882, a group of several black ministers, including William Jefferson White, one of the three founders of Morehouse College, organized the Baptist Educational Society to establish a building fund for the school. Each member contributed five cents a month to the fund and the students were encouraged to recruit members. In less than three months 25 dollars was raised, representing the first fundraising effort by students.

In February 1883, the school relocated to its new nine-acre site, which included five frame buildings with both classroom and residence hall space.

A model school was opened and served a dual purpose. It provided practical experience for those pursuing a teaching career while also providing an elementary education to younger students, many of whom would later attend the Seminary School.

During this period, Dr. Morehouse and the American Baptist Home Mission felt that the society could not afford to pay for separate properties for men and women and hoped to con-

Howe Hall Chapel Service, ca. 1887.
(Courtesy Spelman College Archives)

solidate the Seminary School with the Atlanta Baptist Seminary. However, he told Packard that the new site could be devoted to the exclusive use of the women's school if they would take over the mortgage. Teachers volunteered their services, and gifts of furnishings, supplies, and clothing were sent from the North, but despite these contributions and cost-saving measures, in April 1884, on the third anniversary of its founding, the school found itself in dire straits.

During these darkest of days John D. Rockefeller arrived unannounced with Mrs. Rockefeller, her sister, and her mother, Mrs. Lucy Henry Spelman. Rockefeller was so impressed with the seminary that in yet another miraculous act, he settled the debt on the property. At Packard's suggestion to its governing boards, the school's name was changed to Spelman Seminary in honor and recognition of the Spelman family's longtime activism in the antislavery movement. The home of Mr. and Mrs. Buel Spelman had served as a station on the underground railroad for slaves on their journey north in search of freedom. At the school's three-year anniversary Mrs. Spelman would recall that the only meals she ever prepared on the Sabbath were for slaves journeying northward.

* * *

*"Every day of the week is filled full, from six in the morning to nine at night. . . .
The day begins with the rising bell at six, the devotion bell at half past and
breakfast at seven. The girls are busy before and after breakfast till school time,
with their room work and work in the kitchen, for the boarders take regular turns
in doing the entire housework of the establishment.*

*"At a quarter before nine all are expected to be in school. The first hour is spent in
devotional exercises, led by the Principal; then come recitations which last till two,
with a short recess and lunch at noon.*

*"Immediately after school, those taking music go to the music room, those whose
turn it is to wash to the laundry, others to the sewing room, and the remainder to
study hall excepting those who are taking lessons in type-setting and consequently go
to the printing office.*

*"Dinner comes at four, and at half past five the girls have a prayer meeting by
themselves, followed by general devotions in the chapel at six."*

—Sophia Packard, *The Spelman Messenger,* 1885

Spelman High School graduates, 1887.
(Courtesy Spelman College Archives)

As a result of their hard work and prayer, another milestone in the school's history was reached when diplomas were given to the first six women to complete the Higher Normal and Scientific Course. The first graduates from Spelman Seminary, members of the class of 1887, were Ella N. Barksdale, Clara A. Howard, Lou E. Mitchell, Adeline J. Smith, Sallie B. Waugh, and Ella L. Williams.

Even as Spelman progressed toward becoming a women's college, it continued to offer an industrial curriculum in an attempt to make education practical. Included in the department offerings were sewing, millinery, housekeeping, laundering, printing, and cooking. By 1901 Miss Giles could boast, "Certificates are given on the successful completion of a course in cooking which covers three years, with one lesson of an hour and a half each week. The equipment is good. In a large room there are sixteen sets of individual cooking outfits and eight small gas stoves. . . . "

During the school's early years the cooking classes, in addition to educating students, also prepared the students' meals. Staples such as flour and sugar were ordered from Atlanta. However, white delivery men refused to deliver them to the buildings. Instead, they threw them over the fence, forcing students and teachers to carry them to the kitchen.

In the kitchen students turned the offensive acts into sweet delight by creating delectable treats such as the following Ginger Cookies and Mother's Cake.

Cooking class in Laura Spelman Hall, ca. 1917.
(Courtesy Spelman College Archives)

Recipes from the Spelman Cooking School

GINGER COOKIES

1	cup shortening	2	teaspoons ginger
1	cup sugar	1	teaspoon cinnamon
2	eggs, well beaten	2	teaspoons soda
1	cup molasses	$^1/_2$	teaspoon salt
1	cup sour milk		Flour to roll

Cream the shortening, add the sugar and the eggs and beat well, then add the molasses and milk. Sift the spice, soda, and salt with three cups of the flour, add to the first mixture, and then add just enough more flour so that a small quantity can be handled at a time, on a well floured board. Do not roll too thin. Cut out and place some distance apart on a greased pan. Bake in a moderate oven.

MOTHER'S CAKE

$^3/_4$	cup butter	1	teaspoon mace
$1^1/_2$	cups sugar	$^2/_3$	cup milk
3	eggs, beaten separately	3	cups flour
1	teaspoon lemon or vanilla extract	4	teaspoons baking powder

Cream the butter, add the sugar gradually, then yolks of eggs and flavoring [extract]. Sift the mace, flour and baking powder and add alternately with the milk a little at a time, and then the stiffly beaten whites. Beat thoroughly.

If baked in a loaf it will require nearly an hour in a moderate oven. If baked in layers, about 20 minutes.

This cake may be varied by adding a cup of chopped nuts or raisins, or half a cup of chopped dates.

Frankie Quarles
(Courtesy Spelman College Archives)

When Frankie Quarles was first presented by her mother, an alum of the school and the widow of Reverend Frank Quarles, Miss Packard, perhaps in remembrance of all the Quarles family had done for them, refused to "receive a dollar for her education." From that root of loyal friendship and academic excellence, five generations of Spelman women would grow and experience the leadership of strongly committed Spelman presidents. Among them were leaders for a new era such as Lucy Hale Tapley.

New Leaders for a New Era

LUCY HALE TAPLEY

Before being elected to the presidency in March of 1910, Lucy Hale Tapley worked with the founders for twenty years. As president she specifically adopted Miss Packard's five aims for Spelman students:

Florence Read *(left)* **and Lucy Tapley** *(right)*
(Courtesy Spelman College Archives)

To train the intellect, to store the mind with useful knowledge, to induce habits of industry and desire for general information, to inspire a love for the true and the beautiful, to prepare the pupils for the practical duties of life—the hallmark of a liberal education.

During her administration, Tapley focused on industrial and teacher training, largely based on the fact that 99 of the 113 students enrolled in the first-year high school class elected a course of study in teacher preparation. Additionally, Tapley believed that Spelman students would make best use of their education by returning to their homes in rural communities to teach. According to Camilla Weems, '01, one of Tapley's students, she believed "that a teacher of clean habits, good character, high ideals, and having a noble aim in view, is one of the greatest assets for good that a community can have." In returning to their communities to teach, these students could exert an educational and Christian influence, which would gradually elevate their race and eventually improve upon the quality of students coming to Spelman. But as time changed, the programs changed.

Graduating Class, 1910.
(Courtesy Spelman College Archives)

During this period Spelman began moving toward its destiny as an institution of higher education for African-American women. Students pursuing a liberal arts education would receive degrees, while those majoring in secondary education and home economics education received diplomas, striking a balance between those seeking an academic education and Tapley's desire to see the school produce teachers as a means of bettering communities. On June 1, 1924, the name was officially changed to Spelman College.

FLORENCE MATILDA READ

"The most precious heritage left by Miss Read was her genuine concern with cultural values. Some of the most brilliant people throughout the world were brought to Spelman under Miss Read's aegis. There were scholars . . . scientists and explorers . . . lecturers and authors . . . and musicians. She was indeed wise because she did not bid us to enter the house of her wisdom, but led us to the threshold of our own minds."

—Millicent Dobbs Jordan (Spelman College '33)

Florence Read, former Executive Secretary of the International Health Division of the Rockefeller Foundation, was the first president without a close affiliation with the school, but she suc-

Spelman campus, ca. 1910.
(Courtesy Spelman College Archives)

cessfully developed Spelman into a strong liberal arts college. Recognizing that a strong endowment was fundamental to the success of this objective, she boldly made that a condition of her acceptance, and the trustees in turn used that condition as leverage in soliciting funds that eventually totaled more than $3,000,000. The board also voted to narrow the school's academic focus by eliminating departments that were outside of the college division.

The most significant event of Read's administration was the Agreement of Affiliation between Spelman College, Morehouse College, and Atlanta University in April 1929, which ultimately became the largest consortium of black colleges, later renamed the Atlanta University Center (AUC).

Read brought noted performers and other outstanding figures to the campus, among them Ralph Bunche, Sterling Brown, Margaret Walker, Vladimir Nabokov, Walter White, Langston Hughes, Mary McLeod Bethune, Julius Rosenwald, W.E.B. Du Bois, and Mordecai Johnson. "This kind of exposure broadened and enriched student attitudes toward themselves and their relationship to the universe, not just as black people but as individuals living in and contributing to a *world* community." —Albert E. Manley, fifth president of Spelman College.

Two male presidents succeeded Read. The first was Dr. Albert E. Manley, a graduate of Johnson C. Smith College, who earned his Ed.D. at Stanford University. During his tenure opportunities for black women increased, and as a result, Spelman women were academically prepared and encouraged to enter doors previously closed to them. These included the fields of medicine, law, international affairs, engineering, business, and industry. They were also encouraged to enter the best graduate and professional schools in the country.

In 1976 Manley was succeeded by Dr. Donald M. Stewart, the sixth president of the college. Dr. Stewart, with an A.B. from Grinnell, A.M. from Yale, and M.P.A. and D.P.A. from Harvard, brought a new perspective and academic focus to Spelman. As opportunities for black women of excellence and achievement increased, Stewart ensured that Spelman women were prepared to meet the challenges of a more competitive and complex professional environment by enhancing the college's academic offerings. A thorough review of the curriculum resulted in the development of a writing workshop to improve critical thinking and writing skills. The honors program, continuing education program for nontraditional students, and computer literacy program were initiated. The women's studies program, initiated under the Stewart administration, offered courses in women's studies, presented conferences and symposia, and published a journal. Finally, the endowment was increased from nine to 41 million dollars.

DR. JOHNNETTA BETSCH COLE

On April 25, 1987, Dr. Johnnetta B. Cole became the first black woman president in Spelman's 107-year history. Affectionately referred to as "Sister President" by Spelman students, the former professor of anthropology at Hunter College and director of Latin American and Caribbean studies at the City University of New York, Dr. Cole brought a wealth of scholarly achievement and demonstrated leadership to the college. At her inauguration, Drs. Bill and Camille Cosby made a 20-million-dollar donation to the college for the construction of the Camille O. Hanks Cosby Academic Center, representing at the time the largest single gift from individuals to any historically black college and university. Under Dr. Cole's leadership, Spelman received a coveted number one rating by *U.S. News and World Report* in its 1992 "Best College Buys" issue. Additionally, she spearheaded the most successful major capital campaign in the history of the college and also served on president-elect Clinton's transition team as cluster coordinator for education, labor, and the arts and humanities.

Dr. Cole also ushered in a new era of commitment to the community. "No one is free from the kind of community service that leads to both stronger communities and a just nation. Spelman was born for service." With this philosophy, she established the Johnnetta B. Cole Institute for Community Service and Community Building as an integral part of life at Spelman College.

AUDREY FORBES MANLEY, M.D.

In 1997, Dr. Audrey Manley, the first alumna to lead the college, was inaugurated as the eighth president of Spelman College. In the words of sister Spelman alum and chairwoman of the Spelman Board of Trustees June Gary Hopps, "Dr. Manley has improved our academic standing considerably. . . . She has been responsible for the recruitment of new faculty, initiating an increase in merit pay and adjusting salaries of faculty members to bring them within the 50 percentile of Baccalaureate I Institutions.

"We've also seen more outstanding students enter Spelman College in the last four years, and last year, we recruited the largest freshman class in the college's history. In addition, we have expanded the number of Phi Beta Kappa graduates, and established the Epsilon Georgia Chapter of Phi Beta Kappa Honor Society.

"As a result of her visionary leadership, we have acquired as much land as we could possibly get in adjoining communities that will someday house more recreational facilities for students.

"I think history will record Dr. Manley's tenure as one of the most prolific fund-raising administrations of our time. She has introduced us to new sources of revenue for the college, generating more than 60 million dollars through fund-raising initiatives in the past four years."

DR. BEVERLY DANIEL TATUM

In the spring of 2002, Dr. Beverly Daniel Tatum was appointed the ninth president of Spelman College. She has initiated a strategic plan for Spelman that includes five goals—academic excellence, leadership development, improving the infrastructure, improving the visibility of accomplishments of the campus community, and exemplary [staff] customer service—all designed to create a vision for Spelman of "Nothing Less than the Best."

"I believe in the school and the women who have charge of it."

—John D. Rockefeller to Sophia Packard in a letter dated January 1884

FRESH PEACH LEMONADE

Georgia peaches never tasted so good! This delicious drink, which celebrates the marriage of Georgia peaches and southern lemonade, produces a wonderfully unique beverage.

3 peaches, peeled and chopped	Peach slices
1¹/₂ cups granulated sugar	Mint sprigs
4 cups water	
1 cup freshly squeezed lemon juice	

Combine the peaches, sugar, and water in a saucepan; mix well and bring to a boil over medium-high heat. Reduce heat and allow mixture to simmer until the sugar dissolves, approximately 10 minutes. Remove from heat and cool before straining into a large pitcher by pressing through a sieve to extract as much juice as possible.

Stir in the lemon juice, adjust flavor to taste, chill, and serve in tall, ice-filled glasses. Garnish each glass with a peach slice and a mint sprig.

Makes 8 servings.

PEACH NECTAR LEMONADE

Peach nectar is a sweet contrast to the pucker-up tartness of lemons, and it provides a new twist to this summertime favorite.

2	cups water	$^3/_4$	cup fresh lemonade
$^3/_4$	cup sugar		Spearmint sprigs for garnish
4	12-ounce cans peach nectar		Rock candy stirrer

In a saucepan combine the water and sugar, bring the mixture to a boil over medium-high heat, stirring until the sugar dissolves. Reduce the heat and simmer for an additional 5 minutes. Allow the mixture to cool, pour into a serving pitcher, and refrigerate to chill. Stir in the remaining ingredients and pour into tall, freezer frosted, ice-filled glasses. Garnish with a fresh sprig of mint. To frost glasses, set them on a tray in the freezer compartment until covered with frost. For an even more delightful presentation, dip the rims in tinted sugar and fill with beverage or return unfilled glasses to the sugar to set properly. Throw in a matching rock candy stirrer for a little added pizzaz. Go ahead, you've got plenty!

Makes 4 servings.

PEACH NECTAR IN A MASON JAR

If you have plenty, a Mason jar is as acceptable as Waterford crystal when the offering is as delicious and refreshing as this one.

3	12-ounce cans peach nectar		1	quart carbonated lemon-lime
$1/3$	cup sugar			soda
$1/2$	cup fresh lemonade			

Combine the first three ingredients in a two-quart serving pitcher. Mix well until the sugar dissolves and refrigerate to chill. Just before serving, add the carbonated lemon soda. Stir well and pour into tall, ice-filled Mason jars.

Makes 4 to 6 servings.

SPARKLING LEMONADE

Club soda adds a bubbly, refreshing new twist to this perennial favorite.

2	cups water		1	14-liter bottle club soda
$3^1/4$	cups sugar			Lemon slices
$3^1/4$	cups lemon juice			

Combine water and sugar in a large saucepan and cook over medium-high heat while stirring until the sugar dissolves. Remove from heat and cool slightly. Stir in lemon juice; cover and refrigerate until well chilled. Pour mixture into a pitcher and gradually stir in the club soda. Garnish with lemon slices and serve in tall, ice-filled glasses.

Makes 10 cups.

"When you are inducted into the Spelman sisterhood in a candlelight ceremony, you are given the power to change your life and to light the world. When you graduate, you walk into the Oval and through the Arch, the same path past graduates have taken. For 120 years now, Spelman has sought to develop the total person: to instill in our students a sense of responsibility for bringing about positive change in the world. This is our heritage and our calling."

—Spelman Admissions Brochure

Spelman students under the arch, ca. 1915.
(Courtesy Spelman College Archives)

"What follows are the stories of ordinary women who were early inductees into the Spelman Sisterhood. With extraordinary hearts and hands committed to labor and service, they blazed trails and made a difference in their local communities, country and global community. In doing so, they defined what we know today as the 'Spelman Woman.' We celebrate the women of that era—we know those still living as Golden Girls and Diamond Daughters who set a standard of excellence as Spelman women."

—Dr. Beverly Daniel Tatum

A Tale of Three Spelman Sisters and Their Missions

NORA ANTONIO GORDON (H.S. 1887)

Nora Antonia Gordon, the first Seminary student to enter missionary service in Africa, was born in Columbus, Georgia, on August 25, 1866. After graduating from Spelman, she received a teaching position in Atlanta, which she soon resigned to embark on the great work of her life—missionary work in Palabala in the Congo.

Before departing for Africa, she stopped in Washington, D.C., and then traveled north to Boston and Wollaston, Massachusetts, the founder's hometown. The visit prompted her to write to Miss Giles that "I see what pleasant surroundings you had to leave and somewhat of the sacrifice that you have made. I have always appreciated my teachers, but more so now than ever."

For two years Nora labored at Palabala. However, in early 1891 Nora, very much in need of a rest, visited Lukungu, a station 220 miles from the mouth of the Congo. While in Africa, she frequently wrote letters home

Nora A. Gordon
(Courtesy Spelman College Archives)

and occasionally sent a box of curios back to her beloved Spelman. It is likely that Spelmanite Clara Howard was privy to Nora's letters describing her missionary work, and that these communications from Nora as well as Clara's own interest in missionary work fueled her desire to enter the field with an appointment from the Foreign Mission Board.

CLARA A. HOWARD, SPELMAN SEMINARY 1887, VALEDICTORIAN

Upon graduating from Spelman Seminary in 1887, class valedictorian Clara A. Howard immediately received a position in Atlanta's school system, but continued to board at Spelman Seminary. However, in 1890 she received a long-awaited appointment and left for Lukungo where she pioneered missionary work on the French Congo from 1890 to 1895. While there she was also reunited with her Spelman sister Nora Gordon.

On September 25, 1891, Clara wrote to her friends back home: "Doubtless Nora has told you of my change to this place. You can not imagine how glad we are to be together here. I have charge of the printing-office and help in the afternoon school. I am well, happy, and am enjoying my work. In the office I have few conveniences and really not the things we need. Mr. Hoste has written the first arithmetic in this language and I am now putting it up. I was obliged to stop work on it to-day because my figures in type gave out, and you know we have no shops in this land. My boys in the office are doing nicely."

Clara was enthusiastic about her work, and of her service Nora would write: "Miss Howard is in charge of one of the best primary schools in the Congo. She has about 100 pupils . . . [and] has the sole care of thirty little boys whose ages range from three to thirteen. In the morning she looks after their baths and clean suits, gives them food, takes them to the chapel for service, has them in the primary schools; in the afternoon she sends them out to do gardening, and at night gathers them about her and tells them the

Clara A. Howard
(Courtesy Spelman College Archives)

story of Jesus and His love. It is impossible to describe the transformation which has taken place in these little lives during the past two years."

By 1895 poor health forced her friend, Nora's return to America, accompanied by two native girls. "Two years later Clara was forced to end her missionary work, due to frequent bouts with malaria. Nevertheless, she left behind a legacy of international service to Spelman College as a long-term staff member, and service to the Atlanta community. Both distinguished themselves in their professions as well as in their daily lives." —From *Black Women in America,* Vol. 1 by Elsa Barkly Brown

EMMA B. DELANEY

Despite political unrest, disease, and other hardships, at least three other graduates followed Nora and Clara to Africa, but for many generations to follow, other Spelman women would emulate their example of unselfish service and sacrifice. Among them were Ada Jackson And Emma B. Delaney, who became the fifth Spelmanite to venture forth on the missionary field when she sailed to Nyasaland in British East Africa. Her completion of Spelman's nurses training course helped her provide medical assistance to the natives. However, of almost greater significance was the school she established to train native leaders. It was in full operation three years later, when poor health forced her return to America. A sixteen-year-old boy with whom she had become acquainted in Africa ran away and followed her stateside, determined to receive an American education. They were both guests of Clara Howard while visiting Spelman for several days. During this visit, Emma's ward, Daniel Malekebu, met Flora Zeto, a young African girl who had returned to America with Miss Howard. During their time together they shared their dreams of someday returning to Africa and working toward effecting change.

After Daniel received his medical degree in 1919, the pair were married in Spelman's chapel. A year later they set sail for Nyasaland, where they

Emma B. Delaney
(Courtesy Spelman College Archives)

built a mission on the ruins of one previously started by Emma. Eventually the eleven-building mission would include a church, a hospital, and three school buildings, one of which was named Spelman Hall because Spelman had provided the first money for the building program. In this way the work of Clara Howard and Emma Delaney continued through the next generation, and their work continues to this day as the mission remains in operation.

WATERMELON LEMONADE

8   cups watermelon, cubed and
        seeded
$^1/_2$ cup raspberries
$^1/_4$ cup water

$^1/_2$ cup sugar
$^3/_4$ cup fresh lemon juice
$^1/_4$ cup pineapple juice

Process the watermelon, raspberries, and water in a food processor until they are blended smooth. Strain the mixture through a fine mesh strainer into a serving pitcher. Stir in sugar, lemon juice, and pineapple juice until sugar dissolves. Refrigerate until thoroughly chilled, approximately 1 hour. Serve in tall, chilled, ice-filled glasses.

Makes 4 to 6 servings.

BLUEBERRY LEMONADE

Matchless!

5 cups water, divided	Zest and juice from 6 large lemons
1¼ to 1½ cups sugar, or to taste, divided	1¼ cups fresh blueberries

In a medium saucepan, combine 2 cups of the water with 1¼ cups of the sugar and bring to a boil over medium heat, stirring until the sugar dissolves and forms syrup. Increase the heat to medium-high and cook an additional 5 minutes, or until the syrup begins to thicken slightly. Stir in the remaining 3 cups of water, lemon zest, and juice; remove from heat and set aside.

Purée the berries and add them to the syrup. Allow the mixture to cool at room temperature for at least 1 hour. Adjust taste with the remaining sugar, and strain the lemonade into a large pitcher to remove the seeds and skins. Chill until ready to serve. Pour into tall, ice-filled glasses.

Makes 4 to 6 servings.

Our Sewing School

"This part of our work is by no means least. The girls are all required to learn this very necessary branch of education.

"We invite you to enter the Industrial Hall at three o'clock P.M., after the regular school work is over for the day. The girls are all at work and the room is full to overflowing as are all the rooms at Spelman Seminary.

"To describe the different kinds of sewing, upon which these pupils are engaged, would be a difficult task. Some are just learning, and of course their work is suitable for beginners. Others have such work as they are qualified to perform. Some are cutting garments, some sewing on the machine and all are as busy as bees.

Students in sewing class, ca. 1920.
(Courtesy Spelman College Archives)

Most of the pupils prefer using the machine, but they are required by their teacher to become quite proficient in the art of hand-sewing first.

"Three prizes have been offered for the best samples of the following—sewing, button hole making and darning, to be given at the close of school. Naturally the pupils are all striving for one of the three."

—Sophia B. Packard, *Spelman Messenger,* 1885

"Some students were more successful than others as indicated by the following: A member of my class had a terrible accident one day. She cut two sleeves for the same arm, as if the person had two right or two left arms. Miss ——— had to cut a waist one day and she forgot that the young lady had a neck, so she sewed the place completely up. The worse luck I ever had was—I went to cut a collar fourteen inches and made it only seven, but the teacher never knew anything about this you know."

—Lula Eberhardt, *Spelman Messenger,* June 1900

Victoria Maddox Simmons

"No person can ever tell how much the world owes to its mothers and good guardians. They . . . can never think too highly of that grand work of training children, for they never know for what glorious work they are training them. The mother, grandmother and Spelman Seminary have given to Georgia, in the person of Victoria W. Maddox, a woman in which the race might be justly proud."

—Reverend E. R. Carter, *The Black Side of Atlanta*

Victoria was the first of many Spelman women who would return to their alma mater to teach. She entered the basement school in 1881 as a member of the first class. Later when the school was moved to the barracks, she was among the first boarding students. While still a student, she taught at the Model School. During this period she also set type for the *Spelman Messenger.* After her graduation in 1888, she taught in the Model School for one year prior to accepting a teaching position at the Howe Institute of Memphis, Tennessee.

Victoria Maddox Simmons
(Courtesy Spelman College Archives)

Two years later she returned to Spelman to take the missionary training course, which she completed in 1893. She later married a preacher and the couple raised eight children. After her husband's death she returned to full-time teaching, and taught until her retirement in 1946. Ten years later an Atlanta public elementary school was named in her honor.

PINEAPPLE LEMON-LIMEADE

Surprise your guests with this classically tasty, yet unique lemonade!

2 cups sugar	$1/2$ cup fresh lemon juice
2 cups water	$1/2$ cup lime juice
2 cups unsweetened pineapple juice	5 lemon slices
2 cups seltzer or sparkling water	5 lime slices
	8 mint sprigs

Combine sugar with water and bring to a boil over medium-high heat. Stir until sugar dissolves, reduce heat and allow mixture to simmer undisturbed for 10 minutes. Cool syrup to room temperature and stir in pineapple juice, seltzer, and remaining juices. Pour into tall, ice-filled glasses. Garnish with lemon and lime slices and mint sprigs.

Makes 6 servings.

CRANBERRY PINK LEMONADE

Pretty in pink!

2	cups white sugar	2	cups fresh lemon juice
9	cups water	1	cup cranberry juice, chilled

Combine the above ingredients in a large pitcher. Stir mixture until the sugar dissolves and refrigerate to chill. Pour into tall, ice-filled glasses and garnish with fresh mint.

Makes 12 servings.

Students in benchwork class, ca. 1890.
(Courtesy Spelman College Archives)

GEORGIA PEACH TEA

This refreshing tea is a delicious reminder that Georgia is the peach tree state!

4	11.5-ounce cans peach nectar	1¼	cups sugar
2½	quarts brewed tea, chilled	¼	cup lemon juice

Combine the above ingredients, mix well, and refrigerate to chill. Serve in tall, chilled, ice filled-glasses.

Makes approximately 1 gallon (10 servings).

SWEET GEORGIA PEACH ICED TEA

Sweet, sweet Georgia peach tea. Peaches are the golden child of summer, and this refreshing drink is the liquid gold standard of Southern hospitality.

8	cups boiling water	2½	cups cold water
8	tea bags		Fresh peach slices (choose one
	1-inch cinnamon stick		or two that are slightly
1	cup sugar		under-ripe and firm)
48	ounces peach nectar		Fresh basil to garnish

In a large heat-proof container, pour boiling water over the tea bags and cinnamon stick; steep for 5 minutes. Remove and discard the tea bags. Refrigerate the tea to chill. Before serving, add the sugar, nectar, and water; mix well until the sugar dissolves. Transfer the tea to a serving pitcher, and pour into ice-filled glasses. Garnish with a fresh Georgia peach slice and a sprig of basil.

Makes 8 to 10 servings.

Margaret Nabrit Curry
(Courtesy Spelman College Archives)

Margaret Nabrit Curry

A year after graduating from Spelman in 1924, Margaret returned to the school as the first black to be appointed to the Spelman College faculty. (Victoria Maddox Simmons [1888, MT 1893] was the first Spelmanite to teach at Spelman Seminary before it became a college.) Except for leaving for short periods to pursue advanced degrees, she remained on staff for more than forty years.

One of her first duties was to organize the history department, which she eventually chaired for twenty years. She also served as dean of women. Her success and drive are not surprising as she came from a family of achievers. Her father and two brothers all graduated from Morehouse College. One brother was a member of the legal team that successfully argued *Brown v. Board of Education.*

My First Impression of Spelman

"During my summer vacation I was dreaming of Spelman, wondering what kind of school it was and how it looked. I asked many girls who had been here before about Spelman. They told me how interesting it was. I wanted to come and see for myself.

"On September 20, 1927, I came to the beautiful place. When entering the gate I noticed the beautiful campus and the lovely driveway. I think the old girls were very glad of their driveway. I did not look at the buildings very much. That was because I was very tired. The lady brought me to Morehouse Hall. The first thing that I saw was an interesting sign: 'Welcome ye Freshies' in green letters.

My room was a very nice room.

"The next morning was a lovely morning at Spelman. . . . The chapel hours every

morning during Freshman week were very sweet and touching. I began to like Chapel hours. I was always glad for the night to pass so morning would come for Chapel. . . . If heaven is as beautiful as the Sisters Chapel, I do hope that I shall get there. When Miss Glode led us into the Chapel, I thought I was in another world. I wanted to sit in there all day and look. Last week when school opened I dressed early, and wanted 8 o'clock to hurry up, so I cold hear the pipe organ. When the music started tears came into my eyes at the sound of the sweet music."

—Rosa Strickland, 1931

"When you enter Sisters Chapel, you immediately feel the spirit of hundreds of thousands of people who have gathered here for over seventy-five years for various occasions. Something there is about Sisters Chapel that blurs lines that separate our lives into the past, the present and the future. Something there is about Sisters

Sisters Chapel
(Courtesy Spelman College Archives)

Chapel that gives us clarity about the present, appreciation for the past, and direction for the future. Something there is about Sisters Chapel that makes it a place in which memories resound with harmony."

—Author unknown

"Of all the things that we have done as a family, Spelman stands among the best."

—John D. Rockefeller, on the occasion of Spelman's fiftieth anniversary

SUMMERTIME TEA

Summer living is definitely easy with this cool invigorating tea. Try this Southern summertime classic for a jubilantly refreshing celebration of the season. Enjoy!

5	cups water		1/2	teaspoon ground cinnamon
2 1/2	cups pineapple juice		1/4	teaspoon ground cloves
1	cup fresh orange juice		5	tea bags (black, orange pekoe)
1/2	cup granulated sugar or to taste			

Bring water to a boil over medium-high heat; stir in juices, sugar, and spices. Bring to a second boil; reduce heat and simmer until the sugar dissolves. Remove saucepan from heat and add tea bags. Steep the tea for 4 to 5 minutes. Remove and discard the tea bags and allow mixture to cool to room temperature before refrigerating to chill. Serve over ice in 4 tall, chilled, ice-filled glasses.

Makes 4 servings.

TROPICAL FRUIT TEA

Relive your escape to the tropics with every tasty sip.

1	10-ounce package frozen raspberries, thawed
3	cups water
1/3	cup sugar
1	family size tea bag
2	cups red grape juice
1/4	cup lime juice

1	lemon, sliced
1	lime, sliced
1	orange, sliced thin
7	strawberries, hulled and sliced thin
1	16-ounce bottle sparkling orange drink, chilled

Purée raspberries and press through a fine wire-mesh strainer into a large container, discarding remaining pulp. Set puréed mixture aside and bring water and sugar to a boil over medium-high heat, stirring often to prevent scorching. Remove from heat and add the tea bag. Cover and steep 5 minutes. Remove the tea bag with a slotted spoon, squeezing gently. Allow the tea mixture to cool. Combine the tea mix-

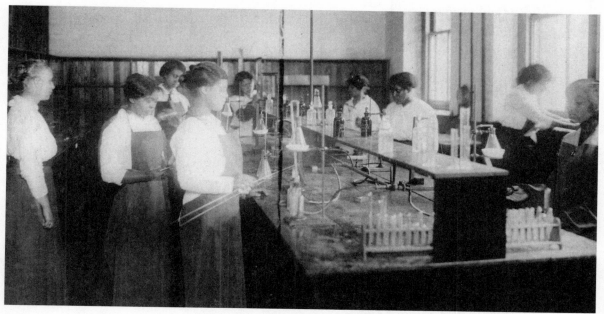

Students in chemistry class, ca. 1890.
(Courtesy Spelman College Archives)

ture with the remaining ingredients except orange drink; mix well and chill. Add orange soda immediately before serving in tall, ice-filled, chilled glasses.

Makes 8 to 10 servings.

Romae Turner Powell, Spelman '47

In 1973 Romae Powell became the first black in Georgia history to be named to a full judgeship of a Georgia Court of Record, and she served as a Fulton County juvenile judge from 1973 to 1990. Her keen legal skills and professionalism were recognized by Governor Busbee, who appointed her to the state crime commission where she chaired the Committee on Serious and Repeated Offenders. A graduate of Howard Law School, she specialized in juvenile law and justice, presided over the Georgia Council of Juvenile Court Judges, and dedicated her life and career to serving children. Atlanta's Judge Romae T. Powell Juvenile Justice Center & Mechanicsville Library Branch Complex was named in her honor and memory.

SUMMER HIBISCUS TEA COOLER

Reminiscent of the rose-colored iced drinks served during Caribbean street carnivals, this tea is best made 12 to 24 hours before serving.

8 tea bags (choose Red Zinger or any other tea containing hibiscus flowers)
1 cinnamon stick
4 cups boiling water
1 quart chilled pineapple juice

1 quart chilled sparkling water
1 1/2 cups orange juice
1 tablespoon fresh squeezed lemon juice
Orange slices for garnish

Add tea bags and cinnamon stick to the boiling water and steep 30 minutes. Remove and discard the tea bags and cinnamon stick; refrigerate the tea for approximately 12 hours or overnight.

Combine the tea with the pineapple juice, sparkling water, orange juice, and lemon juice. Stir. Adjust flavor to taste by adding additional water and/or sugar. Serve over ice in tall, chilled glasses and garnish with orange slices.

Makes 18 servings.

JAMAICAN HIBISCUS DRINK

8 cups water	1¼ teaspoons grated fresh ginger
2 cups dried hibiscus blossoms (sometimes called sorrel blossoms, they can be found in Jamaican or Mexican markets)	1¼ cups sugar, or to taste Jamaican rum to taste (optional)

Bring water to boil in a 4-quart stainless steel or other non-reactive pot. Add the hibiscus and ginger. Remove from heat; cover and steep for 4 hours before straining and sweetening to taste. Chill and serve just as it is or add very good rum, according to your taste.

Makes 2 quarts.

CRANBERRY TEA

Equally enjoyable year-round and a surprising eye-opener, this tangy cranberry drink is a great accompaniment to Thanksgiving dinner—or great heated as a winter drink.

1 gallon water	2 cups orange juice
1 cup granulated sugar	2 tablespoons lime juice
15 tea bags	
1 12-ounce can frozen cranberry juice concentrate, partially thawed and undiluted	

Bring water to a boil; add sugar and stir until dissolved. Add tea bags and steep 4 to 5 minutes, or to taste. Stir in juices and allow the tea to cool at room temperature before refrigerating. Serve in six tall, ice-filled glasses.

Makes 6 servings.

Spelman and Morehouse baccalaureate service, 1928.
(Courtesy Spelman College Archives)

Christine King Farris, Spelman '48

For more than forty-five years Christine King Farris has been an associate professor of education and director of the Learning Resources Center at Spelman College. In addition, she is founder and chair of the Martin Luther King, Jr., Child Development Center. Mrs. Farris is also vice chair and treasurer of the Martin Luther King, Jr., Center for Non Violent Social Change, Inc. In building a living memorial to her brother, Professor Farris recalls, "I didn't realize until I looked back what kind of leadership it took to get the job [of raising funds] done. . . . When I was out there going to banks, foundations, and corporate offices to raise money, many times I was the only female in the room. But Spelman prepared me because you had a sense of self and you didn't think anything was impossible. You just went on and moved on."

The last surviving sibling of Dr. Martin Luther King, Jr., she has introduced a new generation of children to her brother's life and legacy in *My Brother Martin: A Sister Remembers.* She depicts him not as a martyred civil rights leader with a dream, but as a young boy who loved games, hated piano lessons, and grew up in segregated Atlanta. Professor Farris stresses how everyone can pursue the dream. "Were Martin alive today, he would still be pushing for it, knowing that we still do not have a level playing field. [He gave us the] blueprint; we have to carry it out." And that "we" means everyone.

WATERMELON PUNCH IN A WATERMELON SHELL

Cool, ruby red slices of watermelon set in dew-kissed emerald shells are almost emblematic of summer. It's a shame to just eat them when they also make delicious drinks. When selecting a melon look for one that feels heavy for its size. The rind should be bright green, without bruises, dents or cuts, with a cream-colored or buttery yellow underside. The stem should be green and fresh looking. And finally, it should produce a resonant sound, not a dull thud, when thumped.

1   large watermelon
1³/₄   cups sugar
1¹/₄   cups water
1   tablespoon fresh lime juice

1   33.8-ounce bottle sparkling
     lemon-lime drink
     Fresh mint leaves (optional)

Cut a thin slice of melon from the bottom (buttery yellow side) of the melon, just enough to stabilize it when you turn it over. Turn melon over. It should sit flat on the table or counter without rolling or tilting. Slice the top ¹/₃ of the melon away. The pink flesh should be exposed with sufficient shell left to form a bowl once the pulp has been scooped from it.

Scoop pulp from the melon, remove the seeds, and mash the pulp. Measure 1 gallon of juice from the pulp and set aside. Next, use a paring knife to scallop or make other decorations to the edge of the watermelon shell.

Combine sugar, water, and lime juice in a saucepan; bring the mixture to a boil over medium-high, reduce heat, and simmer 5 minutes. Add the mixture to the reserved watermelon juice and chill. Before serving, add the lemon-lime drink and mix gently. Pour the punch into the watermelon shell and sprinkle the top with 5 to 7 fresh mint leaves.

Makes 18 ¹/₂-cup servings.

GOLDEN PEACH NECTAR PUNCH

As light and refreshing as morning dew, this sweet nectar is absolutely delectable.

2   liters lemon-lime soda
2   quarts peach nectar

2   quarts pineapple juice
¹/₂   cup lemon juice

Combine the above ingredients. Mix well and pour into an ice-filled punch bowl just before serving.

Makes 24 servings.

LEGACY & LACE: A LAVENDER TEA PUNCH

2   cups water
$^2/_3$ cup sugar
3   tablespoons snipped fresh
       mint
1   large stem of unsprayed fresh
       lavender

$^1/_2$ cup orange juice
1   cup pineapple juice
$^1/_4$ cup lemon juice
2   cups strong brewed tea
1   1-liter bottle club soda, chilled

Combine the water, sugar, mint, and lavender in a large stainless-steel or non-reactive pan. Bring the mixture to a rapid boil over medium-high heat before removing from heat and allowing it to steep for 20 minutes. Next, strain mixture through a cotton cheesecloth-lined colander.

Add the juices and tea to the lavender infused water and chill. Immediately before serving add the club soda.

Makes 16 servings.

A SUMMER REUNION FRUIT PUNCH FOR FIFTY

As refreshing as it is delicious! And remember this tip: When planning your event, count on 350 cubes of ice for 50 people, or seven per person.

$3^1/_2$ cups sugar
1   pint hot tea
2   cups fresh lemon juice
3   quarts orange juice
1   quart pineapple juice
3   quarts ice water

1   quart ginger ale
1   cup sliced strawberries
1   cup pineapple chunks with
       juice
1   cup sliced white grapes

Commencement reception, 1961.
(Courtesy Spelman College Archives)

Combine the above ingredients and mix well. Store in batches in the refrigerator until needed to fill or refill the punch bowl. To serve, pour into ice-filled punch bowl.

Makes 50 servings.

Marian Wright Edelman, Spelman '60

"Education remains one of the black community's most enduring values. It is sustained by the belief that freedom and education go hand in hand. . . . "

—Marian Wright Edelman in *Black America,* 1989

"When I was sitting where you are, we were getting thrown out of the gallery of the legislature where Julian Bond, Grace Hamilton, and others sit today. We were going

to jail. . . . We were picketing Rich's and Davison's, whose lunch counters and jobs
were closed to us even with a Spelman degree."

—Marian Wright Edelman, in a 1980 speech to the graduating class of Spelman

Marian Wright Edelman, founder and president of the Children's Defense Fund, was the youngest of five children and credits her Baptist preacher father with instilling in her an obligation to right wrongs. When African Americans in her hometown were not allowed to enter city parks, her father built a park for African-American children behind his church.

Edelman is a graduate of Spelman College and Yale Law School. As director of the NAACP Legal Defense and Education Fund office in Jackson, Mississippi, she became the first African-American female admitted to the Mississippi bar. She also was nationally recognized as an advocate for Head Start at this time. In 1968, Edelman moved to Washington, D.C., and became counsel to the Poor People's Campaign organized by Dr. Martin Luther King, Jr. She founded the Washington Research Project, where she lobbied Congress for child and family nutrition programs and expanding Head Start. In 1973, the Washington Research Project became the Children's Defense Fund (CDF), the United States' leading advocacy group for children. As president of the CDF, Edelman has worked to decrease teenage pregnancy, increase Medicaid coverage for poor children, and secure government funding for programs like Head Start.

Marian Wright with Charles Merrill, 1959.
(Courtesy Spelman College Archives)

Edelman has served as director of the Center for Law and Education at Harvard and is the first African-American female on the board of Yale. Her publications include *The Measure of Our Success: A Letter to My Children and Yours*. Edelman's awards include the Albert Schweitzer Humanitarian Prize, the Heinz Award, the Ella J. Baker Prize, the MacArthur Foundation Fellowship Prize, and the Presidential Medal of Freedom, the nation's highest civilian award.

"Service is a rent you pay for living."

—Marian Wright Edelman

PINEAPPLE PUNCH

This is a wonderful punch to serve to younger children because, when spilled, it is less likely to stain than other fruit punches. When serving it to the very youngest partygoers, however, omit the cherries; toddlers or other young children may choke on them.

1	46-ounce can pineapple juice	10	ounces Maraschino cherries with juice (optional)
1	liter lemon-lime soda		

Combine the above chilled ingredients in a bowl, mix well, and add ice. While not necessary, chilling your punch ingredients before serving permits the use of less ice to chill the punch and also slows its melting time, making for a less watery punch.

Makes 30 servings.

WHITE GRAPE PINEAPPLE PUNCH

As delicious as it is lovely!

1	16-ounce can white grape juice	1	6-ounce can frozen lemonade juice concentrate
2	12-ounce cans pineapple juice concentrate	¼	cup lime juice Ice

Combine grape juice, pineapple juice, lemonade concentrate, and lime juice in a punch bowl. Mix well until concentrate is thoroughly blended. Add ice and mix well to chill at least 15 minutes before serving, allowing the ice to dilute the fruit concentrates. Add water to taste, if necessary, just before serving.

Makes 24 servings.

Ruby Doris Smith Robinson

"The civil rights movement of the 1950s and 1960s was largely carried by women whose organizing skills and political consciousness evolved from years of unflagging involvement in social change. The success of the Black freedom struggle was a result of the courageous leadership and selfless commitment of women who dedicated their lives to the vision of a free and just society."

—Ella Baker, civil rights activist

One of those women who dedicated her life to the cause was Ruby Doris Smith Robinson. She was born in Atlanta, Georgia, on April 25, 1942, to Reverend and Mrs. James Smith.

Ruby Doris Smith
(Courtesy Spelman College Archives)

Upon being accepted by Spelman College, she became a member of another community of women and heir to a legacy of social activism in action.

"By the spring of 1960, Ruby Doris was caught in a struggle which would change the world forever—the civil rights movement. As a freshwoman at Spelman College, Ruby—along with Julian Bond and others—organized the Atlanta Committee on Appeal for Human Rights. She was one of the original freedom riders in Jackson, Mississippi. In 1963 Ruby Doris withdrew from Spelman and devoted full time service to S.N.C.C. Like many other sisters of all kinds, Ruby Doris managed to maintain a very active role in the civil rights movement while continuing her education and maintaining her family life. Returning to Spelman in 1964, she completed a bachelor of science degree. Ruby Doris died of a rare cancer on October 7, 1967, at the age of 25. A news release from S.N.C.C. said this: 'During her 7 years in the movement, she was the heart of S.N.C.C. as well as one of the committee's dedicated administrators. . . . ' Now there are many 'sheroes' of the Civil Rights Movement . . . But none stands out more for me than a Spelman student. Her name: Ruby Doris Smith . . . We must never forget her story."

—Dr. Johnetta Cole at the fifth meeting of President's Commission on the
Celebration of Women in American History, held on January 15, 1999,
at the Martin Luther King, Jr. Center in Atlanta, Georgia

All gave some. Some gave all!

FESTIVE CRANBERRY PUNCH

A lovely holiday punch; it is chilled by the fruit concentrates without being diluted by melting ice.

64 ounces cranberry juice	1 quart carbonated lemon-lime
1 quart pineapple juice	soda
1 cup granulated sugar	

Combine cranberry juice, pineapple juice, and sugar. Stir mixture until sugar dissolves and freeze. Prior to serving, thaw juice in covered punch bowl until it forms a solid slush, approximately 1 hour. Add soda just prior to serving, mix well.

Makes 36 servings.

EVERYTHING RASPBERRY PUNCH

2 12-ounce cans frozen concentrated raspberry-kiwi juice, partially thawed	1 gallon raspberry sherbet Fresh raspberries, washed
2 2-liter bottles raspberry crème soda, chilled	

Combine raspberry-kiwi juice concentrate and raspberry soda in a large punch bowl. Use an ice cream scoop to gently add large scoops of sherbet to the mixture. Add ice to taste or as necessary to keep mixture chilled. Garnish with fresh raspberries just before serving.

Makes 48 servings.

Bernice Johnson Reagon

A specialist in African-American oral history, performance, and protest traditions, in 2002 the multifaceted Dr. Bernice Johnson Reagon returned to Spelman College as the first alumna to be named a William and Camille Olivia Hanks Cosby Endowed Professor. An historian, scholar, composer, and song leader, she is renowned for her scholarly work as a folklorist, curator, and founding director of the Program in Black American Culture at the Smithsonian Institution National Museum of American History in Washington, D.C. She is equally recognized as the founder of the internationally acclaimed, award-winning a cappella quintet, Sweet Honey in the Rock.

Reagon entered Albany State College in 1959 as a music major but was suspended in her junior year for marching with the movement in Albany, Georgia, for which she spent three days in jail. "When I got out of jail in '61, I went to a mass meeting and I was hoarse because I sang all the time in the jail. I opened my mouth to sing . . . I never heard that voice before. It was very similar to the way people describe religious conversion. . . . I started to talk, and I had a new talk. I started to walk, and I had a new walk. For the first time I really understood what was in that singing that I had heard all my life."

Reagon transferred to Spelman College, where she studied voice and history. There she was encouraged to use songs as historical documents in a research paper. She then began to appreciate her experiences in jail and fully realized that songs came out of life experience and could articulate collective experiences as well as historical events.

Reagon was the primary researcher for African-American cultural history at the Smithsonian until 1993. *Wade in the Water,* a major Smithsonian exhibition on sacred music, eventually became a Peabody Award–winning 26-hour radio series. Her publications include *We'll Understand It Better By and By: Pioneering African-American Gospel Composers.* She produced *The Songs Are Free,* an hour-long Emmy-nominated TV production with Bill Moyers, and served as music consultant, composer, and performer for such celebrated projects as the TV series *Eyes on the Prize* and the Emmy winner *We Shall Overcome.*

SIMPLY FRUIT PUNCH

1   46-ounce can pineapple juice,
    chilled
1   46-ounce can apricot nectar,
    chilled
1   6-ounce can frozen limeade
    concentrate

2   liters lemon-lime soda, chilled
10 ounces Maraschino cherries
    with juice, chilled

Combine the above chilled ingredients in bowl; mix well and add ice. While not necessary, chilling your punch ingredients before serving permits the use of less ice to chill the punch and also causes the ice to melt more slowly, making for a less watery punch.

Makes 30 servings.

TROPICAL ISLAND PUNCH

1   64-ounce bottle fruit punch,
    chilled
2   15-ounce cans pineapple
    chunks, chilled
1   pint strawberries, stemmed,
    hulled, and sliced

2   bananas, sliced
2   pints lemon sherbet
1   2-liter bottle lemon-lime soda
    Ice

Pour fruit punch into a large bowl, add fruit, scoops of the sherbet, and slowly pour soda over the mixture. Add ice to taste or as necessary.

Makes 30 servings.

SPIKED FRUIT PUNCH

2   16-ounce cans frozen
      pineapple juice concentrate
12 ounces spiced rum
2   2-liter bottles lemon-lime
      soda, chilled

1   10-ounce jar maraschino
      cherries, chilled
4   oranges, sliced into rounds
2   trays frozen pineapple juice
      cubes

Combine pineapple juice concentrate and rum in a large punch bowl. Add lemon-lime soda and maraschino cherry juice; stir to combine. Float cherries and orange slices on top. Add frozen pineapple cubes before serving.

Makes 48 servings.

"One of the things that astounded me about Spelman was that if something major happened in the world, they canceled classes and we all went to Sisters Chapel to discuss it. I remember when President Kennedy was confronting Russia, which then had ships in the water headed for Cuba. Well, we . . . discussed it pro and con, including whether this kind of challenge would lead to war. I was very impressed by a school that felt it was training leaders."

—Bernice Johnson Reagon

Ambassador Ruth A. Davis, Spelman, '66

"It was wonderful to serve under Madeleine Albright, the first female secretary of state who smashed the glass ceiling for women in diplomacy. . . . And then to have her followed by Colin Powell was absolutely fantastic for me. This showed that women and minorities can succeed at the very top of the State Department."

—Ruth A. Davis

Ambassador Ruth A. Davis was the first African-American female career ambassador, serving as ambassador to the Republic of Benin from 1992 to 1996. She is credited with playing a significant role in the organization of the 1992 Barcelona Olympic Games and in Atlanta's successful bid for the 1996 games. She is the recipient of several prestigious awards including a Presidential Distinguished Service Award in 1999 and again in 2002. In 2003, Davis was awarded The Secretary's Distinguished Award by Secretary of State Colin Powell.

Aerial view of Spelman College.
(Archives and Special Collections: Robert Woodruff Library at the Atlanta University Center)

Ambassador Aurelia Brazeal, Spelman '65

After graduating magna cum laude from Spelman in 1965, Ambassador Brazeal became one of the first Spelman graduates to earn a master's degree in international affairs and pursue the profession of a career diplomat. She is also the first African-American female career foreign service officer to be promoted into the Senior Foreign Service of the United States and currently holds the personal rank of career minister, the second highest in the United States Foreign Service. A career member of the U.S. Senior Foreign Service, she assumed her position as U.S. ambassador to Ethiopia in November 2002.

A GEORGIA PEACH CHAMPAGNE PUNCH

4	11½-ounce cans peach nectar	½	cup peach brandy
1	6-ounce can frozen orange juice concentrate	¼	cup grenadine syrup
¼	cup lemon juice	4	750-milliliter bottles champagne
1	tablespoon lime juice		

Chill all ingredients before using them. In a large punch bowl combine peach nectar, concentrated orange juice, lemon juice, lime juice, brandy, and grenadine. Mix well and add champagne. Serve immediately.

Makes 24 servings.

STRAWBERRY CHAMPAGNE PUNCH

Perfect for a bridal shower or other special event.

1   750-milliliter bottle
      champagne, chilled
2   liters ginger ale, chilled
1   10-ounce package frozen
      strawberries, thawed and
      puréed

1   pint fresh strawberries, washed,
      stemmed, hulled, and sliced

In a large punch bowl, combine champagne, ginger ale, and strawberry purée. Stir gently, add the fresh strawberry slices, and serve immediately.

Makes 14 servings.

Alice Walker

Alice Walker, one of the leading voices among black American women writers, attended Spelman from 1961 to 1963 before transferring to Sarah Lawrence College. By age 38 she had produced a large body of work, critically acclaimed for its frank and insightful portrayal of the black cultural experience in America and that of black women in particular. Her most famous work, *The Color Purple,* portrays the lives of Southern black women as they overcome sexism and racism through nurturing and empowering female friendships. The winner of both the Pulitzer Prize and the American Book Award, *The Color Purple* was made into a popular motion picture that received several Academy Award nominations and a Broadway musical. Her books have been translated into more than two dozen languages.

Alice Walker, ca. 1964.
(Courtesy Spelman College Archives)

The youngest of eight children born to impoverished Southern sharecroppers in Eatonville, Georgia, Walker was especially influenced by her parents' storytelling, especially that of her mother, whom she described as "a walking history of our community." Perhaps as a reflection of Walker's view of her mother as a community griot, the preservation of black culture through strong black female characters is a dominant theme in her work.

DAIQUIRI PUNCH

The thirst-quenching, fresh, delicious flavor of this punch makes all the added effort very much worthwhile. If you don't have an electric juicer or access to free labor (family and friends), plan ahead, juice in increments, and freeze.

2	quarts fresh lemon juice		1	pound confectioners' sugar
4	quarts fresh lime juice		4	quarts club soda
4	quarts orange juice		2½	fifths light rum

Combine the fruit juices and confectioners' sugar and mix well; refrigerate to chill for several hours. Add club soda and rum just before serving in tall glasses, filled with cracked ice and garnished with fresh mint.

Makes 75 servings.

WHISKEY SOUR PUNCH

This is a wonderful punch to serve at events ranging from weddings to barbecues. Remember this tip: Your ice will melt away slower if you make large cubes in muffin cups.

1 quart lemon juice	3 quarts sparkling water
1 quart orange juice	Sugar to taste
1 quart whiskey	

Combine the above ingredients; pour over large cubes or a block of ice and garnish with slivers of fresh pineapple.

Makes 50 servings.

Tina McElroy Ansa, Spelman '71

Novelist Tina McElroy Ansa calls herself part of a writing tradition, one of those little Southern girls who always knew she wanted to be a writer. She grew up in middle Georgia in the 1950s hearing her grandfather's stories on the porch of her family home and strangers' stories downtown in her father's juke joint. Those stories were the inspiration for Mulberry, Georgia, the mythical setting of her four novels.

After graduating from Spelman, Ansa became the first black woman to work at the *Atlanta Constitution*. Her novels include *Baby of the Family*, named a Notable Book of the Year by the *New York Times*, and *You Know Better*, which addresses the contemporary issues of children today, the tenuous ties we are building with them, and how we can reclaim them. Ansa was a writer-in-residence at Spelman in 1990, where she also taught creative writing.

Pearl M. Cleage, Spelman '71

An essayist, poet, and journalist, Cleage gained national prominence in 1992 with the production of her play *Flyin' West*, which premiered at the Alliance Theatre in Atlanta and was produced at a number of regional theatres across the nation. *Flyin' West* was soon followed by *Blues for an Alabama Sky* and *Bourbon at the Border*. Her bestselling novel *What Looks Like Crazy on an Ordinary Day*, which deals with the ups and downs of living a truthful life, was selected as an Oprah Bookclub selection in 1998. Cleage has served as a playwright-in-residence at Spelman College, as editor of *Catalyst,* a literary magazine which she co-founded, and as artistic director of Just Us Theater Company.

PIÑA COLADA PUNCH

3   cups well-blended cream of
     coconut, chilled
7$\frac{1}{2}$ cups unsweetened pineapple
     juice, chilled

4$\frac{1}{2}$ cups light rum
5   trays frozen pineapple juice
     cubes

Blend together the cream of coconut, pineapple juice, and rum in batches. Transfer to a large punch bowl and add frozen pineapple cubes just before serving.

Makes 24 servings.

WEDDING PUNCH

2   12-ounce cans frozen
     lemonade concentrate
2   12-ounce cans frozen
     pineapple juice concentrate
2   quarts lemon-lime soda,
     chilled

Up to 2 bottles champagne,
     chilled
Fresh strawberries
Mint leaves

Combine juices and 1 quart of the lemon-lime soda in a large punch bowl; mix well. Immediately before serving, add remaining lemon-lime soda, ginger ale, and champagne to taste. Stir to blend. Garnish with strawberries and a sprig of mint.

Makes 30 servings.

LaTanya Richardson, Spelman '74

Married to Samuel L. Jackson, a fellow thespian and a Morehouse man, Richardson is an accomplished actress whose feature film credits include *Hangin' with the Homeboys*, *The Super*, *Fried Green Tomatoes*, *Malcolm X* (directed by Morehouse graduate Spike Lee), *Lorenzo's Oil*, *Sleepless in Seattle*, *When a Man Loves a Woman*, *Losing Isaiah*, *Lone Star*, *U.S. Marshals*, and *The Fighting Temptations*. Her television credits include *Law & Order*, *Cheers*, *Party of Five*, *Chicago Hope*, *NYPD Blue*, *Ally McBeal*, *Judging Amy*, *Once and Again*, and *Boston Public*.

RED VELVET PUNCH

8   cups cranberry juice cocktail
2   cups brandy
1   6-ounce can frozen orange
     juice concentrate, thawed
1   6-ounce can frozen pineapple
     juice concentrate, thawed

1   6-ounce can frozen lime juice
     concentrate, thawed
2   fifths chilled champagne
     Lemon and/or lime slices

Mix cranberry juice cocktail, brandy, orange juice, pineapple juice, and lime juice in a large punch bowl over a block of ice. Just before serving, add chilled champagne. Garnish with slices of lemon and/or lime.

Makes 25 servings, allowing 3 cups per guest.

Note: For non-alcoholic punch, substitute 2 quarts of ginger ale for the champagne and 2 cups of grape juice for the brandy.

COSMOPOLITAN PUNCH

Smooth and urbane, this punch is definitely not for kids, but it may make you giggle like one.

60	ounces or 40 1.5-ounce jiggers vodka		8	cups cranberry juice
2¹/₂	cups Cointreau		1	10-ounce jar Maraschino cherries and juice
³/₄	cup + 2 tablespoons fresh lime juice		1	2-liter bottle lemon-lime soda, chilled

Combine the first four ingredients in a large punch bowl. Strain maraschino cherry juice into the bowl, mix well, and add ice just before serving. Garnish individual servings with a cherry or float all of them on top of the punch in the bowl.

Makes 40 servings.

Mattiwilda Dobbs, Spelman '46, Valedictorian

One of the great coloratura sopranos of our time, Mattiwilda Dobbs has sung in virtually every major concert hall in the United States and abroad, and she has appeared with the Bolshoi Opera, the Vienna State Opera, Glyndebourne, the Paris Opera, and the Stockholm Royal Opera, often breaking the color barrier. Her 1953 debut at La Scala as Elvira in Rossini's *L'Italiana in Algeri* was the first performance by a black artist on that stage. She desegregated the San Francisco Opera Company and became the first black soprano to sing at the Metropolitan Opera House as well as the first black female to sing regularly under contract with that house. Her debut as Gilda in Verdi's *Rigoletto* followed Marian Anderson's and Robert McFerrin's barrier-breaking debuts by one year. In breaking these racial barriers, Dobbs was simply following in the footsteps of her father, early civil rights leader and the unofficial mayor of Auburn Avenue John Wesley Dobbs. She was one of six Dobbs daughters to graduate from Spelman.

Dobbs was the artist-in-residence at Spelman in 1974 and 1975, received an honorary doctorate from the college in 1979, and currently lives outside of Washington, D.C.

Dobbs family at a Mattiwilda Dobbs concert, ca. 1952.
(Courtesy Spelman College Archives)

KITCHEN SINK PUNCH

Aptly named because it contains everything except the kitchen sink.

1 10-ounce package frozen sliced strawberries in syrup	2 cups brewed black tea
1 12-ounce can frozen orange juice concentrate	2 cups white sugar
	$3^1/_2$ cups light rum
1 12-ounce can frozen lemonade concentrate	3 trays frozen orange juice cubes
8 cups water	2 2-liter bottles lemon-lime soda, chilled

Combine strawberries, orange juice concentrate, lemonade concentrate, water, and tea in a large punch bowl. Add sugar and rum and stir until sugar dissolves. Add orange juice cubes and soda immediately before seving.

Makes 34 servings.

PEACH & STRAWBERRY SANGRIA

1 750-ml bottle dry white wine	3 peaches, pitted and quartered
1³/₄ cups Essenia (a sweet dessert wine)	1 large orange, cut crosswise into six slices
1¹/₄ cups strawberries, washed, hulled and sliced	1 lime, cut crosswise into six slices
1¹/₄ cups peach liqueur	

Combine the above ingredients, bruising the orange slices slightly by pressing against the side of the pitcher. Allow the sangria to stand at room temperature for two hours or chill for four hours before serving in tall, ice-filled glasses.

Makes 8 servings.

ROOTS & WINGS: GEORGIA SANGRIA

With roots strongly anchored in the Mediterranean, traditional sangria has taken wing and headed to Georgia where peaches create a new sangria tradition.

1 750-ml bottle white zinfandel	6 tablespoons thawed lemonade concentrate
¹/₃ cup sugar	4 peaches, peeled, pitted, and sliced
³/₄ cup peach-flavored brandy	
1¹/₄ cups peach nectar	

Academic graduates, 1895.
(Courtesy Spelman College Archives)

Combine wine, sugar, brandy, nectar, and lemonade concentrate; mix until well blended. Add the sliced peaches and refrigerate overnight. Serve the next day from a large, ice-filled pitcher.

Makes 6 to 8 servings.

WATERMELON DAIQUIRI

Summer's signature fruit is blended to perfection in this refreshing offering. Cool and sweet, it's simply delicious!

4¼ cups ³/₄-inch seedless watermelon cubes	3 tablespoons sour watermelon liqueur (such as Puckers, sold at most liqueur and grocery stores)
½ cup light rum	
1 tablespoon Cointreau	
¼ cup powdered sugar	½ cup fresh strawberries, sliced Fresh mint
2½ tablespoons fresh lime juice	

Seal the watermelon in a zip-top plastic freezer bag and freeze for 8 hours to form frozen melon cubes. Process the frozen watermelon and remaining ingredients (except mint) in a blender or food processor until smooth, stopping to scrape down the sides often. Pour into martini glasses, garnish with fresh mint, and serve immediately.

Makes 4 servings.

STRAWBERRIES & CREAM

A snappy pairing of ruby-red strawberries and velvety smooth cream.

1 ounce strawberry schnapps	2 cups crushed ice
1½ tablespoons sugar	4 whole strawberries
2 ounces half and half	Fresh strawberries to garnish

Giles Hall faculty, ca. 1895.
(Courtesy Spelman College Archives)

Blend ingredients except strawberries with 2 cups crushed ice at high speed. Add strawberries and blend for 10 seconds. Serve in a parfait glass with a straw and garnish with a fresh strawberry.

Makes 1 serving.

Peaches & Cream

A piña colada with a distinctive Southern accent.

4 fresh peaches, pitted, peeled and quartered	3 ounces light rum
1 cup chilled peach nectar	15 ice cubes
¹/₂ to 1 cup cream of coconut, chilled	

Select one quartered peach and set aside. Place remaining three quartered peaches in a blender or food processor, blend until smooth. Add remaining ingredients except peach slices and blend until slushy. Pour into glasses and decorate rim with peach slice. Serve immediately.

Makes 2 large drinks.

Note: Cream of coconut can be found in most liquor stores or in some grocery gourmet sections.

Amaretto Ice Cream Cappuccino

It wouldn't be morning in the South without a steaming hot cup of coffee. Now, enjoy an invigorating cup of coffee on even the hottest Southern day with this rich and frosty drink. Delicious any time of year.

2 cups strong brewed Amaretto coffee, chilled	3 to 4 cups vanilla ice cream
²/₃ cup chocolate syrup, chilled	Whipped cream
¹/₂ cup Amaretto liqueur	Cinnamon

Combine coffee, chocolate syrup, and Amaretto. Combine with ice cream in a blender and blend smooth. Pour mixture into four tall, chilled glasses and garnish with whipped cream and cinnamon before serving.

Makes 4 servings.

"If there is any nobler achievement in the annals of American womanhood than the founding of Spelman College . . . We confess that we know not of it."

—*Opportunity,* May 1931

Open house in Laura Spelman Hall, 1965.
(Courtesy Spelman College Archives)

MORRIS BROWN COLLEGE

Knowledge is like a garden: If it is not cultivated, it cannot be harvested.

—African proverb

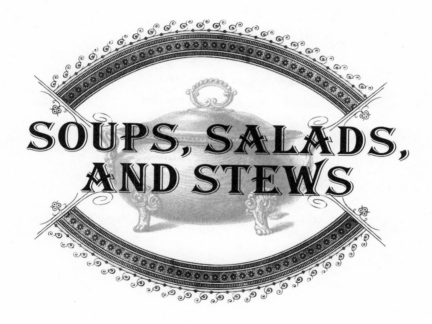

SOUPS, SALADS, AND STEWS

MORRIS BROWN COLLEGE HYMN

Alma Mater, pride of earth,
Gav'st to me another birth,
Haven for all hungry souls,
Feeding them shall be Thy goal,
Ever let thy banner be,
Emblem of the brave and free,
A welcome true to everyone,
Until Thy work is done.

Hail to Thee, maker of men,
Honor to Thee once again,
Sacred truths on firmest ground,
Hail to Thee, Dear Morris Brown.
To her precepts praise accord,
To them may we w' e'er be bound,
And bow and thank the gracious Lord,
For Dear Old Morris Brown

—Milton Randolph, Morris Brown College, '33

A Church and College Built upon
Principles of Independence and Self-Reliance

Founded in 1881 "for the Christian education of Negro boys and girls in Atlanta," Morris Brown College was named to honor the memory of the second consecrated bishop of the African Methodist Episcopal (AME) Church. The AME Church is Methodist in its basic doctrine and order of worship but broke away from the Methodist Church under Richard Allen, born a slave in 1760, because black Methodists could not receive communion until after all white members had been served.

One Sunday Allen and some black companions were led to an upstairs section of St. George's church, which was now the black section. It is likely that this segregated seating arrangement was devised because whites were nervous and perhaps even threatened by the worshipful ways of many black members, who often incorporated call-and-response, dance, weeping, and shouting in their prayers to God. Some members proceeded to the front pews of the gallery but were advised that they could no longer sit in the front pews of the area designated for their use. And as they knelt to pray, they were actually pulled from their knees and told to go to the seats farther back in the gallery. Insult was added to injury when Absalom Jones was physically removed from St. George's by the trustees while he was in the act of prayer, and the congregation supported the act of the trustees. On April 12, 1787, with the assistance of Absalom Jones, William White, and Dorus Ginnings, Richard Allen organized the Free African Society (FAS)

Richard Allen
(Private collection)

in Philadelphia. This independent black organization was the first of its kind in America to dedicate itself to abolishing slavery and fostering self-help and self-dependence among people of color. From this Society came two groups: the Episcopalians and the Methodists. The leader of the Methodist group was Richard Allen, who wanted to be rid of the humiliation of segregated worship. The AME church is unique among religious denominations in the Western world in that its founding originated from sociological rather than theological differences. Fervently committed to the education of blacks, the church founded several AME schools, beginning in 1856 with Wilberforce University, the first private black college in America.

Following the Civil War, the congregation of Old Bethel, founded by slaves in 1840 and the oldest predominately African-

Reverend Wesley J. Gaines and his wife,
Mrs. Julia A. Gaines
(Private collection of Mr. Herman Mason)

American congregation in Atlanta, affiliated with the AME Church and would eventually become known as Big Bethel Church. According to tradition the founding of Morris Brown followed an appeal in 1880 to Reverend Wesley J. Gaines, as presiding elder of the Atlanta district of the African Methodist Episcopal Church, to furnish a room at Clark College. At a meeting to consider the request, according to Annie B. Thomas, who would later become the first assistant principal of Morris Brown College, "One Steward Wiley, an officer of Big Bethel, arose and said, 'Mr. Chairman, if we can furnish a room at Clark University, why can't we build a school ourselves?' To this Wesley J. Gaines responded, 'We can,' and this thought caught fire and in a few moments the matter of furnishing a room at Clark University was tabled, the meeting adjourned, but so impressed was Wesley J. Gaines, the founder, that he said, 'by God's help we'll build a school of our own.'" —Reverend E. R. Carter, *The Black Side of Atlanta*

In 1881, during the North Georgia Annual Conference at Big Bethel, the Reverend Wesley John Gaines introduced a resolution calling for the establishment in Atlanta of an institution for the "moral, spiritual, and intellectual growth of Negro boys and girls." In May 1885 the state of Georgia granted a charter to Morris Brown College of the AME Church. It is only fitting that Morris Brown College, the only college in Georgia started exclusively by African Americans, was a child of the AME church, a denomination started exclusively through the efforts of African Americans who refused to be segregated and treated as second-class citizens in their wor-

The Boys of Summer—Morris Brown Baseball Team, ca. 1910.
(Private collection of Mr. Herman Mason)

ship of a just God. The church wanted more education for their children than they had received, and felt it their duty to sacrifice in providing for it.

On October 15, 1885, 107 students and nine teachers walked into a crude wooden structure at the corner of Boulevard and Houston Streets in Atlanta. This occasion, which occurred just twenty years after the ratification of the 13th Amendment to the U.S. Constitution, marked the formal opening of the first educational institution in Georgia founded for and by African Americans. The school operated on the primary, secondary, and normal school levels until 1894, with a regular academic program and courses in tailoring, dressmaking, home economics, nursing education, commerce, and printing. A theological department for the training of ministers was established in 1894. The College Department began, graduating its first students four years later. The college changed its status to university in 1913, and as a result it was granted the right to establish and operate branch institutions of learning. The heavy financial burden imposed by the branches, however, made it necessary to discontinue them in 1929. And the present name, Morris Brown College, was restored. In 1932 Morris Brown College became the fourth member of the Atlanta University Center.

Morris Brown Bulletin, 1917.
(Private collection of Mr. Herman Mason)

From its earliest days Morris Brown College sought to meet the educational needs of students from low socioeconomic backgrounds. The college, at that time, was largely dependent on a denomination whose constituency was primarily unskilled, untrained, and economically unstable. In order to survive, the college had to enroll a large segment of underachieving students whose parents were loyal supporters of the church that kept its doors open. What began as survival strategy for Morris Brown in 1881 became the liberation cry for black masses and the country at large in the 1960s. While Morris Brown has moved and grown since that time, its basic mission is still to serve as a place that welcomes all students, including those who might not be admitted into other schools for academic or economic reasons.

THE FOUR PRINCIPALS

The first principal of Morris Brown College was Miss Mary McCree, an 1880 graduate of Atlanta University, who resigned as principal after one year but continued teaching at the college. She was succeeded by Mrs. Alice Dugged Carey, who also held the position of principal for one year;

Mrs. Alice Dugged Carey, former principal of Morris Brown.
(Private collection of Mr. Herman Mason)

she then chaired the English department until 1921. Before her death on the campus of Morris Brown College, she had realized her dream of establishing a home for delinquent black girls in Macon, Georgia.

The third principal was the Reverend E. W. Lee, who in 1881 became the third president and the first male to head Morehouse College. Under his administration the first Morris Brown catalogue was published. He also served for one year, but would later return to the college as its fourth college president. A. St. George Richardson, a layperson, was the fourth and the last of principals to lead Morris Brown College, serving from 1888 until 1892. During his tenure Morris Brown experienced considerable growth, with six new teachers and an enrollment of 320 students. In 1892 Richardson was named as the first president of Morehouse College and served in that position until 1896.

The school operated on the primary, secondary, and normal school levels until 1894, with a regular academic program and courses in tailoring, dressmaking, home economics, nursing, education, commerce, and printing. A theological department for the training of ministers was established in 1894. That same year the College Department began, graduating its first students four years later. As the coursework became increasingly demanding the term *president* was applied

Reverend Edward W. Lee, third principal of Morris Brown, 1887–88, and fourth president, 1908–11.
(Private collection of Mr. Herman Mason)

Professor A. St. George Richardson
(Private collection of Mr. Herman Mason)

to the school's leaders. A succession of college presidents followed, each bringing to the presidency their own strengths and vision.

In 1896 Reverend James M. Henderson was named the second president of Morris Brown College. His administration, which spanned eight years, was characterized by expansion and growth. Following a successful appeal to the ministers of the African Methodist Episcopalian Church of Georgia, Dr. Henderson received funds to construct a central building, Turner Hall, and during his tenure the first four-year college students would graduate from the school in 1898. Another first was that Dr. Henderson taught the first law classes to be offered by the college.

Dr. James M. Henderson, second president of Morris Brown, 1896–1904.
(Private collection of Mr. Herman Mason)

The third president was the Reverend Joseph Simeon Flipper, brother of the first black cadet to graduate from West Point Academy. During his presidency the college experienced the highest enrollment in its history, perhaps due in part to the "High Normal Course" instituted by Flipper to provide alternative education and training opportunities for its students, many of whom were from impoverished homes. This course of study prepared students who sought to pursue a teaching career with the academics necessary to enter college, while providing straight normal classes to other students.

In 1908, following Reverend Flipper's appointment to the bishopric, former principal E. W. Lee accepted the mantle of leadership for the second time. By now, 23 years after Lee's first service, the student body had increased to 993 students and the teaching staff had grown from two to 28 teachers. From its grammar school beginnings it had grown into a college, with normal and classical departments. President Lee embarked on a program to improve facilities and the physical appearance of the campus.

To succeed Lee, the Board of Trustees elected Bishop William Alfred Fountain, Sr., as the first alumnus president of the college in 1911. He improved academic standards, introduced a Business Department, and organized a Department of Military Science and Tactics.

Bishop Joseph Simeon Flipper
(Private collection of Mr. Herman Mason)

The next president was the Reverend John H. Lewis, who served in this capacity twice. During his first tenure, 1920–1928, he continued to enhance the curriculum and academic standards while establishing goals of accreditation. He also sought to enhance school spirit by initiating a search for a new school song with a prize of ten dollars to the winner. Andrew W. Clark, a native of Jamaica, penned the following winning song, later popularized by the Morris Brown marching band as a victory song played at football games:

The Early Years, ca. 1900
(Private collection of Mr. Herman Mason)

Bishop William
Alfred Fountain
*(Private collection of
Mr. Herman Mason)*

Professor John H. Lewis,
sixth president of Morris
Brown, 1920–28.
*(Private collection of Mr. Herman
Mason)*

Loyalty to our college, the school we love so dear,
Honor to her standards that never speak of fear
Bulwark of protection, a shelter from all woe,
So victory shall be her guard against unnumbered foe

CHORUS
Dear old Morris Brown, victory for thee,
In thy precepts true we shall ever be,
Firm as one, united are we,
We will keep thy standards high
Ever in achieving sky
Rah for our college dear.

Our hearts with love grow warmer as we linger here,
Our school years are not lonely but filled with holy cheer.
Rising to thy colors and bearing them ahead,
We'll meet the foe where'er we go, fighting till they've fled.

Thy mission to a people shall be met and must,
Thy slogan to all races is "God our shield and trust."
So we'll proclaim thy message, our Alma Mater dear,
Till freedom's sons thy praise shall sing in thy strength and fear.

Morris Brown College band—the beginnings of the Marching Wolverines.
(Private collection of Mr. Herman Mason)

Then breaking forth in anthems we thy fame shall sing,
Till the song of victory, angels convey on wing,
He who sitteth regnant as king upon his throne
Shall join the living chorus praising Morris Brown

In 1928 the school was forced to declare bankruptcy, and Lewis tendered his resignation. The Reverend William A. Fountain, Jr., son of the head of the board of trustees, was named the seventh president of Morris Brown College. He appealed to the board members to take a greater role in the mammoth task of redeeming the school's debt, and Morris Brown emerged from bankruptcy. During this same period the Atlanta University Center was designed as an academic

**The Wolverines, who marched in at least two Rose Bowl parades,
were later featured in the motion picture *Drumline*.**
(Private collection of Mr. Herman Mason)

cooperative intended to cut costs and improve the quality of education without impeding the independent identity of any of its member educational institutions. Under the terms of the agreement of affiliation with Morehouse and Spelman, Morris Brown phased out its undergraduate program to focus exclusively on graduate studies and moved from the corner of Boulevard and Houston Streets to West Hunter and Tatnall Streets.

In 1935 the college was admitted to the Association of American Colleges and the Association of Colleges for Negro Youth. In 1936, for the first time in its history, Morris Brown accepted assistance from white friends in the Atlanta community, in particular the Rosenwald Fund. In 1937 President Fountain and his father, Bishop Fountain, secured a permanent home for Morris Brown by negotiating the deeding of 14 acres of land and three buildings from Atlanta University and raising funds for the purchase by selling land the school held. A new curriculum was introduced and massive renovations were completed before the fall 1939 academic term.

Morris Brown students, ca. 1921.
(Private collection of Mr. Herman Mason)

Beta chapter of Zeta Phi Beta sorority, ca. 1921.
(Private collection of Mr. Herman Mason)

Morris Brown students in chapel.
(Private collection of Mr. Herman Mason)

The school's bright future was reflected in the lyrics of the new school hymn:

> *Alma Mater pride of earth,*
> *Gav'st to me another birth,*
> *Haven for all hungry souls,*
> *Feeding them shall be Thy goal*
> *Ever let Thy banner be,*
> *Emblem of the brave and free,*
> *A welcome true to everyone,*
> *Until thy work is done. . . .*

In 1953 Dr. John H. Lewis returned as president, focusing his attention on raising academic standards so that Morris Brown could qualify for full admission to the Southern Association of Colleges and Secondary Schools. He passed away before this occurred, and Dr. Frank Cunningham was elected acting president in 1958. Within the first few months of his admin-

At the Ready—Morris Brown gridiron warriors.
(Private collection of Mr. Herman Mason)

Alpha Kappa Alpha sorority, ca. 1930.
(Private collection of Mr. Herman Mason)

Morris Brown College girls basketball squad, 1935–36.
(Private collection of Mr. Herman Mason)

istration Morris Brown College had received its long awaited and highly coveted admission into the Southern Association of Colleges and Secondary Schools!

Soups and Stews

Soup is a wonderfully versatile dish. Served hot or cold, it can take you from early spring to late winter. Hearty or light, it's equally filling. From the deliciously cool chilled soups of spring and summer to the more substantial soups of winter, there are so many great recipes that you will never tire of it.

SOUTHERN PEANUT SOUP

$1/3$ cup coarsely chopped celery
$1/3$ cup coarsely chopped carrot
$1/4$ cup chopped onion
$3/4$ cup chicken broth
  1 chicken bouillon cube
  2 cups water, divided
$1/2$ cup creamy peanut butter

$1/4$ teaspoon black pepper
$1/8$ teaspoon cayenne pepper
    Pinch nutmeg
  1 tablespoon cornstarch
$1/2$ cup half and half
    Chopped peanuts
    Sliced scallions

Combine the first four ingredients in a saucepan and bring to a boil over medium-high heat. Reduce heat, cover and cook over low heat until the vegetables are soft and the onion is translucent, approximately 3 to 5 minutes. Add the bouillon cube and $1^1/2$ cups water; cook uncovered until the bouillon cube dissolves. Remove saucepan from heat and allow to cool for 10 minutes before placing its contents into an electric blender or food processor and blending or pureeing it smooth. Return the pureed mixture to the saucepan; add peanut butter, black pepper, cayenne pepper, and nutmeg. Stir until smooth and well blended. Combine the cornstarch and the remaining water and stir until it is well blended before stirring into the soup mixture. Bring to a rapid boil; reduce heat to low, and cook one minute. Stir in half and half. Cook over low heat uncovered, stirring constantly, until thoroughly heated. Garnish with chopped peanuts and scallions.

Makes 4 servings.

WEST AFRICAN PEANUT SOUP

This version of the traditional West African dish is puréed smooth rather than leaving the vegetables in chunks. It tastes wonderful and presents beautifully. Enjoy!

2 tablespoons olive oil
2 cups chopped onion
1 cup chopped yellow bell pepper
2 jalapeño peppers, seeded and chopped
3 large cloves of garlic, minced
1 teaspoon grated, peeled fresh ginger
1 cup chopped carrots

2 cups chopped sweet potatoes
4 cups beef stock
1 28-ounce can chopped tomatoes with juice
Up to 2 teaspoons of sugar
1 cup smooth peanut butter
Cayenne pepper to taste
Chopped green onions
Chopped roasted peanuts

The *Georgia African Methodist*, June 1938 issue, William A. Fountain, Jr. *(center)*, William A. Fountain *(right)*.

(Private collection of Mr. Herman Mason)

Heat olive oil in a large stock pot over medium-high heat. Sauteé the onion, yellow pepper, jalapeño peppers, and garlic in the olive oil until it is translucent. Stir in ginger. Add carrots and sauté for an additional 2 to 3 minutes. Add sweet potatoes and stir in beef stock and tomatoes. Bring the mixture to a boil, reduce heat, and simmer 15 minutes or until the vegetables are fork tender. Allow mixture to cool sufficiently to handle without being burned. Add the vegetables and some of the cooking liquid to a blender or processor and purée in batches, if necessary. Return the purée to the cooking pot, stir in the sugar, and gently reheat as you add the peanut butter and stir until smooth. Add additional sugar to taste. I prefer less sugar and use only up to 1 tablespoon of sugar as opposed to the 1 tablespoon or more called for by some recipes. Add additional stock, water, or even tomato juice if a thinner soup is preferred. Garnish with plenty of chopped green onions and roasted peanuts.

Makes 4 to 6 servings.

CREAM OF PECAN SOUP

This delicious Southern favorite will soon be your favorite, too, no matter where you live.

2 tablespoons unsalted butter	$^1/_8$ teaspoon ground nutmeg
$^1/_4$ cup finely chopped onion	$1^1/_4$ cups pecans
1 tablespoon all-purpose flour	1 teaspoon minced celery leaves
2 cups chicken stock	$1^3/_4$ cups half and half
$^1/_2$ teaspoon salt	4 small sprigs mint
$^1/_8$ teaspoon white pepper	

Melt butter in heavy medium saucepan over medium heat. When foam subsides, add onion and reduce the heat to low. Sauté the onion, stirring frequently, and continue to cook until the onion is soft but not browned, about 5 minutes. Stir in flour until thoroughly blended; cook, stirring, over low heat 1 minute. Gradually add the chicken stock while stirring constantly. Stir in the salt, pepper, and nutmeg. Next, add the pecans and celery leaves. Increase heat to medium and bring the soup to a rolling boil. Reduce heat to low and simmer the soup gently for 10 minutes, stirring occasionally. Stir in cream; simmer over very

Morris Brown students, ca. 1940.
(Private collection of Mr. Herman Mason)

low heat 5 minutes to allow the cream to warm through. Adjust seasonings to taste. Ladle soup into individual warmed bowls. Garnish each bowl with a sprig of mint and serve at once.

Makes 4 servings.

GEORGIA PEACH SOUP

A summertime sonata! It is the perfect prelude to a memorable meal. I have never seen a recipe to which I did not want to add a personal touch. This is an adaptation of a delicious recipe I found in *Coastal Magazine*.

2	quarts chopped fresh peaches	$^1/_8$	teaspoon ground nutmeg
1	cup dry white wine		Pinch of allspice
$1^1/_4$	cups peach schnapps	2	cups half and half
$^1/_2$	cup sugar	$^1/_2$	cup heavy whipping cream
$1^1/_4$	teaspoons chopped fresh mint		Mint leaves
$^1/_2$	teaspoon ground cinnamon		Fresh raspberries

Combine first 8 ingredients in a large saucepan and cook over medium heat for 15 minutes or until the peaches are fork tender and the liquid is reduced. Remove from heat and allow the mixture to cool before processing it in a blender or food processor until smooth, stopping intermittently to scrape down the sides. Cover and chill. Just prior to serving, add the half and half and mix well. Return soup to the refrigerator, then whip cream until stiff peaks form. Ladle soup into individual serving bowls and garnish with a dollop of whipped cream, two or three mint leaves, and a raspberry.

Makes 4 to 6 servings.

Morris Brown students, ca. 1950.
(Private collection of Mr. Herman Mason)

Reverend Hosea Williams, Morris Brown '51

"From his bravery in the fields of battle in World War II, to his leadership in the civil rights struggle at home, Hosea Williams was a profile in courage."

—President William Jefferson Clinton

Hosea Williams, a pioneer of the civil rights movement and one of the major architects of the New South, served in an all-black unit of Patton's Third Army during WWII, where he worked as a weapons carrier and was the sole survivor of a 13-man platoon hit by a shell in France. Hospitalized for more than thirteen months, he was permanently disabled by his injuries. Soon after returning home, Williams was beaten so brutally for drinking from the only water fountain in a segregated bus station that doctors did not expect him to live. With an eye to the future however, Williams completed high school at age 23, earned a bachelor's degree in chemistry from Morris Brown College, and earned a master's from Atlanta University. He became the first black research chemist to work south of the Mason-Dixon Line when he was employed by the U.S. Department of Agriculture.

In the 1950s Williams was a middle-class civil service worker living in Savannah. One day his sons asked him to buy them a sandwich and a Coke from a segregated lunch counter at a local drugstore. The pain and humiliation of explaining racism to his young sons awakened a sleeping giant within him. He began delivering civil rights speeches in a downtown park during his lunch hours, and began leading marches and sit-ins in Savannah that attracted the attention of King and others in the Southern Christian Leadership Conference. In 1963 they invited him to join their efforts to mobilize the civil rights movement across the South. An active participant in the Freedom Summer voting registration campaign, Williams was arrested more than 125 times.

As the chief organizer of King's marches and demonstrations, Williams recalled that he "would . . . mobilize the street people in the black communities . . . Jesse Jackson would come in later and deal with the middle-class blacks and Andy Young would negotiate with the white power structure."

On March 7, 1965, he and John Lewis led the Selma-to-Montgomery protest march, known as "Bloody Sunday," across the Edmund Pettus Bridge, but not without opposition. "I am Maj. John Cloud of the Alabama state troopers," boomed an amplified voice. "This is an unlawful march, and it will not be allowed to continue. You are ordered to

Morris Brown College, class of 1958.
(Private collection of Mr. Herman Mason)

disperse. You have two minutes." Rather than trying to turn the marchers around, which would have caused a panic or confronting the police, marchers knelt to pray. This angered the police, who attacked the marchers with clubs, bullwhips, and tear gas.

Williams escaped the initial onslaught by vaulting over the backs of troopers bent over with the effort of clubbing their victims. Lewis, who was beaten unconscious by a trooper, suffered a skull fracture. Both men would march again. Lewis would go on to take a seat in Congress. And Williams, who was with Martin Luther King, Jr., when he was assassinated on April 4, 1968, was elected to the Georgia General Council in 1974. He worked among the poor for more than thirty years, organizing holiday dinners that fed as many as 40,000 homeless and hungry people in a day. Hosea Williams will long be remembered for his efforts to feed the hungry, his trademark denim overalls and red shirt, and his courageous confrontation of social injustice.

OLD-FASHIONED POTATO SOUP

Nothing says home more eloquently or makes coming home more pleasant than home-made soup.

8 cups boiling chicken broth	$1/2$ cup butter
1 teaspoon salt	2 tablespoons flour
8 cups raw potatoes, pared and chopped fine	2 cups table cream
	6 cups milk
$1/4$ cup chopped onion	2 tablespoons minced parsley
1 leek, thinly sliced	Parsley (optional)

In a large pot, combine the broth and salt, and bring to a boil over medium-high heat. Add the potatoes, onion and leek. Reduce heat to medium and continue to cook until the mixture thickens, approximately 15 to 20 minutes. In a second large pot, melt butter over medium-high heat and stir in the flour until it is smooth. Add the cream and milk and cook until the mixture is thickened and smooth. Add the cream mixture to the potato mixture; add minced parsley and mix well. Serve piping hot with a garnish of additional chopped parsley.

Makes 6 to 8 servings.

GARDEN FRESH PEA SOUP

1 pint water	3 tablespoons flour
$1/8$ teaspoon sugar	$1/2$ teaspoon salt
3 cups fresh peas (may substitute frozen)	$1/8$ teaspoon pepper
	3 cups milk
$1/2$ cup chopped onion	$1/2$ teaspoon minced fresh mint
3 tablespoons butter	$1/8$ teaspoon nutmeg

Combine water and sugar in a saucepan and bring to a rapid boil; add peas and onion, and cook over medium heat until the peas are soft but still bright green, 5 to 7 minutes. Allow peas to cool for 10 minutes before processing them smooth in a blender or food processor. Melt butter in the top of a double boiler, add flour, salt, and pepper; and then cook over medium-high heat until the butter mixture begins to bubble. Add milk and cook while continuously stirring over the hot mixture until it is smooth. Combine the pea mixture and cream sauce in the top of the double boiler. Stir in mint and nutmeg approximately 10 minutes before serving.

Makes 6 servings.

CREAM OF CORN SOUP

The pimento adds a festive touch to this delicious Southern favorite.

3	strips bacon, finely chopped		2	cups milk
1/4	cup finely chopped onion		1	teaspoon salt
2 1/4	cups fresh or frozen corn		1/2	teaspoon pepper
3	tablespoons butter		1/3	cup chopped pimento
3	tablespoons flour		2	cups table cream

Fry the bacon until crisp; add the onion and sauté until the onion is tender. Process the corn through a food processor or blender until finely chopped, but not pureed. Transfer to a saucepan, add corn to the bacon and onion mixture, and cook until the corn begins to brown. Reduce heat; add the butter and stir in the flour; cook slowly for 3 minutes. Add the milk, salt, and pepper and cook until thickened. Next, add the pimento and cream and heat and stir until smooth for 2 to 3 minutes.

Makes 6 servings.

CHICKEN VELVET SOUP

This soup and the one that follows call for cooked chicken. As a result, it provides a great opportunity to use leftover chicken or even turkey in a new and delicious way.

$^1/_3$ cup butter	$1^1/_4$ cups warm table cream
$^3/_4$ cup flour	$1^3/_4$ cups finely diced cooked
6 cups hot chicken broth, divided	chicken breast
1 cup warm milk	Salt and pepper to taste

Melt butter over medium-high heat. Stir in flour and continue to stir and cook until the mixture is smooth and well blended. Add two cups of hot chicken broth and the warm milk and cream. Reduce heat and cook slowly, stirring frequently until the mixture thickens. Add remaining broth and chicken and increase heat to bring soup to a boil. Season to taste and enjoy!

Makes 6 servings.

CHICKEN & CORN SOUP

A quick and nutritious meal can be made from leftovers and some ingredients from your pantry. During the winter I try to keep on hand plenty of soup "fixins," such as broth, pasta noodles, tomato paste, etc., so when the soup opportunity presents itself, I am ready for the challenge.

1 quart chicken broth	$^1/_3$ cup creamed corn
$^1/_2$ cup alphabet noodles	1 hard cooked egg, finely grated or mashed
$^3/_4$ cup cooked chicken, finely diced	1 teaspoon chopped parsley

Heat chicken broth to boiling and add the noodles; bring to a second boil and cook an additional 3 minutes. Add chicken and corn; reduce heat to medium and cook an additional three minutes. Add remaining ingredients, cook an additional minute or two and serve with a few homemade croutons, if you are so inclined and have them on hand.

Yields 4 servings.

CHICKEN & RICE SOUP

I love this soup on a cold winter afternoon. It is truly comfort food. And its heady fragrance competes with its flavorful, warm broth to soothe you.

1	3- to 3^1/$_2$-pound chicken, with neck and giblets (omit liver)	2	quarts chicken broth, divided
4	cloves of garlic, peeled and crushed	1^1/$_2$	cups long-grain rice
1	small onion, finely chopped	3	carrots, peeled, trimmed and sliced crosswise
^{1}/$_2$	cup chopped green pepper	3	stalks celery, trimmed and sliced crosswise
1	teaspoon salt		Pinch of saffron threads

Place chicken, garlic, onion, green pepper, salt and 8 cups of the chicken broth into a large, heavy-bottomed pot and bring to a boil over high heat. Reduce heat to medium-low, cover, and simmer until the chicken is tender, approximately 1 hour. Use a slotted spoon to transfer the chicken to a plate and set aside to cool. Strain chicken broth into a large bowl, discard solids, and return broth to a clean pot. Add rice, carrots, celery, and saffron and bring to a boil over high heat. Reduce heat to medium and cook, uncovered, stirring occasionally until the rice is tender, approximately 15 minutes.

When the chicken is sufficiently cool to handle, remove the skin and bone and discard. Cut the meat into large chunks. Return the chicken to the pot with remaining broth. Season to taste with salt and pepper

Makes 6 to 8 servings.

CHICKEN, RICE & MUSHROOM SOUP

This light and easy-to-prepare version of chicken and rice soup can be appreciated anytime. However, its light flavor is especially enjoyable in early spring or fall.

$1/2$	stick butter	3	cups cooked chopped chicken
$1^1/_4$	cups mushrooms	$1^3/_4$	cups cooked rice
$1^1/_4$	cups sliced leeks		Salt and pepper to taste
9	cups chicken broth		

Melt butter in a large stockpot and sauté mushrooms and leeks over medium heat until tender. Add remaining ingredients; stir well, and simmer for 30 minutes.

Makes 10 to 12 servings.

CHICKEN VEGETABLE SOUP

As pleasing to the eye as it is to the palate!

1	3- to 4-pound chicken, cut up into 8 or 9 pieces	1	cup chopped carrots
3	quarts chicken broth	1	cup fresh green beans cut into bite-size pieces
1	tablespoon salt	$1/2$ to 1	cup frozen corn kernels
$1/2$	teaspoon garlic powder	5	new potatoes, quartered
1	teaspoon onion powder	$3/4$	cup finely chopped onions
$1/3$	cup chopped parsley	2	tablespoons minced garlic
$1/4$	cup chopped dill	3	bay leaves
1	cup chopped celery		

Wash chicken thoroughly under cold running water and remove all visible fat. Place chicken and broth in a large stockpot and bring to a full boil over high heat. Skim off foam as it forms. Reduce heat to low and simmer an additional hour, skimming fat as it forms on the surface of the soup. Remove chicken and any skin or bones from the pot. Remove remaining skin and bone from the chicken pieces and discard. Chop chicken meat and add to the pot along with the remaining ingredients. Bring to a rolling boil, then reduce the heat to medium and continue to cook an additional 30 minutes or until the vegetables reach the desired degree of tenderness. For crisper vegetables reduce cooking time.

Beverly Harvard, Morris Brown '72

Beverly Harvard, appointed Atlanta's chief of police in October 1994, was responsible for the overall operation of the largest municipal law enforcement agency in the state of Georgia. She was the first African-American to hold this position in the nation.

Amen!
(Private collection of Mr. Herman Mason)

DOWN-HOME CHICKEN STEW

If it grows on the land, swims in the water, or is hunted or herded, you will find it in Southern soup or stew.

2	3- to $3^1/_2$-pound broiler fryers, washed under cold running water	1	cup frozen cut okra
3	quarts chicken broth	7	new potatoes, halved
2	16-ounce cans chopped tomatoes, undrained	2	large onions, chopped
$4^1/_2$	cups whole kernel corn	1	tablespoon sugar
$2^1/_2$	cups fresh butter beans	1	tablespoon salt
		1	teaspoon pepper
		$^1/_2$	cup butter

Combine the chicken and broth in a large Dutch oven and bring to a boil. Cover, reduce heat, and simmer for 1 hour. Remove the chicken from the Dutch oven and allow the chicken to cool completely. Remove and discard the skin and bone from the chicken. Chop the chicken.

Combine 4 quarts of the reserved broth, chicken, and remaining ingredients in the Dutch oven; resume boiling. Reduce heat to low and simmer, uncovered, 4 to 5 hours, stirring often and adding additional broth or water as necessary to prevent scorching or burning

Makes approximately 1 gallon.

ALPHABET BEEF SOUP

This vegetable-laden alphabet soup says "back to school" so deliciously that your children will gladly heed its call. Start it when they leave for school and it will be ready when they come in from the cold.

1 pound beef stew meat, cubed
8 cups beef broth
2 16-ounce packages frozen
    mixed vegetables
1/2 cup diced onion
2 14 1/2-ounce cans Italian-style
    diced tomatoes

2 8-ounce cans tomato sauce
1 beef bouillon cube (I use it
    instead of salt for added beef
    flavor)
1 cup alphabet noodles,
    uncooked

Combine meat, beef broth, vegetables, onion, tomatoes, tomato sauce, and bouillon in a slow cooker; cover and cook on low 6 to 8 hours or until meat is tender. Turn control to high. Add noodles. Cover and cook on high 15 to 20 minutes or until noodles are cooked through. Serve hot.

Makes 6 to 8 servings.

BEEF, BARLEY & MUSHROOM SOUP

This tasty blend of fresh vegetables and grains makes for an excellent "cold weather" meal when paired with your favorite green salad and fresh baked whole grain bread. It's early September and my mouth is watering at the thought of it!

1 pound beef stew meat, cut in
    small pieces
3 14 1/2-ounce cans beef broth
2 cups thinly sliced carrots
2 ribs celery with tops, sliced
2 small onions, diced
1 1/2 cups fresh green beans cut
    into bite-size pieces

1 14 1/2-ounce can diced tomatoes
1 cup frozen lima beans
1 1/2 cups sliced mushrooms
2 teaspoons salt
2 cloves garlic, minced
2 bay leaves
1/4 cup fresh parsley, chopped
1/4 cup barley

Place meat and beef broth into a large stockpot and bring to a rapid boil. Reduce heat and simmer for 2 hours. Add remaining ingredients except barley and cook an additional 30 to 40 minutes. Add additional broth as needed to allow ingredients to boil freely without sticking. Add barley and cook until barley is tender. Check package directions for approximate cooking time. Serve with green salad and crusty bread.

Makes 6 to 8 servings.

VEGETABLE BEEF SOUP

This hearty beef stew–like soup will quickly become a favorite with your family and friends. Serve it up hot with a wedge of sour cream cornbread or one of the other delicious cornbreads featured in the Hot from the Oven section.

3	tablespoons all-purpose flour		1	28-ounce can stewed tomatoes, undrained
1	tablespoon paprika		2	quarts beef broth, divided
2	teaspoons salt		1	bay leaf
$1/2$	teaspoon black pepper		2	tablespoons tomato paste
$1/4$	teaspoon ground cumin		7	unpeeled new potatoes, halved
1	3- to $3^1/2$-pound boneless beef chuck cut into 1-inch cubes		4	medium carrots, sliced
$1/4$	cup vegetable oil		1	11-ounce can whole kernel corn, drained
2	medium onions, chopped		1	cup French cut green beans
1	cup chopped green pepper			
3	cloves garlic, peeled and finely chopped			

In a large, zip top plastic bag, combine the flour, paprika, salt, black pepper, and cumin. Seal and shake to mix. Add the beef a few pieces at a time and shake to coat. In a large heavy-bottomed pot or soup kettle, heat the vegetable oil over medium-high heat. Brown the beef in small batches, on all sides, for approximately five minutes. Stir in the onions, green pepper, and garlic; stir and sauté for five minutes or until onion is softened. Add stewed tomatoes; four cups of the beef broth, scraping up any brown sediment stuck to the bottom of the pot; and bay leaf. Bring to a boil and reduce heat, partially cover and simmer for thirty minutes, stirring occasionally. Stir in the tomato paste. Reduce heat to medium, partially cover the pot, and simmer until meat is fork tender, approximately 30 minutes.

Morris Brown football team, ca. 1940.
(Private collection of Mr. Herman Mason)

Add potatoes, carrots, corn, green beans, and remaining broth to the pot, reduce heat to medium-low, and continue to cook with the pot partially covered until the potatoes are soft, approximately 35 to 40 minutes. Add additional seasoning to taste.

Makes 8 to 10 servings.

Eula L. Adams, Morris Brown '72

"You never know where one path may lead you. Don't be afraid to take on new assignments. A lot of doors have been opened to me because of my willingness, flexibility, curiosity, and ambition."

—Eula L. Adams

Recognized by *Fortune* magazine in August 2002 as one of the "50 Most Powerful Black Executives," Eula L. Adams has spent more than thirty years in financial services and accounting. Currently vice president of Data Management Group/Delivery Services for

Sun Microsystems, he was vice president of Global Services for StorageTek before that company was acquired by Sun Microsystems. From 1991 to 2003, he was associated with Atlanta-based First Data Corporation, a 6-billion-dollar credit card issuer. Adams managed 11,000 employees in the U.S., the U.K., and Australia and was also president of the corporation's Omaha-based Card Issuing Services division, which processed 2 trillion dollars' worth of electronic payment transactions a year.

Adams was the first in his family to attend college, winning a football scholarship to Morris Brown, where he won academic honors that gained him acceptance into Harvard's MBA Program.

NAVY BEAN SOUP

This soup is a tradition in my family. My dad could be counted on to prepare it at least once a week.

1   pound dried navy beans
2   meaty ham hocks
2   tablespoons bacon drippings or vegetable oil
1   medium onion, peeled and finely diced

1   large clove garlic, finely minced
2   quarts chicken broth
    Salt and freshly ground pepper

Pick over beans and remove any stones or any other foreign objects. Rinse beans, place them in a large non-reactive container with sufficient water to cover by 2 inches, and soak overnight. Rinse ham hocks and place them in a large Dutch oven with chicken broth and sufficient water to cover. Bring ham hocks to a rapid boil, reduce heat to low, cover, and simmer for one hour. Meanwhile, heat drippings or vegetable oil in a medium skillet over medium heat; add the onions and garlic and cook, stirring frequently, until the onions are just beginning to brown, 3 to 5 minutes. Drain the beans and rinse again before adding them to the Dutch oven. Add onions and remaining ingredients to the pot; reduce heat, and simmer beans over low heat until they are tender, stirring occasionally. When beans are tender, remove ham hocks and allow them to cool before cutting the meat from the bones, chopping, and returning it to the pot. Discard skin, bone, and excess fat. Use a large cooking spoon to mash some of the beans against the side of the pot and stir to thicken the soup and make it creamier. Season this heart-warming soup to taste with salt and pepper and serve piping hot with a side of cornbread.

Makes 8 to 10 servings.

THREE-BEAN SOUP

A confetti of colorful beans and riotous color makes this soup as beautiful as it is delicious. Enjoy!

2 cups dried navy beans	1 cup sliced celery
1 cup dried red beans	2 large cloves garlic, finely minced
1½ cups dried black beans	1 tablespoon minced parsley
2 ham hocks	1 teaspoon salt
3 10½-ounce cans chicken broth	1 teaspoon finely minced fresh basil
3⅔ cups water	1 teaspoon dried oregano
2 large onions, finely chopped	3 cups chopped turnip greens
1 cup sliced carrots	

Pick over beans and remove any stones or other foreign objects. Rinse beans, place them in a large non-reactive container with sufficient water to cover by 2 inches, and soak overnight. Rinse ham hocks and place them in a large Dutch oven with chicken broth and sufficient water to cover. Bring ham hocks to a rapid boil, reduce heat to low, cover, and simmer for one hour. Drain the beans and rinse again before adding them to the Dutch oven. Add onions and next 7 ingredients to the pot; reduce temperature and simmer beans over low heat until they are tender, stirring occasionally. When beans are tender, remove ham hocks; cut meat from the bones, chop, and return it to the pot. Add greens during the last 30 minutes of cooking time, stirring occasionally.

Makes 8 to 10 servings.

RED BEAN SOUP WITH SMOKED TURKEY

This delicious soup is a great source of protein. The addition of the chunks of turkey makes it a one-pot meal that your family will really enjoy. With a more demanding writing and speaking schedule I have rediscovered the many benefits of one-pot and crock-pot cooking.

1	pound dried red beans	$2\frac{1}{2}$	cups smoked turkey, cut in 1-inch cubes
$\frac{3}{4}$	cup chopped onions		Salt and pepper to taste
$\frac{1}{2}$	cup chopped green peppers	4	cups cooked rice
3	cloves garlic, minced		
2	quarts unsalted chicken broth		

Place all ingredients except rice and seasonings, in crock-pot; cover and cook 6 hours on the "High" setting or overnight on the "Low" setting. Check pot often and add additional broth as necessary to prevent sticking. When beans are finished add salt and pepper to taste. Just prior to serving, stir in the rice and adjust seasoning to taste.

Makes 8 servings.

JAMAICAN RED PEA SOUP

Some of the best Jamaican food, outside of the islands, must be in Atlanta. Usually my first stop after arriving in the city is one of the plethora of Jamaican restaurants located there. I am particularly fond of those near the AUC. However, timing is everything, so arrive slightly ahead of the lunch and dinner hour rush. I love the flavor and intensity of this soup. The Scotch bonnet pepper called for in the recipe is extremely hot. Extreme diners, enjoy! All others beware.

2	cups dried kidney beans, soaked and drained	6	green onions
10	cups water	1	large carrot, diced
2	tablespoons vegetable oil	1	sweet potato, peeled and cubed
2	medium onions, diced	2	teaspoons thyme
1	large green pepper, diced	1	cup coconut milk
4	cloves garlic, minced	$^1/_2$	teaspoon allspice
1	Scotch bonnet pepper, seeded and minced	$^1/_2$	teaspoon black pepper
		1	teaspoon salt

Pick over beans to remove foreign objects and soak overnight in sufficient cold water to cover beans by 2 inches. Drain and rinse beans before cooking. Place in a large soup pot and add water. Bring beans to a quick boil and reduce heat to medium. Cook for 1 hour, adding additional water as necessary to prevent the beans from sticking. Drain beans, reserving 5 cups of the liquid, and set aside. Sauté the onions, green pepper, and garlic in the oil for 5 to 7 minutes. Return beans to the pot containing the sautéed vegetables. Add cooking liquid and remaining ingredients except salt. Simmer for 1 to 1$^1/_2$ hours over low heat. Add salt to taste.

Makes 8 servings.

Lt. General Albert J. Edmonds, Morris Brown '64

In 1996, the Career Communications Group recognized Albert J. Edmonds as Black Engineer of the Year. In 2001, *Washington Techway* magazine named General Edmonds one of the region's ten most admired managers. In 2002, *Fortune* magazine recognized him as one of the top 50 most powerful black executives. In November 2002, Edmonds was appointed by President Bush to serve as a member of the National Infrastructure Advisory Council. And in 2004, he was named among the 50 most important African Americans in technology by *US Black Engineer* magazine and Blackmoney.com.

Albert J. "Al" Edmonds, Lt. Gen. USAF (Ret.), president of U.S. government accounts for EDS Operations Solutions line of business, is responsible for ensuring that U.S. federal, civilian, military, state and local clients—which include Medicaid programs in eighteen states—achieve unparalleled results in the digital economy. He oversees all aspects of the company's relationships with the government, from strategic growth planning to delivery of the corporate services portfolio.

JAMAICAN PEPPER POT SOUP

There are as many versions of Jamaican pepper pot soup as there are cooks. This one, made simply with shrimp, is one of my favorites.

1¼ cups green bell pepper, seeded and chopped	1 ripe Scotch bonnet pepper, whole
¾ cup minced onion	6 cups chicken stock
3 tablespoons vegetable oil	1 10-ounce package frozen okra, sliced
3 cloves garlic, minced	
1 teaspoon salt	1 cup chopped fresh spinach
½ teaspoon thyme leaves, crushed	2 pounds (50 to 60) small shrimp, peeled and deveined
½ teaspoon marjoram, crushed	1 cup canned cream of coconut
½ teaspoon rosemary, crushed	10 lime slices

Combine green pepper, minced onion, oil, and minced garlic in a large stockpot; sauté over medium heat until the onions are limp and transparent. Add salt, thyme, marjoram, rosemary, pepper, and chicken stock and heat to boiling. Reduce heat; simmer, covered, 30 minutes. Add okra and spinach and cook an additional 30 to 40 minutes. Add shrimp and coconut milk. Simmer until shrimp are cooked, about 5 minutes. Ladle into individual serving dishes and garnish with lime slices.

Note: The Scotch bonnet pepper is extremely hot. Take care that it does not burst during cooking, and remove it from the pot immediately after the soup is done.

Makes 10 servings.

CHICKEN PEPPER POT SOUP

For the chicken lover in you!

1 3- to 3$\frac{1}{2}$-pound chicken, cut into 8 pieces	$\frac{1}{2}$ teaspoon black pepper
10 cups chicken broth	1 15-ounce can chickpeas, rinsed
8 whole cloves	4 tablespoons unsalted butter
2 bay leaves	3 cloves of garlic, minced
3 thin slices peeled fresh ginger	4 tablespoons all-purpose flour
2 tablespoons turmeric	1 cup canned coconut milk
$\frac{1}{2}$ teaspoon cayenne pepper, to taste	$\frac{1}{2}$ cup heavy cream
1 tablespoon curry powder	Lemon wedges
	Fresh cilantro
	Hot cooked white rice

In a large enamel or stainless steel soup pot combine chicken and broth, bring to a rapid boil, reduce heat, and simmer for approximately 1 hour or until the chicken is tender and falls from the bones. While the chicken is simmering, add the cloves, bay leaf, ginger, turmeric, cayenne, curry powder, and black pepper. Skim away foam as it rises to the surface, then cover partly and simmer for about 1 hour or until chicken is tender and falling from the bones. Remove chicken and discard skin and bones. Pull chicken meat into bite-size pieces and set aside. Skim and strain soup and return to rinsed pot.

Purée chickpeas in blender or food processor with 1 to 2 cups of soup as needed. Pour puréed chickpeas with their liquid back into soup and return to a simmer with the pot partially covered.

Recipe can be prepared up to this point and stored, covered, in the refrigerator for 1 day.

About 30 minutes before serving, add chicken pieces to soup and bring to a simmer; add additional broth if the soup becomes too thick. Melt butter in a small skillet and when hot, sauté garlic for 3 to 4 minutes or until it just begins to brown. Sprinkle flour over the mixture, stirring and sautéing for about 5 minutes until it turns bright yellow. Beat into simmering soup with a whisk and cook 10 minutes.

Stir in coconut milk and cream and simmer gently for approximately 5 minutes. Adjust seasonings to taste, and then simmer for 5 minutes.

Serve in small bowls or cups garnished with lemon wedges and cilantro. If serving as a main course, mound portions of rice on side plates.

Makes 4 to 6 servings.

CARIBBEAN PUMPKIN & BLACK BEAN SOUP

High in fiber, this hearty and flavorful soup is perfect for fall!

2	teaspoons ground cumin	2	cups canned vegetable broth
2	15-ounce cans white pumpkin purée	8	tablespoons chopped fresh cilantro, divided
2	15-ounce cans black beans, drained	4	teaspoons fresh lime juice
2	14-ounce cans light unsweetened coconut milk	1¹/₂	teaspoons grated lime peel
			Salt or salt substitute to taste
			Pepper

Stir cumin in heavy medium saucepan over medium heat 30 seconds to release the flavor. Add pumpkin, beans, coconut milk, broth, and 5 tablespoons of the cilantro. Bring soup to a boil, stirring constantly. Reduce heat to medium-low and simmer 3 minutes to blend flavors. Mix in lime juice and lime peel. Season the soup to taste with salt (or salt substitute) and pepper. Ladle soup into bowls. Sprinkle with remaining 3 tablespoons of the cilantro.

Makes 4 servings.

JAMAICAN CREAM OF PUMPKIN SOUP

2	tablespoons butter		Salt and black pepper to taste
2	large onions, finely chopped	1	cup light cream
2¹/₄	pounds pumpkin, peeled and cut in chunks		Dash of Tabasco
4	cups chicken stock		Finely minced parsley
			Roasted shelled pumpkin seeds

Heat the butter in a saucepan and sauté the onion until transparent. Add pumpkin and chicken stock and simmer, covered, until the pumpkin is tender. Cool slightly and put through a sieve or process for a few seconds in an electric blender. Return the soup to the saucepan and season it with salt and pepper. Add the cream and Tabasco and gently reheat. Garnish with parsley and roasted pumpkin seeds.

Makes 6 servings.

Salads

Salads—cool, crunchy, and delicious—are often the perfect accompaniment to soup. And as with soup there is an endless variety from which to select. We'll start with a marinated Vidalia onion and sliced tomato salad and end with an adaptation of an African salad. While our adaptation is slightly saucier than the peach salad, it's not impertinent.

MARINATED VIDALIA ONION & SLICED TOMATO SALAD

Ummm ummm good. One taste and I am seated at my grandmother's table again, saying grace and asking my cousin to pass the salad.

2	medium Vidalia onions, sliced thin		$1/8$	teaspoon celery seeds
1	cup warm water		$1/8$	teaspoon cayenne pepper
$1/2$	cup sugar		1	large tomato, sliced thin
$1/4$	cup white vinegar			Mayonnaise
$1/4$	cup mayonnaise			Paprika
				Bread and butter pickles

Separate onion slices into rings. Combine water, sugar, and vinegar, stir until sugar dissolves. Pour mixture over onion rings and refrigerate to marinate for 3 to 4 hours or overnight. Drain and reserve marinade from onion rings. Arrange onion rings in a shallow serving dish with tomatoes. Stir mayonnaise and celery seeds into $^3/_4$ cup of the reserved marinade and pour over salad. Garnish with a small dollop of mayonnaise, paprika, and a scattering of bread and butter pickles before serving.

Makes 6 servings.

VIDALIA ONION & CUCUMBER SALAD

3 cups peeled, seeded, and thinly sliced cucumbers	$2^1/_2$ tablespoons fresh dill, chopped fine
$1^1/_2$ cups thinly sliced Vidalia onions or 2 small onions	$^1/_2$ teaspoon salt
$^2/_3$ cup grated carrot	$^1/_4$ teaspoon ground black pepper
$^1/_2$ cup white vinegar	6 $^1/_4$-inch slices of vine ripened tomatoes
$^1/_4$ cup sugar	6 boiled egg wedges

In a medium-sized bowl combine the cucumbers, Vidalia onions, and carrot. Set aside. Prepare dressing by combining the next five ingredients, mix well, and pour over the vegetables. Toss to coat and refrigerate three to four hours or until ready to serve. Using a slotted spoon, place a heaping mound of cucumber salad on a tomato slice and garnish with an egg wedge. The cucumber salad is also excellent when served alone.

Makes 6 servings.

OLD-FASHIONED CUCUMBER SALAD

I love cucumbers and this recipe is among my many favorites.

2 medium unpeeled cucumbers, scored and very thinly sliced	2 tablespoons chopped onion
	1 tablespoon lemon juice
	1 teaspoon celery seeds
1 small white onion, very thinly sliced	$1/4$ teaspoon minced dill
	$3/4$ teaspoon salt
$1/4$ cup white vinegar	$1/8$ teaspoon pepper

Arrange cucumber and onion in a shallow serving dish. In a separate bowl, combine the remaining ingredients, mix well, pour over cucumbers, cover, and chill 4 to 6 hours before serving.

Makes 6 servings.

CUCUMBER & ONION SALAD

This is a great side salad spring, summer, winter, or fall! It complements almost everything without being overpowering.

1 large cucumber	$1/4$ cup fresh squeezed lime juice
1 medium red onion	$1/4$ cup olive oil
1 large tomato	Salt and pepper
$1/4$ cup finely chopped parsley	

Cut up cucumbers, onion, and tomato into small cubes. Place in a salad bowl, add parsley, and lightly toss together. Combine remaining ingredients and use to dress the salad. Salt and pepper the salad to taste; and refrigerate to chill.

Makes 4 to 6 servings.

Isaac Blythers, Morris Brown '73

Isaac Blythers, named president of Atlanta Gas Light and Chattanooga Gas in June 2002, is responsible for executive oversight of these two regulated utilities. Before that, he served as vice president of operations, directing the management and operation of the customer care center, service centers, and field operations throughout the state of Georgia and in Chattanooga, Tennessee.

Blythers is active in the local community and is a member of several organizations including the Atlanta Chamber of Commerce (life member), DeKalb Alumni Chapter of Morris Brown College, Leadership Atlanta, Atlanta Rotary Club, and the Atlanta Chapter of 100 Black Men. In addition, Blythers serves on the board of directors for the Boys and Girls Club of Metro Atlanta, Junior Achievement, Communities in Schools, Emory University Board of Visitors, DeKalb County Zoning Board of Appeals, Senior Citizens Services Foundation, and the John C. and Dorothy J. Tucker Foundation.

MARINATED GARDEN-FRESH TOMATOES

Nothing is as delicious as garden-fresh tomatoes. The fresh parsley and basil only enhance their appeal. Don't refrigerate your tomatoes. Once refrigerated, tomatoes stop ripening and lose their taste. Keep this in mind when bringing tomatoes home that are underripe when they are shipped in order to reach their destination in an unspoiled condition.

4	large tomatoes		$1/4$	cup red wine vinegar
$1^1/_2$	tablespoons chopped fresh parsley		1	teaspoon salt
$1^1/_2$	tablespoons chopped fresh basil		$1/2$	teaspoon sugar
$1/3$	cup vegetable oil		$1/4$	teaspoon coarsely ground black pepper
			1	clove garlic, finely minced

Slice tomatoes $^{1}/_{2}$-inch thick and arrange in a shallow dish. Set aside. Garnish tomatoes with parsley and basil. Combine the remaining ingredients, mix well and pour over the tomato slices. Cover and marinate in the refrigerator for several hours or overnight.

Makes 6 servings.

SWEET PEPPER & ONION SALAD

1 medium green pepper, thinly sliced	1 clove garlic, minced
1 medium yellow pepper, thinly sliced	$^{1}/_{2}$ cup cider vinegar
1 medium red pepper, thinly sliced	$^{1}/_{2}$ cup water
1 red onion, sliced thin and separated into rings	$4^{1}/_{2}$ teaspoons vegetable oil
	2 tablespoons minced fresh basil
	$2^{1}/_{4}$ tablespoons sugar
	$^{1}/_{4}$ teaspoon salt
	$^{1}/_{8}$ teaspoon black pepper

Arrange the pepper and onion slices in a shallow serving dish. In a separate, small mixing bowl, combine the garlic, vinegar, water, and vegetable oil, mix well and pour over the salad. Refrigerate overnight. Just before serving, add the basil, sugar, salt, and pepper and mix well.

Makes 6 servings.

MARINATED CORN SALAD

The variety of color and flavor make this a particularly inviting summer salad. This old school favorite receives an A+ for its eye and taste appeal.

2 cups yellow corn cut from the cob (approximately 4 to 5 ears)

$^1/_3$ cup water

$^1/_3$ cup chopped red pepper

$^1/_4$ cup chopped onion

$^1/_2$ cup chopped celery

3 tablespoons thinly sliced green onion

1 tablespoon chopped fresh parsley

$^1/_4$ cup vegetable oil

1 tablespoon cider vinegar

$^1/_2$ teaspoon sugar

$^1/_2$ teaspoon salt

$^1/_2$ teaspoon dry mustard

$^1/_4$ teaspoon pepper

Combine corn and water in a medium-sized saucepan. Bring to a boil over medium-high heat and simmer 8 to 9 minutes or until the corn is crisp-tender. Drain, combine the corn with the pepper and the next four ingredients. Set aside. Combine the remaining ingredients and mix well. Dress salad, cover, and marinate for 4 hours or overnight before serving.

Makes 6 servings.

ZESTY BLACK-EYED PEA SALAD

Saucy but not impertinent, its zesty flavor demands notice. So do include it in a salad and bread supper. It pairs well with the Marinated Corn and Tomato and the Vidalia Onion salads.

2 16-ounce cans black-eyed peas

$^1/_2$ cup chopped celery

$^1/_3$ cup finely chopped Bermuda onion

1 green pepper, stemmed, seeded, and chopped

1 large tomato, peeled, seeded, and chopped

1 jalapeño pepper, stemmed, seeded, and chopped

3 cloves garlic, minced

3 green onions, sliced, include the tops

1 8-ounce bottle zesty Italian salad dressing

Combine the above ingredients in a large non-reactive bowl and toss together to blend. Cover and chill 8 hours, stirring occasionally. Drain and serve well chilled. Save marinade and add it and another can of beans to any remaining salad. Your family is sure to want more!

Makes 8 servings.

James A. McPherson, Morris Brown College '65

The work of novelist and short-story writer James Alan McPherson has appeared in twenty-seven journals and magazines, seven short-story anthologies, and *The Best American Essays.* He won the 1978 Pulitzer Prize for fiction for his short-story collection *Elbow Room,* as well as several prestigious grants and fellowships, including a Guggenheim Fellowship (1972 to 1973) and a MacArthur Foundation Award (1981). In 1995, McPherson was inducted into the American Academy of Arts and Sciences. He was educated at Morris Brown College, Harvard Law School, The University of Iowa Writers' Workshop, and Yale Law School. He is currently a professor of English at the University of Iowa. Other works include *A World Unsuspected, The Prevailing South, Confronting Racial Differences,* and his memoir, *Crabcakes.*

HONEYED HARVEST CARROT SALAD

Even your children will enjoy eating vitamin A–rich carrots prepared in this manner.

1	pound shredded carrots		¹/₂	cup raisins
1	8-ounce can crushed pineapple, drained		3	tablespoons sour cream
³/₄	cup miniature marshmallows		3	tablespoons lemon juice
¹/₂	cup flaked coconut		3	tablespoons honey
				Chopped toasted pecans

Combine first 5 ingredients in a large mixing bowl and set aside. Combine the remaining ingredients except the toasted pecans, pour over the carrot salad, and mix well. Cover and refrigerate 8 hours or overnight. Garnish with toasted pecans immediately before serving.

Makes 6 servings

TURNIP SLAW

Turnips elevate this delicious Southern favorite to new heights. Fresh turnips should have a smooth, firm appearance and feel heavy for their size.

3 cups shredded turnips	$^3/_4$ cup mayonnaise
$1^3/_4$ cups shredded carrot	1 tablespoon lemon juice
$^3/_4$ cup raisins	1 tablespoon sugar
2 tablespoons sour cream	

Combine the above ingredients in a large bowl. Mix the salad well, and refrigerate to chill before serving.

Makes 6 to 8 servings.

FESTIVE APPLE SLAW

Apples are a tasty and healthy addition to this slaw.

¼ cup sour cream	1½ cups grated cabbage
½ cup mayonnaise	1¼ cups grated red cabbage
¼ teaspoon celery seeds	½ cup grated carrots
1¼ teaspoons sugar	1 unpeeled apple, cored and
1 teaspoon white vinegar	coarsely chopped
Pinch of salt	

Combine the first six ingredients and mix well to make the salad dressing. In a large bowl, combine the dressing and remaining ingredients and refrigerate before serving.

Makes 6 to 8 servings.

WALDORF SALAD, GEORGIA STYLE

The peach preserves offer the perfect twist to this classical favorite!

5 medium Red Delicious apples, unpeeled	½ cup raisins
Juice of 1 lemon	⅓ to ½ cup mayonnaise
½ cup sliced celery	¼ cup peach preserves
½ cup chopped pecans	Lettuce leaves

Wash apples and pat dry before coring and cutting them into ½-inch cubes. Sprinkle with lemon juice to prevent discoloration. Combine apples with celery, pecans, and raisins. In a separate bowl combine mayonnaise and peach preserves. Mix well and add just enough to salad mixture to reach the desired consistency. Salad should be firm and chunky, not soupy. Serve apple salad on lettuce leaves.

Makes 6 servings.

GEORGIA PEACH SALAD WITH RASPBERRY VINAIGRETTE DRESSING

This luscious peach salad is perfectly at home on a formal dinner table or at a private alfresco dinner for two beneath Georgia's star-strewn sky.

4 peaches, sliced	$^1/_3$ cup raspberry preserves
Mixed greens	$2^1/_4$ tablespoons red wine vinegar
$^3/_4$ cup coarsely chopped pecans, toasted	1 tablespoon vegetable oil

Arrange peaches on serving plate over a bed of mixed greens. Sprinkle with pecans. Combine remaining ingredients and mix well. Drizzle over fruit.

Makes 4 to 6 servings.

CHICKEN PECAN FAN SALAD WITH PEACH VINAIGRETTE

The hand that the lady fans with may be otherwise occupied if this tasty salad is served at your next summer luncheon or garden party. Enjoy!

$4^1/_4$ cooked chicken, cubed	$^1/_4$ cup Peach Vinaigrette (recipe follows)
$1^3/_4$ cups toasted pecans, chopped	3 peach wedges, peeled
$^1/_3$ cup sliced green onions	Salad greens
$^1/_3$ cup raisins	
$^1/_2$ cup mayonnaise	

Combine the first four ingredients in a large bowl and mix gently to combine. In a separate bowl, combine the mayonnaise and peach vinaigrette and pour it over the chicken mixture and toss gently. Refrigerate for at least 2 hours before serving. Arrange beds of lettuce leaves on individual salad plates. Arrange a "fan" of three wedges of sliced peaches on the salad greens with half of it extending onto the plate. Spoon approximately ³/₄ cup of salad on each bed, taking care not to completely cover the fan. Drizzle an additional teaspoon of vinaigrette over the salad before serving.

Makes 6 servings.

PEACH VINAIGRETTE

1 cup peach preserves	1 teaspoon seasoning salt
¹/₄ cup peach nectar	1 teaspoon Italian seasoning
¹/₄ cup white vinegar	

Combine all of the above ingredients in a blender or food processor and puree until well blended. Refrigerate until ready to use.

Makes 1¹/₂ cups.

CHICKEN, PINEAPPLE & PEPPERED PECAN SALAD

I love the crunchy texture and subtle interplay of flavors in this salad, which is perfect luncheon fare.

1	teaspoon salt	1/2	cup mayonnaise
1/2	tablespoon coarsely ground black pepper	1/4	cup sour cream
1/8	teaspoon onion powder	1/2	cup sliced green onions, include tops
1/4	cup sugar		Salt
1	cup pecan pieces		White or black pepper, to taste
4	cups cubed, cooked chicken		Lettuce leaves
1	cup cubed pineapple pieces, well drained		

Lightly oil a cookie sheet and set aside. Combine salt, pepper, onion powder, and sugar and stir to blend. Heat heavy cast-iron skillet and add pecans. Place pan over high heat and stir pecans for 1 minute while pan is heating. Sprinkle half the sugar mix on pecans and continue to stir for 1 minute. While cooking, add remaining sugar mixture and continue to stir until sugar mixture is completely melted. Remove nuts and immediately place on pre-oiled cookie sheet. Set pecans aside and allow them to cool completely. Combine chicken, pineapple, mayonnaise, sour cream, and green onions in a large bowl; mix to combine and add salt and pepper to taste. Add pecans and toss well to coat and serve immediately. If desired, serve salad on a bed of lettuce leaves.

Makes 6 to 8 servings.

Thomas J. Byrd, Morris Brown College '74

In his twenty-year career, Byrd has starred in numerous film, stage, and television productions. Film credits include *The Kudzu Christmas, MacArthur Park, Bamboozled, Trois,*

Bulworth, He Got Game, Get on the Bus, Set It Off, Clockers, Young Guns 2, Out Cold, Wet Gold, Death Ride to Osaka, and *Young Doctors in Love.* He has performed at numerous regional theaters, including the San Diego Repertory Theater, the Alliance Theater, Indiana Repertory, Brooklyn Academy of Music, and the Long Wharf Theater. He made his Broadway debut as the erudite piano player Toledo in August Wilson's *Ma Rainey.* Playing opposite Whoopi Goldberg and Charles S. Dutton, he recalls thinking, " 'Hey, that's Whoopi Goldberg up here!' And I'm like . . . I'm the happiest person in town. I'm on stage next to Whoopi!"

JAMAICAN JERK CHICKEN SALAD

If you like a little drama, you will love this spicy salad drama queen.

1 head Belgian endive lettuce	Dressing (recipe follows)
2 15-ounce cans black beans, rinsed and drained	2 cups coarsely chopped Jerk Chicken Breast (recipe follows)
1/3 cup each red, yellow, and orange pepper, chopped	1 ripe mango, peeled, seeded, and sliced
1/2 cup ripe papaya, peeled and diced	1 ripe avocado, sliced into 8 wedges
1/3 cup chopped red onions	
1/3 cup sliced celery	

Wash lettuce and set aside to drain. Arrange a bed of lettuce on each of four plates. In a medium bowl combine the remaining ingredients except chicken, sliced mango, and avocado. Prepare dressing (see recipe below), pour 1/3 cup of it over the black beans, and toss lightly. Divide the salad among the four plates by spooning it on top of the lettuce. Top each individual salad with 1/2 cup of the chopped chicken. Garnish the side of each plate with the mango slices and two avocado wedges.

DRESSING

$1/2$	teaspoon salt		$1/4$	teaspoon fresh thyme
$1/4$	teaspoon ground cumin		1	teaspoon fresh ginger, grated
$1/4$	teaspoon allspice		$1/4$	cup vegetable oil
$1/8$	teaspoon chili powder		1	tablespoon + 2 teaspoons fresh lime juice
	Pinch ground nutmeg		1	tablespoon honey
	Pinch ground cinnamon		$1/4$	teaspoon ground red pepper
1	clove garlic, minced			

Combine the beans, peppers, papaya and red onion in a salad bowl, and mix gently. Combine the remaining ingredients in a tightly covered jar, shake well, and pour over salad just before serving.

Makes 4 to 6 servings.

JERK CHICKEN BREAST

1	tablespoon ground allspice		$1/2$	cup white vinegar
1	tablespoon dried thyme		$1/2$	cup orange juice
$1^3/4$	teaspoons cayenne pepper		$1/4$	cup lime juice
$1^1/2$	teaspoons freshly ground black pepper		2	Scotch bonnet peppers (habañero), seeded and finely chopped
$1^1/2$	teaspoons ground sage		5	green onions, finely chopped
1	teaspoon ground nutmeg		$1^1/4$	cups onion, finely chopped
1	teaspoon ground cinnamon		2	tablespoons grated ginger
2	tablespoons minced garlic		4 to 6	chicken breasts, washed and trimmed of fat
1	tablespoon sugar			
$1/4$	cup olive oil			
$1/4$	cup soy sauce			

In a large bowl, combine the first nine ingredients and mix to blend. Slowly add the olive oil, soy sauce, vinegar, orange juice and lime juice to the bowl while beating the mixture with a wire whisk. Add the peppers, onions and grated ginger to the bowl and mix well. Place chicken breasts in the marinade and turn once to coat. Marinate for at least 2 to 3 hours, longer if possible, turning once at the midway point.

Remove the breasts from the marinade and cook on a preheated grill for approximately 6 minutes on each side or until fully cooked. While the chicken is grilling use the leftover marinade to occasionally baste it. Chicken is done when the thickest part is pierced with a fork and the juices run clear.

BREAD & BUTTER PICKLE POTATO SALAD

It's likely that this recipe will conjure up the old-fashioned taste of your grandmother's "forgotten" potato salad recipe. Grocery store relishes don't quite capture that delicious taste. Take a bite and remember summers in the South or in the country at grandma's house.

4 pounds new potatoes, scrubbed	1 cup mayonnaise
1 small yellow onion, finely chopped	tablespoons cider vinegar
1 cup finely chopped bread and butter pickles plus $^1/_2$ cup of juice from the jar	1 large red pepper, stemmed, seeded, and chopped
	$^3/_4$ cup fresh parsley, minced
	Salt and pepper to taste

Bring potatoes to a rapid boil over high heat; reduce heat and simmer until the potatoes are fork tender, approximately 20 to 30 minutes. Drain well and allow to stand until sufficiently cool to handle.

In a large bowl combine the chopped onion, chopped pickles, pickle juice, mayonnaise, and vinegar. Once your potatoes are cool, cube them and add the red peppers. Pour the salad dressing over the salad and mix gently. Allow the salad to rest at room temperature for 15 minutes before adding $^1/_2$ cup of the parsley. Add salt and pepper to taste, mix well to blend, and transfer salad to a serving bowl. Garnish with remaining parsley and serve.

Makes 12 servings.

BREAD & BUTTER PICKLES

Bread and butter pickles, once only canned in home kitchens, are now available in stores. But if you have a hankering to make your own, here is the recipe:

4	quarts sliced pickling cucumbers		3	cups cider vinegar
8	medium white onions, sliced		2	tablespoons mustard seed
$1/3$	cup pickling salt		$1/2$	teaspoon crushed red pepper
4	cloves of garlic, halved		$1^1/2$	teaspoons turmeric
	Cracked ice		$1^1/2$	teaspoons celery seed
4	cups + 2 tablespoons sugar		18	whole allspice

In a 6- to 8-quart stockpot combine cucumbers, onions, pickling salt, and garlic. Add two inches of cracked ice. Cover the pot and refrigerate pickle mixture for 3 hours. Drain and remove the garlic halves from the mixture.

Add the sugar, vinegar, mustard seed, crushed red pepper, turmeric, celery seed, and allspice to the cucumber mixture and bring to a boil. Pack the hot cucumber mixture with liquid into hot, sterilized (follow manufacturer's directions) canning jars, leaving $1/2$ inch of headspace. Wipe rims, adjust lids, and process in boiling water for 10 minutes. Remove jars and cool on racks for 10 minutes.

Makes 7 pints.

JAMAICAN POTATO SALAD

Yah, mon, it's a little different from its American cousin, which follows, but it's a delicious accompaniment to Jerk Chicken and a multitude of other Caribbean dishes.

4¼	cups cooked potatoes, diced	¼	teaspoon black pepper
3	large boiled eggs, diced	¼	cup chopped celery
¼	cup sliced green onions	¼	cup corn
2	tablespoons butter, melted	¼	cup baby peas, blanched
1	clove garlic	¼	cup chopped carrots
½	teaspoon garlic powder	¼	teaspoon salt
1	cup mayonnaise		

Combine the above ingredients and mix well. Serve warm or cold.

Makes 6 to 8 servings.

ALL-AMERICAN POTATO SALAD

Enjoy this perennial favorite with any food—traditional soul food, barbecue, grilled meats, Southern traditional Sunday dinner favorites like turkey or ham. Are you hungry yet?

1½	pounds baking potatoes, halved	8	large hard-boiled eggs, coarsely chopped
¾	cup finely chopped red onion	½	cup mayonnaise
¾	cup finely chopped green pepper	2	tablespoons cider vinegar
⅓	cup finely chopped celery	1	tablespoon Dijon mustard
⅓	cup sweet pickle relish	½	teaspoon salt

Cook potatoes in boiling water 25 minutes or until they are fork tender; drain and cool completely. Peel and cut potatoes into $1/2$-inch cubes. Combine potatoes, onion, green pepper, celery, relish, and eggs in a large bowl. Combine mayonnaise and remaining ingredients in a small bowl; stir with a whisk. Pour over the potato mixture, tossing gently to coat. Cover and refrigerate at least 8 hours.

Makes 6 to 8 servings.

HOTLANTA SLAW

This flavorful slaw is a favorite at the Hotlanta Festival in Georgia. Crunchy pecans, sweet peaches, and the sizzle of jalapeño and cayenne peppers make it a riot of flavor for your mouth and an excellent pairing for smoked or grilled meats.

1 small head green cabbage, shredded (about 8 cups)	$1/2$ cup lemon juice
5 carrots, shredded (about 3 cups)	$1/2$ cup cider vinegar
1 16-ounce can sliced peaches, drained and coarsely chopped	2 tablespoons poppy seeds
	2 jalapeño peppers, seeded and minced
$1^1/4$ cups chopped toasted pecans	2 cloves garlic, minced
1 bunch green onions, thinly sliced (about 1 cup)	1 teaspoon ground black pepper
	1 teaspoon salt
1 cup mayonnaise	1 teaspoon sugar
	$1/4$ teaspoon paprika
	Pinch of cayenne pepper

Mix together cabbage, carrots, peaches, pecans, and green onions in a large bowl; set aside.

Combine mayonnaise, lemon juice, vinegar, poppy seeds, jalapeño, garlic, black pepper, salt, sugar, paprika, and cayenne pepper. Toss with the cabbage mixture and refrigerate for at least one hour before serving to allow flavors to blend.

Makes 12 servings.

HOT SLAW

Awww yeah! The party's on. Prepare this slaw and know that the "queue"—as in barbeque—will soon follow.

5	slices of bacon, fried crisp (reserve drippings)	4	cups shredded cabbage
1¼	teaspoons sugar	2	cups shredded purple cabbage
¼	teaspoon salt	1¼	cups chopped tomato
¼	teaspoon black pepper	1¼	cups peeled and chopped cucumber
3	tablespoons hot pepper vinegar	¾	cup thinly sliced green onions

Crumble bacon and set aside. Add sugar, salt, pepper, and vinegar to the pan drippings. Stir well and cook over medium heat until the mixture comes to a boil. Combine the cabbage and remaining ingredients in a large bowl; add the vinegar dressing and toss gently to mix. Garnish with bacon and serve immediately.

Makes 8 to 10 servings.

FRESH AVOCADO SALAD

This salad first appeared on my table this summer. It received so many rave reviews that I decided to include it for your enjoyment. It's great with almost any summer food, especially grilled meats. If the ingredients look familiar, they should. It's a salad-size version of almost everyone's favorite—guacamole! To Italianize it, substitute basil or parsley for the cilantro.

4	ripe, but slightly firm avocadoes, peeled, pitted, and quartered	3	large cloves of garlic, minced
		1/4	cup cilantro, finely chopped
		1/4	cup lime juice
2	vine-ripened tomatoes, washed and quartered	1/4	cup olive oil
			Kosher salt

Combine avocado, tomatoes, garlic, and cilantro in a mixing bowl and mix to blend. In a separate container combine the lime juice and olive oil; mix well and dress salad. Refrigerate to chill and add salt to taste just before serving.

Makes 4 to 6 servings.

Graduation.
(Private collection of Mr. Herman Mason)

Interdenominational Theological Center

A wise man who knows proverbs, reconciles difficulties.

—African proverb

Vegetables and Side Dishes

On November 8, 1866, the board of bishops of the Methodist Episcopal Church, assembled at New York City, declared: "The emancipation of millions of slaves has opened at our very doors a wide field of calling. . . . The time may come when the states in the South will make some provision for the education of the colored children now growing up in utter ignorance in their midst. But thus far they have made none, nor perhaps can it soon be expected of them. Christian philanthropy must supply this lack. We cannot turn away from the appeal that comes home to our consciences and hearts. Nor can we delay. The emergency is upon us, and we must begin to work now."

Following the abolition of slavery, many missionaries and ministers from diverse but like-minded church denominations flocked to the South where they established churches and schools to evangelize and educate former slaves. In doing so, they sought to not only educate minds,

Atlanta Baptist Seminary, the early home of the Morehouse School of Religion, which was organized to train black Baptist ministers following emancipation.
(Private collection)

but also to convert grateful hearts to their own Christian denominations. During this period several denominations, such as the American Home Mission Society, converged on Atlanta because, as the gateway to the South, Atlanta was home to a large black populace. They established educational institutions such as Atlanta University, Clark, and Morehouse, among others, to provide secular and religious education to former slaves.

The Interdenominational Theological Center is a collection of six private Christian seminaries founded in 1958 for the purpose of training African American ministers. The schools and their denominations, in order of dates of establishment, include the following: Morehouse School of Religion, Baptist (1867); Gammon Theological Seminary, United Methodist (1883); Turner Theological Seminary, African Methodist Episcopal (1885); Phillips School of Theology, Christian Methodist Episcopal (1944); Johnson C. Smith Theological Seminary, Presbyterian USA (1867); and Charles H. Mason Theological Seminary, Church of God in Christ (1970). This unique consortium of six seminaries is a Bible-centered, social action–oriented center, proficient in the study of black religion, including churches of Africa and the Caribbean. ITC has educated more than 35 percent of all trained black ministers in the world and 50 percent of all black chaplains in the United States military, including the highest-ranking female chaplain.

Each seminary has its own dean and board of directors, and each provides for its own student financial aid and housing. This traditionally black consortium is a United Negro College Fund member and a member of the Atlanta University Center.

The ITC is located on a ten-acre plot in the heart of the Atlanta University Center. The site is a generous gift of Atlanta University. The buildings and all other facilities are modern, providing every resource for effective instruction and comfortable living.

Since its inception, the ITC has welcomed into its enrollment students from denominations other than the six constituent denominations. These students are designated as "At-Large." Currently, At-Large students make up the fourth largest of the individual student segments at the ITC and participate fully in the life of the institution.

Morehouse School of Religion

In February 1867, the Augusta Institute, a school to train ministers and other church leaders, was organized in the Springfield Baptist Church of Augusta, Georgia, under the sponsorship of the American Baptist Home Mission Society. In 1879, the Institute moved to Atlanta, whereupon it was renamed Atlanta Baptist Seminary. Twenty years later, the seminary was authorized to offer college work and the name was changed to Atlanta Baptist College. Theological students continued to outnumber liberal arts students until 1923–24. In 1924, the Divinity School of Morehouse College, named in honor of Dr. Henry L. Morehouse, corresponding secretary of the American Baptist Home Mission Society, became known as the School of Religion and became the Baptist constituent member of the consortium known as the Interdenominational Theological Center.

Gammon Theological Seminary

Gammon Theological Seminary began in 1869–70 as a Department of Religion and Philosophy at Clark University (now Clark Atlanta University). Its benefactor, the Reverend Elijah H. Gammon, offered the school liberal financial support if it would become independent of Clark University, in order to serve the entire Methodist Episcopal Church and all her colleges in the South. In 1998, with the official connection between Gammon and Clark dissolved, the seminary was granted a charter. The seminary offered all students of Christian ministry, without distinction of race, an extensive and well-arranged course of study that is now the exclusive function of the ITC.

Reverend Elijah H. Gammon
(Private collection)

Turner Theological Seminary

Turner Theological Seminary began as a department of Morris Brown College in 1894. The name Turner Theological Seminary was approved in 1900 in honor of Bishop Henry McNeal Turner, the resident bishop of the African Methodist Episcopal Church and senior bishop of the denomination at that time. The seminary remained on the campus of Morris Brown College until 1957, when a building was acquired at 557 Mitchell Street. The Trustee Board of Morris Brown College authorized Turner Theological Seminary to become a founding constituent of Interdenominational Theological Center in 1958.

Turner Theological Seminary remains committed to its motto, "For a Prepared Ministry," in keeping with the aim of its founders to be "an institution for the preparation of young men and women for every department of Christian work." Her graduates can be found in all areas of the church: college and seminary teachers and presidents, pastors, presiding elders and bishops, as well as civic and political officials.

Phillips School of Theology

Phillips School of Theology, founded in 1944, is the only seminary of the Christian Methodist Episcopal (CME) Church. It was named for Senior Bishop Charles Henry Phillips, the twentieth bishop of the CME Church. In 1950, the General Conference of the Christian Methodist Episcopal Church designated the seminary as a connectional school, entitling it to the support of the denomination. Early enrollments at Phillips were across denominational lines. In 1958, Phillips School of Theology moved to Atlanta and became a founding constituent of the ITC.

Graduates of Phillips serve effectively at every level of ministry in the Christian Methodist Episcopal Church—as civilian and military chaplains, professors, and teachers. Phillips prides itself in shaping men and women for a competent, relevant ministry that is priestly, pastoral, and prophetic.

Johnson C. Smith Theological Seminary

Johnson C. Smith Theological Seminary is one of the ten theological institutions of the Presbyterian Church (USA). It was established in 1867 as a part of the Freedmen's College of North Carolina, subsequently named Biddle Memorial Institute, Charlotte, North Carolina. In 1923, Mrs. Jane Berry Smith of Pittsburgh endowed the institution and constructed several buildings on the 75-acre campus in honor of her husband, Johnson C. Smith. In recognition of this gift, the Board of Trustees voted to change the name of the Institute to Johnson C. Smith University. In 1969, the seminary moved to Atlanta and became a member of the ITC.

Charles H. Mason Theological Seminary

Initial plans for Charles H. Mason Theological Seminary began in 1965 when Senior Bishop Ozro Thurston Jones, Sr., convened a planning committee to explore the possibility of the Church of God in Christ organizing a seminary and becoming an affiliate of the Interdenominational Theological Center. He also invited Dr. Harry V. Richardson, president of ITC, to meet with that special committee.

In April 1970, the General Assembly of the Church of God in Christ authorized the Charles H. Mason Theological Seminary, named in honor of the founder of the church, to become a constituent seminary of the Interdenominational Theological Center. The seminary officially opened in the fall of 1970.

SUNDAY COLLARD GREENS WITH RICE & HAM

I remember, and perhaps you do too, when collard greens were a mainstay of plates sold for $1.25 at church fund-raising dinners. Even today their heady fragrance returns me to a time when I prayed, recited my Easter "piece" before the congregation, and received spiritual and physical nurturing in my grandmother's church.

6 to 8	cups cleaned and chopped collard leaves, loosely packed, approximately 1¹/₂ to 2 bunches	2	ham hocks, washed
		2	cups cooked long-grain rice
		1	cup coarsely chopped ham
			Salt and pepper to taste

Clean greens by removing thick stalks and discarding any yellowed or badly blemished leaves. Wash greens under cold running water and rinse any remaining sand from the sink. Fill sink with cold water, add greens, and plunge up and down several times to wash any remaining sand and sediment from the greens. Stack several leaves and roll cigar fashion and slice into horizontal segments slightly smaller than ¹/₄ inch.

Place ham hocks in a large pot and add sufficient water to cover the ham hocks by 3 to 4 inches. Bring to a rapid boil. Reduce heat, cover pot, and allow ham hocks to simmer for 1¹/₂ hours, adding additional water as necessary to prevent scorching. Add the collard greens and cook until tender, approximately 1 to 1¹/₂ hours. Young, tender greens will require less cooking time; older greens will require more cooking time. Remove all except 4 cups of "pot liquor" (liquid) and set aside. Remove ham hocks from the pot and allow to cool, so that they may be safely handled. Remove fat and skin and discard or return to the pot (depending on your dietary habits). Remove the lean meat from the bone, chop it up, and return to the pot. Add rice, ham, and additional liquid as necessary to prevent the mixture from being

In my parents' house, Sunday was a day of family worship.
(Private collection)

too dry. However, it should not be soupy. Stir to combine. Add salt and pepper to taste. Serve hot with homemade hot sauce (see recipe below) and hot corn muffins on the side.

Makes 6 to 8 servings.

HOT! HOT! HOT! HOMEMADE HOT HABAÑERO PEPPER SAUCE

You almost can't serve greens in the South without passing chow-chow, a bottle of hot pepper vinegar, or some hot sauce to top them off! Your family and friends will be amazed when you present them with your own homemade hot sauce, but remember—a dab will do.

½ cup chopped onion
3 cloves garlic, minced
½ cup chopped carrots
14 habañero peppers, stems and
    seeds removed, finely
    chopped

1 tablespoon vegetable oil
½ cup distilled vinegar
¼ cup lime juice
   Small bay leaves

Sauté the onion and garlic in oil until the onion is limp or transparent. Next, add the carrots together with approximately ¼ cup of water. When the water begins to boil, reduce the heat and simmer until the carrots are soft. Place the carrot mixture and peppers into a blender and purée until smooth. Don't allow the peppers to cook, since cooking dilutes the flavor of the habañero. Combine the purée with vegetable oil vinegar and lime juice, and then simmer for 5 minutes. Place a bay leaf in each sterilized jar used, add sauce, and seal.

Makes 2 cups.

Garden Mustards with Fresh Red Tomatoes

As a young child visiting my grandmother in Tampa, Florida, I always attended Tyer Temple United Methodist Church of which she was a founding member. Every Sunday, my cousin Victoria and I sang in the youth choir. . . . Ok, ok, so Vicky sang and I was asked to "simply move my lips." I wasn't offended; I simply continued the exercise at Sunday dinner where my grandmother served one of her delicious greens dishes.

3 pounds mustard greens,
    cleaned and chopped
2 ham hocks
8 cups water
2 teaspoons vegetable oil
2¼ cups chopped onion

3 cloves garlic, minced
2 cups peeled, seeded, and diced
    ripe tomatoes
½ teaspoon red pepper flakes
   Salt and freshly ground pepper
    to taste

Clean greens by removing thick stalks and discarding any yellowed or badly blemished leaves. Wash greens under cold running water and rinse any remaining sand from the sink. Fill sink with cold water, add greens, and plunge up and down several times to wash any remaining sand and sediment from the greens. The curly leaves of mustard greens tend to retain sand so several washings may be necessary. Stack several leaves, roll cigar fashion and slice into horizontal segments slightly smaller than ¼ inch.

Combine ham hocks and water in large pot. Place on medium-high heat. Bring to a boil. Reduce heat and simmer for about 1½ hours, or until liquid has reduced to about 3 cups. Add greens, cover, and simmer for 30 minutes. Remove cover and simmer for an additional 30 to 45 minutes or more.

Heat vegetable oil in large skillet over medium heat. Add onion and garlic. Sauté the onion for 10 minutes or until it is transparent and then stir it into the collard greens. Stir in tomatoes and red pepper flakes and cook an additional 5 to 10 minutes. Add salt and pepper to taste. Serve piping hot with a large wedge of buttermilk cornbread and cucumbers and vinegar on the side.

Makes 4 to 6 servings.

BLAZING JALAPEÑO & TURKEY GREENS

This is equally at home as either a one-pot Sunday meal or a side dish.

5 pounds assorted greens (collard, kale, mustard, and turnip, etc.)	1 quart chicken broth
2 tablespoons vegetable oil	2 smoked turkey wings, approximately 2 to 2½ pounds
1 large onion, chopped	Seasoned salt and ground black pepper to taste
½ cup green bell pepper, chopped	Chopped fresh jalapeno peppers
3 jalapeño peppers, seeded and minced (optional)	Chopped onions

Clean greens by removing thick stalks and discarding any yellowed or badly blemished leaves. Wash greens under cold running water and rinse any remaining sand from the sink. Fill sink with cold water, add greens, and plunge up and down several times to wash any remaining sand and sediment from the greens.

The curly leaves of mustard greens tend to retain sand so several washings may be necessary. Roll leaves cigar fashion and slice into horizontal segments slightly smaller than ¹/₄ inch.

In a large pot, combine the vegetable oil, onions, green bell pepper, and jalapeños; sauté over medium heat until the onions are limp. Add chicken broth and smoked turkey wings; bring to a rapid boil over high heat. Reduce heat, cover, and simmer for 1 hour. Add additional broth as necessary to prevent scorching. Gradually stir in the greens, allowing each batch to wilt before adding more greens. Bury the turkey wings in the simmering greens. Cover and reduce the heat to medium-low. Continue cooking the greens an additional 30 minutes. Uncover the pot and cook an additional 15 to 30 minutes, or until the greens are tender to personal taste, stirring occasionally. Younger greens will require less cooking time; older greens will require more. Remove the turkey wings. Discard the skin and bones, chop the meat, and return to the pot. Season with seasoned salt and pepper to taste.

Every Sunday was also a homecoming celebration when extended family members gathered to share a meal and the traditions that bound us together.
(Private collection)

Using a slotted spoon, transfer the greens to a serving dish. Serve hot with additional chopped peppers and onion on the side for garnish.

A chunk of cornbread and some sliced tomatoes with onions would make this meal a feast by anyone's definition.

Makes 6 to 8 servings.

COLLARD GREENS & CABBAGE WITH SWEET ONION RELISH

What a tasty dish; especially when served with down-home chicken and a skillet of pan bread! Today it seems to be calling my name . . . maybe this Sunday?

3 slices of bacon	4 bunches collard greens, cleaned and cut
1 large onion, chopped	1 head cabbage, cleaned and cut up
1 large green pepper, seeded and chopped	$1/4$ teaspoon crushed red peppers or to taste
3 large cloves of garlic, peeled and chopped	Salt and pepper to taste
2 medium ham hocks	

Place bacon in a large stockpot and fry over medium high heat to render fat. Continue to cook the bacon until it is slightly browned. Add onion, pepper, and garlic and sauté until the onion is limp or transparent. Add the ham hocks, cover with water by 2 to 3 inches or more to allow the ham hocks to boil freely. Place on medium-high heat. Bring to a boil. Reduce heat and simmer for about $1^1/2$ hours. Add the collard greens; cover and cook until tender, approximately 1 hour or to taste. Add the cabbage during the last 20 minutes of cooking time and cook until tender or to taste. Season with salt and pepper to taste. Offer sweet onion relish to garnish (recipe follows).

Makes 10 to 12 servings.

SWEET ONION RELISH

10 pounds Vidalia onions, peeled and quartered	1 teaspoon turmeric
1/2 cup salt	1 teaspoon pickling spice
1 quart cider vinegar	1 4-ounce jar chopped pimento
	4 1/2 cups sugar

Process onions in a food processor to yield 1 1/2 gallons. Add salt and allow to stand for 30 minutes. Squeeze juice from the onions and discard; place onions in a large pot. Add vinegar. Place spices in cheese cloth or tea ball. Add spice ball and sugar to the vinegar. Bring mixture to a boil and simmer for 30 minutes, stirring often. Spoon onions and sufficient liquid to cover into canning jars, which have been sterilized according to manufacturer's directions, leaving 1/2 inch headspace. Remove air bubbles by running a plastic knife to the bottom of the jar several times. Tighten lids and process in a water canner according to manufacturer's directions or for 10 minutes in a boiling water bath.

Makes 8 pints.

Sunday dinner, fragrant and inviting, greeted you warmly at the front door, drew you in with a smile, and wrapped its arms around you.
(Private collection)

BOILED STRING BEANS WITH PIG'S TAILS

Before purchasing string or green beans check for freshness by breaking a bean in half. The bean should snap crisply and have a flavorful taste with just a hint of sweetness. Never select beans that are dull, limp, and flat-tasting.

8	pig's tails	2½	teaspoons salt
2⅓	pounds fresh string beans	1	teaspoon black pepper
½	cup chopped onion	1	teaspoon sugar

Place pig's tails in a large pot with sufficient water to cover the pig's tails by 3 to 4 inches. Bring to a rapid boil over high heat. Reduce heat, cover, and simmer for 1 hour. Add additional water as necessary to prevent scorching. Prepare the green beans while the pig's tails are simmering. Snap the stem at each end of the bean, without severing it from the bean; then pull gently along the length of the bean to remove the string and the stem. (It may not be necessary to remove the string from very young beans.) Rinse the beans in a colander under cold running water and drain. Add the beans and remaining ingredients to the pot and allow to simmer until the beans are tender, 30 to 45 minutes or to taste. Add more seasoning according to taste.

Makes 4 large servings.

POLE BEANS

Nothing beats the taste of garden fresh pole beans. In the middle of winter, I sometimes find myself counting the days until summer when my garden will again produce pole beans! Pole beans are the broad, flat, thick-skinned cousin of conventional string or green beans and they are ideal for slow cooking. In my family we are guilty of slow cooking all beans grouped in this category. However, pole beans simply must be slow cooked.

1	smoked ham hock		$^1/_2$	teaspoon sugar
3	pounds pole beans			Salt and freshly ground black
1	small yellow onion, finely			pepper
	chopped			Pepper vinegar (recipe follows)
1	clove garlic, minced		$^1/_2$	teaspoon cayenne pepper

Place the ham hock in a large pot and add sufficient water to cover by 3 to 4 inches. Place over medium-high heat and bring to a boil. Reduce heat and simmer for about $1^1/_2$ hours. Prepare the green beans while the ham hock is simmering. Snap the stem at each end of the bean without severing it from the bean, then pull gently along the length of the bean to remove the string and the stem. (It may not be necessary to remove the string from very young beans.) Rinse the beans in a colander under cold running water and drain. Add the beans and remaining ingredients to the pot and allow the beans to simmer until tender, 45 to 60 minutes or to taste. Add additional seasoning according to taste.

Serve hot with condiments such as chopped raw onion, pickled hot peppers, and pepper vinegar.

Makes 10 to 12 servings.

PEPPER VINEGAR

My grandfather made his pepper vinegar by pouring about one-fourth of the vinegar out of a cider-vinegar bottle and filling the remaining space with hot peppers from his bush in the yard. He then would allow the peppers to marinate a week or two before serving. As the pepper vinegar was used, he would simply add more vinegar. Just before the peppers became too weak for reuse, he would start another batch. Don't wait too long, though, this vinegar is addicting. You will find yourself using it on greens and other vegetables. If, like me, you don't have a pepper bush, try using small Serrano peppers, but keep in mind they are very hot and you may need fewer of them, or you can divide the batch and dilute it by adding more vinegar.

Makes about 4 cups.

SAUTÉED GREEN BEANS

This excellent recipe is one handed down by my grandmother to my mother and then to me. It's as treasured as any heirloom received from them.

2	tablespoons bacon fat	1	small onion, finely chopped
2	pounds green beans, cleaned and tips removed	1/2	cup water
		1	teaspoon sugar or to taste

What could be more comfortable or comforting than a soft lap to sit on
while enjoying a delicious dessert treat on Sunday afternoon?
(Private collection)

Heat the bacon fat in a large cooking pot. Add the beans, salt, and pepper. Sauté the beans until they are lightly golden, about 3 minutes. Add the onion and sauté another minute. Add just enough water for moisture. Stir in sugar, cover, reduce heat to medium, and cook 20 to 25 minutes or until beans are the desired tenderness. Add additional water as necessary to prevent scorching. Uncover and cook beans down for an additional 10 to 15 minutes or to taste.

Makes 6 to 8 servings.

SAVORY GREEN BEANS

1$\frac{1}{2}$ pounds fresh green beans	$\frac{1}{2}$ teaspoon sugar
3 tablespoons of bacon drippings or vegetable oil	$\frac{1}{4}$ teaspoon beef bouillon granules
2 cloves garlic, crushed	$\frac{1}{4}$ teaspoon black pepper
$\frac{1}{4}$ cup chopped onion	

Wash the green beans, trim ends, and remove the strings. Place the bacon drippings or vegetable oil in a large saucepan and sauté the garlic and onions over medium-high heat. Remove and discard the garlic. Add the remaining ingredients, cover, and cook over medium heat for 30 minutes or until the green beans reach the desired degree of tenderness.

Makes 6 servings.

BAKED OKRA, CORN & TOMATO CASSEROLE

You can almost hear the back screen door slam, the fan humming, chairs scraping against the broom-scrubbed hardwood floor, and red Kool-Aid being poured. Amen?

3	cups sliced fresh okra	1	large onion, thinly sliced
1/3	cup chopped Canadian bacon	1/2	teaspoon salt
1	large tomato, chopped	1/4	teaspoon pepper
1/2	cup frozen corn	2	tablespoons water

Preheat oven to 350°F. Coat a 1 3/4 quart casserole dish with a thin layer of butter. Layer half of the okra, Canadian bacon, tomato, corn, and onion slices. Sprinkle evenly with half of the salt and pepper. Repeat and sprinkle with water. Cover with aluminum foil, place in preheated oven, and bake until the vegetables are tender, 40 to 45 minutes.

Makes 6 servings.

FRESH CORN, OKRA & TOMATO

Savor this Southern summertime tradition. When selecting fresh corn, look for fresh green husks, dry silks, and even rows of plump kernels. If you pop a kernel between your fingers and the milk is watery, the corn is immature. If it is thick and starchy, the corn is old.

3	tablespoons butter	1 3/4	tablespoons tomato paste
3/4	cup chopped green pepper	1/2	teaspoon salt
1 1/4	cups chopped onion	1/4	teaspoon ground black pepper
1 3/4	cups white corn cut from the cob (approximately 4 ears)		Pinch ground nutmeg
3/4	cup water	1/4	teaspoon paprika
2	medium tomatoes, peeled, seeded, and chopped	1 1/2	cups sliced okra

Melt butter in a large skillet over medium-high heat. Add green pepper and onion and sauté until the vegetables are crisp-tender. Reduce the heat to medium, add the corn, water, tomato, tomato paste, salt, pepper, nutmeg, and paprika; cover and continue to cook 10 minutes, stirring occasionally. Add okra, cover, and simmer 5 to 7 additional minutes. Add salt and pepper to taste.

Makes 6 servings.

FRIED CORN

When storing fresh corn, leave it in husks and refrigerate to prevent the sugar from turning to starch.

12 ears fresh white corn	$3/4$ cup water
$1/2$ cup butter	$1/8$ teaspoon ground nutmeg
2 tablespoons bacon drippings	$1/2$ teaspoon salt
$1/2$ cup chopped onion	$1/4$ teaspoon black pepper

Husk and remove the silk from the corn. Cut corn from the cob; forcefully scrape each cob again to remove the milk, and set aside. Combine the butter and bacon drippings in a large skillet over medium-high heat. Add onions and sauté until the onions are tender and translucent. Add corn, stir, and continue to cook for 2 to 3 minutes. Add the water, nutmeg, salt, and pepper. Cook uncovered over medium heat until the mixture comes to a boil. Reduce heat and simmer 10 to 12 minutes or until the liquid is absorbed, stirring frequently.

Makes 10 to 12 servings.

Fresh Corn Fritters

1   pint grated fresh corn,
     uncooked
¹/₂ cup corn milk (scraped from
     the cobs)
2   egg yolks (reserve whites)

¹/₂ cup flour
1   teaspoon salt
1   teaspoon baking powder
1   tablespoon melted butter

Sunny Sunday afternoons also bring back memories of family car rides,
even when Dad was stationed overseas. (My mother is to the left,
I am in the middle, and that's my Uncle Johnny on the right.
Dad is taking the photo with his brand new Kodak camera.)
Note the car plates.

(Private collection)

Place fresh grated corn in a large mixing bowl and set aside. In a separate bowl, collect milk from cobs by forcefully scraping them with a spoon or butter knife. Measure $1/2$ cup of the corn milk and add to the grated corn. Add the egg yolks and mix well. Next, combine flour, salt, and baking powder, mix until well blended. Add flour mixture and butter to the corn mixture and mix to combine. Beat reserved egg whites until stiff and fold into the corn mixture. Drop fritter batter from a tablespoon onto a well-greased, hot griddle or frying pan and cook like pancakes. Serve with melted butter, syrup, and plenty of crispy, fried bacon.

Makes 6 servings.

FRESH BUTTER BEANS

3 tablespoons bacon drippings
    or 4 slices bacon
1 large onion, finely chopped

1 cloves garlic, minced
1 meaty ham hock

Heat bacon drippings in a large pot over medium-high heat or render drippings from bacon and reserve bacon. Add onion and garlic and sauté until the onion is translucent. Rinse ham hock and place it in the pot with sufficient water to cover. Bring ham hock to a rapid boil, reduce heat to low, cover, and simmer for one hour. Rinse beans before adding them to the pot. Bring to a boil. Reduce heat and simmer, stirring occasionally, until beans are tender, 30 to 45 minutes. Add more water as needed to prevent scorching. Cut ham from the ham hock, chop, and return the meat to the pot. Crumble reserved bacon and serve as an optional garnish for the beans.

Makes 6 to 8 servings.

SPICY HOT PINTO BEANS

Spicy hot and deliciously satisfying!

1 pound dried pinto beans	¹/₄ cup firmly packed brown sugar
2 ham hocks	2 tablespoons ground cumin
2 tablespoons bacon drippings or five slices of bacon	1 tablespoon chili powder
1 large onion, diced	1 teaspoon black pepper
³/₄ cup chopped green pepper	1 teaspoon hot pepper sauce
5 garlic cloves, finely minced	1 teaspoon salt
1 jalapeño pepper, stemmed, seeded, and finely chopped	2 small bay leaves
¹/₄ cup Worcestershire sauce	1 16-ounce can undrained, chopped tomatoes
1 pound smoked link sausage, cut into 12-inch slices	

Pick over beans and remove any stones or other foreign objects. Rinse beans and place them in a large non-reactive container with sufficient water to cover by 2 inches and soak overnight. Rinse ham hocks and place them in a large Dutch oven with sufficient water to cover by 3 to 4 inches. Bring ham hocks to a rapid boil, reduce heat to low, cover, and simmer for one hour. Drain the beans and rinse again before adding them to the Dutch oven.

Heat bacon drippings in a large skillet over medium-high heat or render drippings from the bacon and discard bacon. Add onion, green pepper, garlic, and jalapeño pepper to the drippings and sauté until the onion is translucent and the remaining vegetables are tender. Add to the beans. Add Worcestershire and the remaining ingredients except the tomatoes; bring the mixture to a rapid boil, reduce heat, cover and simmer for 2 hours or until the beans are tender, stirring occasionally. Add tomatoes and juice. Cook an additional 30 minutes. Cut lean meat from the ham hock, chop, and return the meat to the pot. Remove bay leaves before serving.

Makes 10 servings.

BLACK-EYED PEAS AND TOMATOES

Dried peas and beans, both rich in nutrients, provide much needed sustenance to people during the winter months when fresh beans and vegetables are too expensive. However, they require soaking to rehydrate. If an overnight soaking is impossible, there is a quicker method: Combine 1 pound dried peas or beans and 2 quarts of water in a large pot and bring to a boil. Place a cover on the pot and cook an additional two minutes before removing the peas from the heat and allowing them to stand 1 hour. Drain, and then cook according to directions.

1 pound black-eyed peas	1 clove garlic, finely minced
2 tablespoons bacon drippings or vegetable oil	2 large meaty ham hocks
1 large onion, chopped	2 bay leaves
1 green pepper, stemmed, seeded, and chopped	1 teaspoon salt
	1^1/$_2$ cups garden fresh chopped tomatoes, undrained

Pick over beans and remove any stones or other foreign objects. Rinse beans and place them in a large non-reactive container with sufficient water to cover by 2 inches and soak overnight. Place bacon drippings or vegetable oil in a large Dutch oven and bring to medium heat. Add onions, green pepper, and garlic to Dutch oven. Cook until onions are transparent. Rinse ham hocks and place them in the Dutch oven with sufficient water to cover. Increase heat to medium-high and bring ham hocks to a rapid boil, reduce heat to low, cover, and simmer for one hour. Drain the beans and rinse again before adding them to the Dutch oven. Add bay leaves and salt, bring beans to a rapid boil, reduce heat, cover, and simmer 2 hours or until the beans are tender. Remove top and cook an additional 20 minutes uncovered to allow the beans to cook down. Add the tomatoes, stir, and cook an additional 15 to 20 minutes.

Makes 6 to 8 servings.

BLACK-EYED PEAS WITH SMOKED PORK

Pass the peas and praise the Lord!

1 pound dried black-eyed peas, rinsed, picked over, soaked overnight	2 bay leaves Salt and pepper to taste
1 smoked pork picnic shoulder, about 5 to 7 pounds	

Pick over the peas to remove any foreign objects and soak overnight in sufficient water to cover by 2 to 3 inches. Place pork in a large pot of boiling water, cover, and bring to a second boil. Reduce heat, add bay leaves, and simmer for 1½ hours. Drain and rinse the peas and add to the pot, and simmer an additional 1½ hours longer, or until pork and peas are tender. Remove pork from pot; trim off skin and fat

Sunday was a day to relax and recreate. Sometimes—after church, of course—the entire family picnicked and fished.

(Private collection)

layers. Slice about half of the pork ¹/₄ inch thick. Season peas with salt and pepper to taste and allow the peas to cook down until liquid reaches the desired consistency. Serve with pork slices, rice, and corn bread.

Makes 6 to 8 servings.

John's Hip-Hoppin' Black-Eyed Peas

Black-eyed peas, thought to have originated in North Africa, were probably introduced to the New World by Spanish explorers and African slaves. Now common in the Southern United States, they are available dried, fresh, canned, and frozen.

1 pound dried black-eyed peas	2 smoked ham hocks
1 large onion, peeled and coarsely chopped	2 bay leaves
1 large green pepper, seeded and chopped	3 teaspoons seasoned salt
3 jalapeño peppers, seeded and chopped	¹/₂ teaspoon onion powder
3 cloves garlic, large	¹/₂ teaspoon ground cumin
3 tablespoons vegetable oil	³/₄ teaspoon dried thyme leaves
	1¹/₂ cups seeded and diced tomatoes

Pick over the peas to remove any foreign objects and soak overnight in sufficient water to cover by 2 to 3 inches. In a large pot, sauté the onions, green pepper, jalapeño pepper and garlic in the vegetable oil until the onion is limp or transparent. Rinse the ham hocks, add to the pot, also adding sufficient water to cover by 3 to 4 inches. Place on medium-high heat and bring to a boil. Reduce heat and simmer for about 1¹/₂ hours. Drain and rinse the peas, add to the pot, and simmer an additional 1 hour. Add the bay leaves, seasoned salt, onion powder, ground cumin, and dried thyme leaves. Remove the ham hocks, coarsely chop the lean meat, and return it to the pot. Add the tomatoes and cook down an additional half hour or until the beans are soft and the liquid slightly thickened.

Makes 4 to 6 servings.

BUTTER BEANS & OKRA

I love all types of beans, prepared in a variety of ways. Butter beans, also known as calico beans or Madagascar beans, are among my favorites.

1¹/₂ pounds dried butter beans	2 tablespoons solid vegetable shortening
1 meaty ham bone or 3 large ham hocks	1 tablespoon sugar
3 cups water	1 tablespoon salt
¹/₂ pound okra, washed and thinly sliced	2 teaspoons freshly ground black pepper

Pick over the beans to remove any foreign objects and soak overnight in sufficient water to cover by 2 to 3 inches. In a large pot combine hambone or ham hocks and sufficient water to cover by 3 to 4 inches. Place on medium-high heat and bring to a boil. Reduce heat and simmer for about 1¹/₂ hours. Remove the ham hocks from the pot and set aside to cool. Meanwhile, drain and rinse the beans and add them to the pot. Cover and allow the beans to simmer for an additional hour. While the beans are simmering, remove the lean meat from the cooled ham hocks, shred it, and return the shredded meat to the pot. Add the okra, cover, and simmer an additional 25 minutes. Uncover the pot and cook down an additional 15 to 20 minutes or until the beans are tender and the liquid is slightly thickened.

Makes 6 to 8 large servings.

TWICE-BAKED HONEY & PECAN SWEET POTATOES

6 medium sweet potatoes, scrubbed	¹/₄ teaspoon salt
3 tablespoons butter	¹/₄ cup pecans, toasted and chopped
3 tablespoons honey	

And then there was Easter Sunday with cousins Deborah, Judy, and Barbara Jeane Quick.
(Private collection)

Preheat oven to 400°F. Prick each potato once with a fork and bake it on a foil lined, rimmed baking sheet 45 to 55 minutes or until it is fork-tender and soft. Remove the potatoes from the oven and set aside to cool. When they are sufficiently cool to handle, cut them in half lengthwise and scoop insides into a medium bowl. Mash together with the next three ingredients until smooth. Spoon potatoes back into skins and garnish with the pecans. Reduce oven temperature to 350°F. Place the potatoes on a foil-lined baking sheet and bake uncovered for 15 minutes.

Makes 6 servings.

SWEET POTATO CASSEROLE

3 cups grated uncooked sweet potato	4 eggs, slightly beaten
1¼ cups sugar	3 tablespoons all-purpose flour
1 cup table cream	¼ teaspoon allspice
½ teaspoon vanilla extract	½ teaspoon ground nutmeg
¼ cup butter	¼ teaspoon ground cinnamon

Preheat oven to 350°F. Lightly butter a shallow, 2-quart baking dish and set aside. Combine the above ingredients and mix well before spooning into the prepared casserole dish. Bake uncovered for 30 minutes. Stir and bake an additional 15 minutes or until a knife inserted in the center comes out clean.

Makes 6 to 8 servings.

CANDIED YAMS WITH BOURBON

Simply delicious!

6 to 8 large sweet potatoes, peeled, boiled, and cubed	3 tablespoons brown sugar
¼ cup light corn syrup	1 teaspoon cinnamon
¼ cup dark corn syrup	¼ cup good Kentucky bourbon
	Chopped pecans, toasted

Arrange sweet potatoes in a buttered casserole pan or dish. Combine remaining ingredients and pour over potatoes. Bake at 350°F until bubbling hot. Garnish with toasted pecans.

Makes 4 to 6 servings.

SWEET POTATO SOUFFLÉ

Can it be Sunday dinner without sweet potatoes? I don't think so, and neither will you once you try this sweetly delicious soufflé.

3 cups cooked sweet potatoes, mashed	½ cup light corn syrup
½ cup sugar	3 eggs
¼ cup melted butter	¼ teaspoon nutmeg
	1¼ teaspoons vanilla extract

Spray a 2-quart baking dish with cooking spray. Preheat oven to 350°F. Mash sweet potatoes and set aside. Combine sugar, butter, syrup, eggs, nutmeg, and vanilla. Beat until creamy. Stir butter mixture into mashed sweet potatoes. Pour potato mixture into prepared dish. Prepare topping (recipe follows) and sprinkle over potatoes. Bake the soufflé in a preheated oven for 35 minutes or until soufflé is lightly browned.

Makes 6 to 8 servings.

TOPPING

1 cup brown sugar, firmly packed	½ cup flour
½ cup butter	½ teaspoon cinnamon
	1 cup chopped pecans

Combine brown sugar, butter, flour, cinnamon, and chopped nuts. Sprinkle over Sweet Potato Soufflé before baking.

Easter Sunday with my cousins and brother Kevin
(note the 45 rpm records behind Kevin).
(Private collection)

OLD-FASHIONED PARSLEY MASHED POTATOES

The rich, old fashioned flavor of this potato dish hearkens to an earlier era when dinner took time to prepare and diners lingered over their meals while sharing memories and traditions.

8	medium white potatoes, peeled and cubed	$^1/_3$	cup butter
1	medium onion, finely chopped	1	teaspoon salt
Up to $^2/_3$	cup of evaporated milk, divided	$^1/_4$	teaspoon sugar
		$^1/_8$	teaspoon white pepper
		2	tablespoons finely minced parsley

Cook the potatoes and onion in enough boiling water to cover for 15 minutes or until the potatoes are fork-tender. Drain the water away, retaining the onion with the potatoes, add remaining ingredients and mash with additional milk as needed until the potatoes reach their desired consistency. Serve piping hot. With gravy or not, these potatoes are delicious either way.

Makes 8 servings.

THREE-CHEESE MACARONI 'N' CHEESE

Mac and cheese is another Sunday favorite in my family. How about yours?

1 pound elbow macaroni	2 cups grated Monterey Jack cheese
¼ stick of butter	¼ cup table cream
8 ounces mild Cheddar cheese, grated	¼ cup sour cream
8 ounces Colby Jack cheese, grated	Pinch of nutmeg
	Salt and pepper to taste

Preheat oven to 350°F. Cook macaroni according to package directions; drain, and add butter and cheese. Stir gently to combine. Add table cream, sour cream, and nutmeg. Continue cooking until cheeses are melted and the mixture is smooth and creamy. Stir constantly to prevent scorching. Add salt and pepper to taste. Pour mixture into a lightly buttered baking dish and bake for approximately 15 minutes.

Makes 4 to 6 servings.

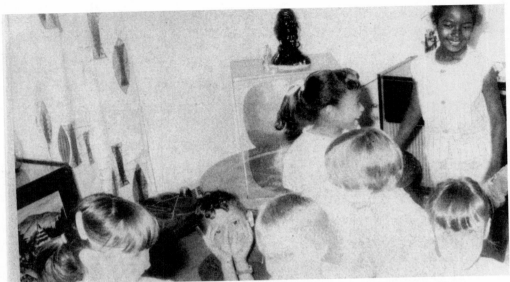

Birthday Sundays were always the best. I am the girl with the ponytail and bangs,
standing excitedly near the stereo and waiting to do the twist.
(Private collection)

EASY JAMAICAN RICE & PEAS

I first tasted Jamaican beans and rice when researching this book in Atlanta. It was love at first taste. I hope you will feel the same!

Fresh gungo peas, otherwise known as "pigeon peas," are used when in season, but dried red beans are usually the "peas" in Jamaican rice and peas—probably one of the island's best loved and most exported dishes!

1   19-ounce can kidney beans,
        reserve liquid
2   cups coconut milk
2   cloves minced garlic
5   green onions, chopped
        (approximately $^1/_2$ cup)
1   jalapeño pepper, seeded and
        minced

$^3/_4$ teaspoon dried thyme
$^1/_2$ teaspoon salt
$^1/_2$ teaspoon black pepper
2   cups rice
1   tablespoon butter

Combine the liquid from the canned peas with the coconut milk, and add additional water, if necessary, to make 3¹/₂ cups of liquid. Pour the liquid into a large saucepan and add the peas, minced garlic, green onions, jalapeño pepper, thyme, salt, and black pepper. Bring to a rolling boil and boil for 3 minutes. Add the rice and butter and stir once. Reduce the heat to low, cover, and simmer for 20 to 30 minutes or until all the liquid is completely absorbed and the rice is cooked. (If the rice is not tender after the water evaporates, add 2 to 4 tablespoons of water, cover, and simmer for another 5 to 10 minutes.)

Makes 4 to 6 servings.

ETHIOPIAN LENTILS

Among the plethora of ethnic restaurants dotting Atlanta's culinary landscape are a number of Ethiopian restaurants. Lentils are served at most. They appeal to my Southern heritage, and in fact, to me they are just another delicious bean.

2	red onions, chopped		2¹/₄	tablespoons Berbere Spice Mix (recipe follows)
3	cloves garlic, minced		1	pound lentils
¹/₄	cup ghee (recipe follows)			Freshly ground black pepper
6	cups water or chicken broth			
6	cups mild green chilies, roasted, peeled, seeded and chopped			

In a 4-quart pot, sauté the onion and garlic in the ghee until the onions are tender. Add the broth, bring to a boil, and simmer 10 minutes. Add chilies and Berbere Spice Mix. Add the lentils and cook covered for another 35 to 40 minutes, or until most of liquid is absorbed. Add additional broth as necessary to prevent sticking. Season with ground black pepper to taste.

This dish is especially delicious when served with brown rice and sliced fresh tomatoes.

Makes 6 to 8 servings.

GHEE

Ghee is basically clarified butter. It's very tasty and excellent for cooking!

1 **pound unsalted butter**	4 **whole cloves**

Place butter in a heavy, medium-size pan and melt over medium heat. Reduce heat and continue to cook until the butter begins to foam and whitish curds begin to form on the bottom of the pot. Keep a close watch on the ghee, as it can easily burn. At this point add your cloves and stir. The cloves aid in clarifying the butter. If it turns brown, or has a nutty flavor, it is burned and must be discarded.

Spoon away the foam to see if the butter is clear. Some people save the foam for use in cooking vegetables or making Indian bread; otherwise, it can be discarded. At this point the butter will smell like popcorn and should be turning a lovely golden color and clearing. Once the ghee has stopped foaming and is clear all the way to the bottom of the pan it is done. Remove from the heat and spoon away any remaining foam. Allow it to sit until it is just warm and then pour it through a fine sieve or layers of cheesecloth into a clean, dry glass container with a tight lid. Discard the curds at the bottom of the saucepan. Each pound of butter requires approximately 15 minutes of cooking time.

Note: Because ghee contains no milk solids, it can be kept safely without refrigeration for an extended period of time. However, be very cautious to keep water out of the stored ghee because bacteria can readily grow in the combination of these liquids.

Makes 2 cups.

BERBERE SPICE MIX (ETHIOPIAN HOT PEPPER SEASONING)

This spice mix is used in many Ethiopian dishes. Make extra; you'll soon find your-self using it in other recipes as well.

1 teaspoon ground ginger	2 tablespoons salt
1/4 teaspoon ground cinnamon	1 tablespoon ground fenugreek
3/4 teaspoon ground cardamom	1 1/4 cups cayenne pepper
1/4 teaspoon ground allspice	2 1/2 tablespoons sweet Hungarian
1/2 teaspoon ground coriander	pepper
1/4 teaspoon turmeric	1/2 teaspoon nutmeg

Even in the face of adversity and oppression, fathers looked toward the future as they loved, guided, and provided for their families.

(Private collection)

SOUTHERN HOMECOMING TRADITIONS

Combine the spices in a small frying pan and toast over medium-low heat for approximately 2 minutes while stirring constantly. Remove from the pan and cool for 5 minutes. Store spice mix in a tightly covered jar.

Makes about 1 1/2 cups.

BERBERE SAUCE (ETHIOPIAN HOT SAUCE)

This North African sauce is named after the Berbers, a tribe noted for their horsemanship. Hot pepper sauce as a flavor enhancer is offered by almost every culture. I hope you will enjoy this delicious offering from Africa.

1 teaspoon turmeric	5 ounces red Mexican dried chilies, seeds removed
1/2 teaspoon garlic powder	2 teaspoons salt
1/2 teaspoon ground cloves	1 teaspoon ground ginger
Mexican dried chilies, seeded	1/2 teaspoon ground nutmeg
2 teaspoons cumin	1/2 cup dried onions
1/2 teaspoon cardamom	1/2 cup salad oil
1/2 teaspoon black peppercorns	1/2 cup red wine
1/4 teaspoon allspice	Cayenne powder
1/2 teaspoon fenugreek	

Toast the spices, chilies, and salt in a hot skillet, shaking constantly, for a couple of minutes, until they start to crackle and pop. Grind or process the spices and dried onion to form a powder. Place the spice blend in a bowl and add the oil and wine. Add cayenne to taste. Stir until thickened and store in a covered plastic container in the refrigerator.

Makes about 2 1/2 cups.

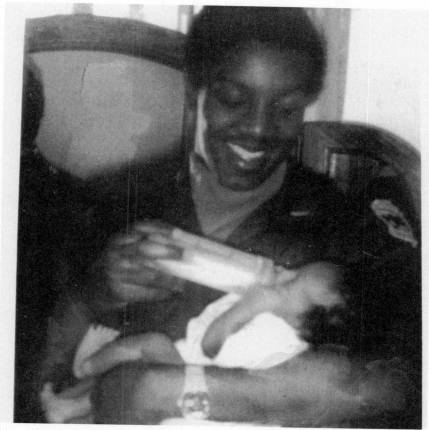

This tradition of unity, love, and strength continues to be handed down in my own family. For that I very gratefully give thanks.

(Private collection)

"Set us free, O heavenly Father, from every bond of prejudice and fear: that, honoring the steadfast courage of thy servants Absalom Jones and Richard Allen, we may show forth in our lives the reconciling love and true freedom of the children of God, which thou hast given us in our Saviour Jesus Christ, who liveth and reigneth with thee and the Holy Spirit, one God, now and for ever."

—A prayer of the African Episcopal Church, founded by Absalom Jones with the establishment of St. Thomas African Episcopal Church in 1794.

MOREHOUSE SCHOOL OF MEDICINE

There is no medicine to cure hatred.

—African proverb

MAIN DISHES

Morehouse: A Small Medical School
with Outrageous Ambition!

U ntil challenged by civil rights activists, hospitals in the North and South were racially segregated. By 1923, about 200 black hospitals had been founded, three-fourths of them in
the South, but they were under white control. Only six provided internships, and none
had residency programs. One black hospital, McVicar, a department of Spelman Seminary, was
considered outstanding, but it too was under white control. Black doctors, even those with excellent credentials from Howard, Meherry, Harvard, or Rush, could not enter city hospital practices until 1953 and were not admitted to many Southern and some Northern medical societies.
Under these conditions it was difficult for doctors to obtain the practical experience required
for professional growth and excellence. Those African-American doctors fortunate enough to
have a practice of their own could not admit a patient to McVicar's segregated facilities without
permission from a white doctor.

The NAACP and other civil rights organizations sought legal remedies and AUC students
protested at the segregated hospitals to draw national attention to the problems experienced by
black Americans when seeking medical care. For instance, when admitted to segregated facilities, African-American patients often found themselves in unheated attics or damp basements
where they received substandard medical care. Wards were frequently ill-equipped and the nursing staff limited. During the 60s, students and other activists began knocking on the door of
America's social conscience by protesting and demanding change. In June of 1962, Spelman student Ruby Doris Smith and seven other plaintiffs filed a federal lawsuit against Grady Hospital
in Atlanta. The suit, brought in Smith's name, charged the hospital with practicing racial discrimination and segregation. Grady, a segregated white hospital, also provided services to blacks,
but in a separate and unequal facility. Until the hospital's later integration the two facilities were
referred to collectively as "The Gradys" Hospital.

While the NAACP and other civil rights organizations sought legal remedies, AUC students continued to protest as a means of drawing national attention to the problems experienced
by black Americans when seeking medical care. In October of 1961 the Committee on Appeal
for Human Rights (COAHR) and the National Association for the Advancement for Colored
People (NAACP) demanded the desegregation of Grady Hospital. The following year 23 students were arrested at Grady Hospital for protesting segregation of its facilities.

As legal battles were fought to extend the holding in *Brown v. Board of Education* to hospital desegregation cases, community activist Xerona Clayton coordinated the activities of Atlanta's black doctors in the Doctors' Committee for Implementation project, which resulted in the desegregation of all of Atlanta's hospitals. Both COAHR and the NAACP supported efforts by Morehouse graduate Albert M. Davis, M.D.; Atlanta University graduate James Ellison, M.D.; Asa Yancey, M.D.; dentist Roy Bell; and a host of Atlanta's other African-American health professionals in their fight to desegregate Grady Hospital. Joining them in this effort were longtime white activists such as Eliza Pachall, executive director of the Atlanta Council on Human Relations.

But some of the earliest and perhaps, in one way, the most important support came at a time when it was least popular to support black political causes. In the 1940s Margaret Mitchell, the author of *Gone with the Wind,* worked behind the scenes with Dr. Benjamin Mays, president of Morehouse College, to anonymously provide scholarships to Morehouse students. Dr. Otis Smith, one of Atlanta's first black pediatricians, was aided by her generosity. In 1949 Mitchell was struck by a taxi and taken to Grady, where she died of her injuries. However, her commitment to civil rights lived on; Dr. Smith was among the cadre of doctors who helped desegregate Grady Hospital. The desegregation of hospitals such as Grady opened new internship and residency opportunities to black medical students, which were previously closed to them as a result of racial discrimination. However, in regards to medical school admissions, they still fought for the limited "quota" or "minority" seats in medical schools sharply focused upon the medical needs of mainstream America.

In 1975 a medical school was established at Morehouse College. The principal teaching hospital for Morehouse is Grady Hospital, which serves a large percentage of the urban minority population in the metropolitan Atlanta area. Morehouse students assume up to half of the responsibility for patient care, medical education, and clinical research at Grady. The goal of the medical school was to address the shortage of physicians among minority communities. The Morehouse School of Medicine remains committed to training doctors who will work in underserved communities and research diseases that disproportionately affect minorities and the poor.

From its very beginning in 1975 under the direction of Dr. Louis W. Sullivan and other Morehouse alumni, Morehouse School of Medicine (no longer affiliated with Morehouse College) has been committed to preparing doctors for careers as primary care physicians—an area of medical practice that continues to be plagued by disparities in service to the African-American community. As part of their commitment to health care in black communities, the medical school focuses upon preventative health care aimed at preventing health care problems such as high blood pressure and diabetes, which have long plagued the black community.

In consideration of the changing times and health and dietary needs of African-American families, including my own, I have included some of my everyday recipes that are lower in fat and higher in fiber. However, on special occasions, I celebrate my heritage with Southern and soul food recipes that have sustained generations of Americans from slavery to freedom and beyond. I'm certain that as families struggled to send children to college or start a new business enterprise in Atlanta some of these recipes strengthened them and sustained them, welcoming them home from their fields of labor. These recipes, lest they be forgotten, are proudly included as well.

Also included are Caribbean recipes. Some may be surprised by their inclusion in an American soul food recipe book, but I am sure most Atlantans won't be. The plethora of Caribbean restaurants in the city, especially around the Atlanta University Center, attest to the fact that Africans formerly enslaved in the Caribbean migrated to the United States, bringing their recipes with them. Their common African roots and tasty spiciness ensured these recipes' adoption into the melting pot of African-American cooking.

Louis W. Sullivan

Dr. Louis Wade Sullivan was born in Atlanta's Grady Hospital in 1933 and graduated from Morehouse College magna cum laude with a B.S. degree in biology. Although he was a resident of Georgia, segregation prevented him from attending an in-state medical school; instead, the state paid the difference in tuition for him to attend medical school outside of Georgia. Dr. Sullivan earned his medical degree, cum laude, from Boston University School of Medicine in 1958. He completed fellowships in pathology in 1960–61 at Massachusetts General Hospital, and in hematology during 1961–64 at Thorndike Memorial Research laboratories of Harvard Medical School at Boston City Hospital.

In 1975 Dr. Sullivan became the founding dean and director of the Medical Education Program at Morehouse College. In 1989 George H. W. Bush appointed him Secretary of the U.S. Department of Health and Human Services, where he managed the federal agency responsible for the major health, welfare, food and drug safety, medical research, and income security programs serving the American people. In that position he battled the tobacco industry and championed victims of HIV/AIDS. In January 1993, he returned to MSM and resumed the office of president. He stepped down in 2002, taking the title president emeritus.

APPLE CIDER-GLAZED PORK TENDERLOIN WITH BAKED SWEET POTATOES & GRANNY SMITH APPLES

What a wonderful dish for an autumn harvest supper with family and friends!

2	tablespoons dried rosemary, crushed		7	garlic cloves, minced
1¼	tablespoons grated orange rind		3	1-pound pork tenderloins, trimmed
1	tablespoon olive oil		3	cups apple cider
½	teaspoon salt		3	whole cloves
¼	teaspoon freshly ground black pepper		2	bay leaves
			1	cup fat-free, less-sodium chicken broth

Combine the first 6 ingredients; rub evenly into pork. Place pork in a dish; cover and chill 2 hours or overnight.

In a large skillet, combine the cider, cloves, and bay leaves and bring to a boil over medium-high heat. Cook until reduced to 1½ cups (about 10 minutes). Add the broth and bring the mixture to a second boil. Next, use a sharp knife to remove and discard any whitish silver skin and visible fat from the tenderloins. Add the pork tenderloins; cover and simmer 20 minutes or until done. Remove pork from pan and keep warm. Bring cooking liquids to a quick boil and continue to cook until the liquid is reduced to ¾ cup, approximately 8 minutes. Strain reduced liquid through a fine sieve to remove solids. Spoon over warm thin-sliced pork and serve with Baked Sweet Potatoes and Granny Smith Apples (recipe follows).

Makes 12 servings.

BAKED SWEET POTATOES & GRANNY SMITH APPLES

5 cups (½-inch) cubed, peeled sweet potatoes (about 1½ pounds)	½ teaspoon salt
1¼ cups coarsely chopped onion	½ teaspoon black pepper
¼ cup packed brown sugar	⅛ teaspoon ground nutmeg
⅓ cup fresh orange juice	3 cups (1-inch) cubed Granny Smith apples (about 1¼ pounds)
2 tablespoons vegetable oil	1 cup raisins
1 tablespoon fresh lemon juice	

Preheat oven to 350°F.

Combine sweet potatoes and onion in a 13 × 9-inch baking dish and set aside. In a separate bowl, combine the sugar and next 6 ingredients. Pour the orange juice mixture over the sweet potato mixture; toss well. Cover with aluminum foil and bake at 350°F for 30 minutes; stir occasionally. Stir in the apples and raisins, replace foil, and bake an additional 15 minutes or until apple is tender. Uncover and bake an additional 5 minutes.

Makes 12 to 14 servings.

CUMIN & SAGE PORK TENDERLOIN

2 tablespoons dark brown sugar	1 onion, sliced thin
1 teaspoon ground cumin	2 large cloves garlic, minced
½ teaspoon ground sage	Dash of salt
1 teaspoon coarsely ground black pepper	1 1-pound pork tenderloin
2 teaspoons cider vinegar	Cooking spray

Combine the first 7 ingredients in a zippered plastic storage bag. Shake to mix and set aside.

Next, use a sharp knife to remove and discard any whitish silver skin and visible fat from the tenderloins. Put the pork in the plastic storage bag, which contains the marinade, and place in the refrigerator for one hour, turning occasionally. Remove pork from the plastic bag and discard the marinade. Place pork on a broiler pan coated with cooking spray. Insert meat thermometer into thickest portion of pork and bake in a preheated 400°F oven for 25 minutes or until thermometer registers 160°F (slightly pink). Cut pork into thin slices before serving.

GRILLED PORK TENDERLOIN

2 pork tenderloins, about 12 ounces each	$^1/_8$ teaspoon paprika
1 tablespoon olive oil	$^1/_4$ teaspoon ground sage
$^1/_4$ teaspoon salt	$^1/_4$ teaspoon freshly ground black pepper
$^1/_8$ teaspoon onion powder	

Preheat grill or broiler to medium-high. Next, use a sharp knife to remove and discard any whitish silver skin and visible fat from the tenderloins.

Rub the tenderloins with olive oil, combine seasoning ingredients, and use the mixture to generously season the tenderloin. Sear the pork on all sides on the grill or under the broiler. Lower the heat to medium and cook for 8 to 12 minutes, or until the tenderloin is just cooked through. Transfer it to a warm platter and let the meat rest for 2 to 3 minutes before slicing.

Makes 6 to 8 servings.

David Satcher

Born in Anniston, Alabama, in 1941, David Satcher graduated from Morehouse College in Atlanta in 1963 and received his M.D. and Ph.D. from Case Western Reserve University in 1970. He became the sixteenth surgeon general of the United States in 1998, and served simultaneously as assistant secretary for health. He is currently the interim president and director of the new Morehouse School of Medicine National Center for Primary Care.

Dr. Satcher is a former Robert Wood Johnson Clinical Scholar and Macy Faculty Fellow. He is the recipient of many honorary degrees and numerous distinguished honors, including top awards from the American Medical Association, the American College of Physicians, the American Academy of Family Physicians, and *Ebony* magazine. In 1995, he received the Breslow Award in Public Health and in 1997 the New York Academy of Medicine Lifetime Achievement Award. He also received the Bennie Mays Trailblazer Award and the Jimmy and Roslyn Carter Award for Humanitarian Contributions to the Health of Humankind from the National Foundation for Infectious Diseases.

HERB-ROASTED CORNISH HENS

3 Cornish hens
Salt (or salt substitute) and freshly ground pepper to taste
5 cloves garlic, sliced
2 tablespoons fresh rosemary leaves
2 tablespoons minced, fresh thyme

1 1/2 bay leaves
3 shallots, roughly chopped
2 carrots, roughly chopped into 1-inch pieces
2 stalks celery, roughly chopped into 1-inch pieces
1 1/2 lemons
Paprika
Finely minced parsley

Preheat the oven to 375°F. Wash the Cornish hens under cold running water and pat dry. Next, season with salt or salt substitute and pepper inside and out. Combine the garlic, rosemary, and thyme. Divide the mixture evenly and use it to stuff the hens. Place half a bay leaf inside each hen. Add some shallots, carrots, and celery to each hen's cavity. Spread any remaining vegetables on the bottom of a roasting pan. Place the hens on top of the vegetables and squeeze lemon juice over the hens then add half a lemon to each hen cavity. Roast in the preheated oven until the hens are golden brown and crisp and the juices run clear when the thigh is pierced with a sharp knife, approximately 45 minutes.

Transfer the hens to a warm serving platter and let rest for approximately 5 minutes. Remove the skin from the hens and cut each one in half. Garnish with paprika and parsley before serving.

Makes 6 servings.

AUTUMN CHICKEN STEW

3	pounds skinless, boneless chicken breasts cut into 2-inch cubes		2	bay leaves
	Salt (or salt substitute) and freshly ground pepper to taste		2	cups red wine
	Flour for dredging		2	cups canned diced tomatoes, with their juices
2	tablespoons olive oil		4	cups low-sodium chicken broth
1	large yellow onion, diced		4	large carrots, peeled and cut into 1-inch pieces
4 to 5	cloves garlic, minced		4	large parsnips, peeled and cut into 1-inch pieces
3	sprigs thyme		2	large russet potatoes, diced

Season the chicken to taste. Dredge it in flour, shake off the excess, and set aside. Heat the olive oil in a heavy soup pot or Dutch oven over medium-high heat. Sear the meat on all sides; adjust the heat if necessary so that the chicken is well browned, but does not burn. Add the onions, garlic, thyme, and bay leaves and cook 2 minutes before adding the red wine. Use a wooden spoon to scrape any caramelized sediment from the bottom of the pan and cook until the wine is almost completely evaporated.

Next, add the tomatoes with their juices and the chicken broth and bring to a boil. Reduce heat to a simmer and cook until the meat is tender, approximately 1 hour.

Add the carrots, parsnips, and potatoes and cook until the vegetables are completely tender, approximately 20 additional minutes. (The potatoes serve as a thickener.) Adjust the seasoning to taste, remove the bay leaves, and serve in a deep tureen. Add a salad and hearty whole wheat or brown bread, if you like.

Makes 8 servings.

While root vegetables were quite common in our grandmother's kitchen, today they are often overlooked. Less popular than other vegetables, root vegetables such as beets, carrots, rutabagas, turnips, parsnips, onions, garlic, daikon, and ginger are packed with nutrition, flavor, and cancer-fighting nutrients. When they are added to almost any dish, such as soup, stews, and casseroles, they are easiest to sneak into the family meal plan.

Economical and plentiful during the fall and winter months, root vegetables are a healthful addition to seasonal soups and stews. When selecting these vegetables look for those that are firm and of medium size. At home store them in a dry and dark place until you are ready to cook them. It is expected that the federal advisory committee will soon increase its daily recommendation for vegetables from five to thirteen servings a day. This increase will require more creative uses for fruits and vegetables in your everyday cooking. For instance, grated carrots add body and nutrients to your spaghetti sauce. And rutabagas may be added to mashed potatoes or stews and casseroles.

WINTER CHICKEN

This is a very easy and very tasty recipe. It warms your heart and lifts your spirits on a cold winter day without being too heavy.

4	boneless skinless chicken breasts		1/2	cup chopped green pepper
3	cloves of garlic, crushed		3	stalks celery, sliced
1	large onion, chopped		1	quart chicken broth
			2	cups frozen mixed vegetables

Combine the above ingredients, except the frozen vegetables, in a large pot and bring to a quick boil, reduce heat to low, and simmer for about an hour or until the meat is fork-tender. Remove meat from pot; and when it is sufficiently cool to handle, dice the meat and return it to the pot. Add mixed vegetables during the last 15 minutes of cooking time. Remove pot top and continue to cook uncovered until the broth cooks down to desired consistency. If you desire thicker gravy, combine 3 tablespoons of flour with 1 cup of water, mix well to remove any lumps, and rapidly stir into your stew while cooking. Serve over rice, if desired, and try substituting brown for white rice. Changing lifetime eating habits is an evolutionary process. If like my husband, you are not quite ready to accept brown rice, try wild rice. Whether you chose white or wild, add chopped steamed vegetables into your rice, gradually using more vegetables and less rice. In this way you add fiber and flavor while hopefully reducing carbs and calories depending on the vegetables used. Add more broth to any that's left over and serve it as soup the next day.

Makes 4 servings

James R. Gavin III, Ph.D.

Dr. James R. Gavin, outgoing president of the Morehouse School of Medicine, graduated from Livingstone College in Salisbury, North Carolina, with a degree in chemistry, and earned his doctorate in biochemistry at Emory University in Atlanta and his medical degree from Duke University School of Medicine. His postgraduate training included an internship in pathology at Duke University School of Medicine, an internship and residency in internal medicine at Barnes Hospital in St. Louis, Missouri, and a clinical fellowship in metabolism at Washington University School of Medicine.

Active in clinical research, Dr Gavin has authored and coauthored more than 180 articles and abstracts for such publications as *Science, Journal of Applied Physiology, Diabetes,* and the *American Journal of Physiology.* He has also served on the editorial board of the *American Journal of Physiology* and the *American Journal of Medical Sciences.* Dr. Gavin is a member of several professional organizations, including the Institute of Medicine of the National Academy of Sciences, the American Diabetes Association (ADA), the American Society of Clinical Investigation, the American Association of Physicians, and the Association of Black Cardiologists. He is a past president of the ADA and was voted Clinician of the Year in Diabetes by the ADA. Additional honors include the Banting Medal for Distinguished Service from the ADA, Internist of the Year from the National Medical Association, the Emory University Medal for Distinguished Achievement, and the Distinguished Alumni Award from Duke University School of Medicine.

The work of Dr. James Ellison, Dr. Albert M. Davis, Dr. Otis W. Smith, and other civil rights pioneers in the field of medicine, is credited with achieving systemic equality in American health care. Georgia Senate Resolution 353, passed on March 17, 1995, commended Otis W. Smith for how he had "doggedly documented the inequities based on race within the American health care system, particularly within the City of Atlanta, and masterfully exposed them to full public view." Georgia Senate Resolution 351, also passed on March 17, 1995, commended the work of Albert M. Davis and helped ensure that tragic episodes such as the one which follows would never be repeated.

A 70-year-old man with white skin and blue-gray eyes was struck by an automobile driven by a white physician who practiced at Grady Hospital. The physician rushed the victim to Grady Hospital, where physicians worked diligently to save the patient's life, during which time the family received notification of the accident. As family members began arriving to the hospital, among them a nationally prominent black man, the attending physicians recognized their error and, in the words of the man's son, his father "was snatched from the examination table lest he contaminate the 'white' air, and taken hurriedly across the street in a driving downpour . . . to the 'Negro' ward." The father of the executive director of the National Association for the Advancement of Colored People, Walter White, died sixteen days later.

Grady Hospital, named for Henry W. Grady, managing editor of the *Atlanta Constitution* in the 1880s, was established to provide health care for low-income families in Atlanta. Opening its doors in 1892 with 18 employees and 100 beds (approximately 50 each for blacks and whites) the hospital featured one operating room with an amphitheater for students and staff. Shortly before World War I the hospital was completely divided into two separate facilities, each featuring their own clinics, nurses' quarters, and emergency rooms. For this reason it would be referred to as "The Gradys" until almost fifty years later when it was desegregated.

After *Brown*, the energies of the NMA, the NHA, and the NAACP focused on applying the same strategy that ended systemic educational discrimination toward achieving systemic change in health care. Once again, the legal team targeted the unequal distribution of federal funds to black and white medical facilities. In short, segregated hospitals did not meet the Supreme Court's previous test of "separate but equal." During that period of time, black medical students struggled for admission to a medical field that often provided disparate treatment to minority communities.

Today, however, the student body of Morehouse Medical School is 81 percent black, 7 percent white, and 12 percent Asian, Indian, and Pakistani. Actively involved in providing service and education to the local community, the students are determined to effect change and make a difference by providing quality medical service and reducing disparities in health care service.

"At this medical school, this is such an important priority for us. We consider it as something that we attack with outrageous ambition. We are determined to make a change and to make a difference."

—Dr. James R. Gavin III, president of Morehouse School of Medicine

Black Bean Stew

1 pound black beans	1 teaspoon ground cumin
10 cups unsalted chicken broth	Pinch cayenne pepper
2 green bell peppers, seeded and coarsely chopped	1 teaspoon salt or to taste
2 bay leaves	Black pepper to taste
4 slices bacon or 3 tablespoons vegetable oil	3 to 4 cups cooked white rice (may substitute brown or wild rice)
1 large yellow onion	$^1/_4$ cup sherry
3 cloves garlic, minced	Hot pepper sauce
1 small pumpkin (2 to 3 pounds), peeled and seeded	

Pick over beans to remove foreign objects and soak overnight in sufficient cold water to cover beans by 2 inches. Drain and rinse beans before cooking. Drain beans, then put about 10 cups of broth in a large pot. Add the beans, half of the green pepper, and the bay leaves to the pot; bring to a rapid boil, reduce the heat to low, and simmer for 1 hour. Remove bay leaves. Cut pumpkin into $^1/_2$- to 1-inch cubes and set aside. Add pepper, onion, garlic, pumpkin, cumin, cayenne pepper, salt, and pepper to the skillet after removing bacon. Cook vegetables about 15 minutes over medium-high heat, or until softened. Add vegetables to beans and cook another hour, uncovered, or until beans are tender. In a separate skillet cook the bacon crisp and remove it to a paper towel to drain. Set the bacon aside for a later use.

Stir in sherry just prior to serving. Serve over rice and garnish with crumbled bacon for a complete meal. Allow each guest to season individual servings with hot pepper sauce to taste.

Makes 6 to 8 servings.

SOUTHERN BUTTER BEANS & CHICKEN

2	cups all purpose flour			Vegetable oil
1	tablespoon salt		1¼	cups chopped onion
1	tablespoon freshly ground black pepper		½	cup chopped green pepper
1	teaspoon paprika		1½	cups chicken broth
½	teaspoon onion powder		3	cups fresh butter beans (frozen may be substituted)
1	3-pound fryer, cut up			

Combine the flour and next four seasoning ingredients in a zip top storage bag, seal the top, and shake to blend. Next, wash the chicken pieces under cold running water, drain, and pat dry. Add the chicken, a few pieces at a time, to the plastic storage bag containing the flour and shake to coat. Repeat until all chicken has been coated with flour. Allow the bag to sit for a few minutes before shaking the chicken a second time to coat well. Remove the chicken from the bag, shaking excess flour back into the bag. Add additional flour mixture to the bag as needed. Next, on a medium-high burner, heat approximately ¼-inch of the oil in a large pot. Lightly brown chicken on all sides, reduce heat to medium, and continue frying, turning regularly, for an additional 10 minutes. Remove chicken from the pot and place on a paper towel–lined plate. Remove all but 3 tablespoons of the vegetable oil from the pot. Sauté onion and bell pepper until the onion is transparent. Add 2 tablespoons of flour from the plastic bag, using additional flour as needed, and sauté, stirring constantly, for approximately 3 minutes. Add chicken broth and butter beans, return chicken to the pot, reduce to a simmer, and cook an additional 35 to 40 minutes, or until the beans are tender and the chickens juices run clear when pierced with a fork.

Makes 4 to 6 servings.

MUSTARD GREENS WITH SMOKED TURKEY

4 bunches of mustard greens
2 quarts low-sodium chicken
  broth
1 cup chopped onion
1 garlic clove, minced
1 tablespoon seasoned salt
  (or to taste)

$^1/_2$ teaspoon ground red pepper
5 thyme sprigs
1 bay leaf
3 8-ounce smoked turkey wing
  drumettes, skinned

Trim thick stems from mustard greens and discard. Coarsely chop leaves. Combine greens, broth, and remaining ingredients in a large stockpot; bring to a boil. Cover, reduce heat, and simmer 45 minutes or until tender. Remove thyme sprigs, turkey wings, and bay leaf.

Place broth and skinned turkey wing drumettes in a large pot and bring to a rapid boil. Reduce heat to low and simmer for 30 minutes. While the turkey is boiling, prepare the turnip greens by removing thick stalks and discarding any yellowed or badly blemished leaves. Wash greens under cold running water and rinse any remaining sand from the sink. Fill sink with cold water, add greens, and plunge up and down several times to wash any remaining sand and sediment from the greens. Several washings may be needed, but are not usually necessary with store-bought greens. Roll leaves cigar fashion and slice into horizontal segments slightly smaller than $^1/_4$ inch.

Next, gradually stir in the greens, allowing each batch to wilt before adding more greens and remaining ingredients. Bury the smoked turkey in the simmering greens. Cover and reduce the heat to medium-low. Continue cooking the greens an additional 30 minutes. Uncover the pot and cook an additional 15 minutes, or until the greens are tender to personal taste, stirring occasionally.

Makes 8 servings.

One thing that I have learned is to occasionally and very judiciously indulge my food cravings. Over time I found that if I ignored them, I ate all of the good foods and nibbled around the bad food until I finally gave in and overindulged in whatever it was that I was originally craving. So now I try to eat less of what it is that I really want from the very beginning. I prefer this more balanced approach, which some call a "lifestyle choice." I prefer "lifestyle adjustment," which allows me to *readjust* as necessary, and I never feel deprived. It's not a diet, so I never have the guilt associated with "cheating." As a result, I still enjoy fried fish and chicken on special occasions; however, I now try to plan for these indulgences. I have included some of my favorite recipes for those of you who, like me, occasionally indulge.

FRIED CHICKEN & WAFFLES

What do Roscoe's of Hollywood and Gladys Knight and Ron Winans' Chicken and Waffles, Atlanta, have in common? Why chicken and waffles, of course. While this delicious dish has migrated to the west coast, its roots remain firmly planted in the South.

FRIED CHICKEN

My friend Cassandra Bethels's delicious recipe for fried chicken appeared in my first cookbook, *The African American Heritage Cookbook.* It is still one of my favorite ways to prepare fried chicken.

1	2¹/₂- to 3-pound fryer, cut up		2	large onions, sliced thin
2	teaspoons onion powder			Solid shortening
1¹/₂	teaspoons garlic powder		¹/₄	cup butter
1¹/₂	teaspoons pepper			Flour
2	teaspoons seasoned salt			

Wash chicken, pat dry, and set aside. Mix together the next 4 seasoning ingredients and use to season chicken. In a large non-reactive bowl, thoroughly combine the chicken and the sliced onions. Cover tightly and (this is the important part) refrigerate overnight. In a large, heavy skillet heat three inches of shortening to approximately 375°F. Add butter to the shortening. Discard onions and coat the chicken with flour, shaking off the excess, and place the chicken in hot oil. Do not crowd the pan. Cook on each side for approximately 15 minutes or until golden. Repeat as necessary. Test doneness by piercing the thickest part of the chicken with a fork. When done, the juices should run clear.

WAFFLES

2	cups all-purpose flour		2	eggs (at room temperature) separated (reserve the whites)
1	teaspoon baking powder			
¹/₂	teaspoon salt		2	cups cold milk
¹/₂	cup sugar		¹/₄	cup butter, melted
¹/₈	teaspoon nutmeg			

Combine the dry ingredients in a large bowl and mix to combine. In a separate bowl, combine the egg yolks, milk and butter. Add to the flour mixture and stir until just moistened. Beat egg whites until stiff peaks form and gently fold into the batter. Bake, according to manufacturer's directions, in an oiled, preheated waffle iron. Separate into 16-inch squares. Serve with butter and cane or maple syrup.

Makes 8 servings.

SUNDAY FRIED CHICKEN & HOMEMADE BUTTERMILK BISCUITS

This chicken is so good and crispy that you won't want to wait until Sunday! Enjoy.

2	3- to 4-pound fryers, cut up		$3/4$	teaspoon dried oregano
$1^1/2$	cups all-purpose flour		$1/2$	teaspoon onion powder
$1/2$	cup cornmeal		1	teaspoon rubbed sage
$1/4$	cup cornstarch		1	teaspoon black pepper
1	tablespoon salt		2	eggs, well beaten
1	teaspoon pepper		$1/4$	cup water
$2^1/4$	teaspoons paprika			Vegetable oil
$1/8$	teaspoon cayenne pepper			

Wash fryer pieces well under warm running water and place in a colander to drain. In a large zip top plastic storage bag add the dry ingredients, shake well to combine, and set aside. Combine egg and water in a shallow dish and mix well. Dip chicken in egg mixture, one piece at a time; place in bag a few pieces at a time and shake to coat. In a cast iron skillet heat 1 inch of oil to 375°F. Add chicken and fry for 3 to 5 minutes on each side or until crispy and golden brown. Place chicken in two ungreased 15-inch × 10-inch × 1-inch baking pans. Bake uncovered at 350 degrees for 25 to 30 minutes or until, when pierced with a fork, the chicken's juices run clear.

Makes 18 pieces.

HOMEMADE BUTTERMILK BISCUITS

2	cups all-purpose flour	$1/2$	teaspoon salt
2	teaspoons baking powder	$1/2$	cup solid shortening
$1/2$	teaspoon baking soda	$3/4$	cup buttermilk

Preheat oven to 450°F. In a large bowl, combine the first four ingredients. Using a fork or pastry blender, cut in shortening until the mixture resembles coarse cornmeal. Blend in the buttermilk until a soft dough is formed. Turn out onto a lightly floured surface and knead lightly for 7 to 8 minutes. Roll to $1/2$-inch thickness and cut out with a floured biscuit cutter. Reroll scraps and cut until all dough is used. Place biscuits on an ungreased cookie sheet, approximately 1 inch apart, and bake until golden, approximately 15 minutes. For a delicious treat, serve these biscuits hot with either homemade fig preserves (see recipe below) or strawberry jam.

Makes approximately 18 to 24 biscuits.

FIG PRESERVES

6	quarts figs	4	pounds sugar
1	cup baking soda	3	quarts water
6	quarts water		

Spread figs on the bottom of a well scrubbed sink and sprinkle with baking soda. Pour 6 quarts of boiling water over the figs and allow them to stand undisturbed for 5 to 7 minutes. Drain the water away from the figs, rinse, and fill sink with cold water. Wash figs in this cold water bath, drain, and repeat.

Next, combine the sugar and 3 quarts of hot water in a large pot to make a syrup. Add the figs to the syrup mixture and bring to a rapid boil, cooking until the figs become transparent and tender. Remove the figs from the syrup and set aside. Continue to cook and boil down the syrup until it thickens to the consistency of maple syrup. Pour syrup over figs, ensuring the figs are completely covered. Allow figs to stand overnight before packing the figs into canning jars and covering with syrup. Process in a water bath canner at 212°F for 25 minutes or according to manufacturer's directions.

Makes 8 quarts.

SPICY FRIED CHICKEN WITH SPICY TOMATO SALAD

This is an adaptation of Caribbean fried chicken. If you like spicy, you will love this chicken.

1   4-pound chicken, cut up
2   medium-size onions, finely chopped
1   tablespoon parsley, finely minced
1½   tablespoons fresh thyme, finely chopped
1   tablespoon fresh marjoram, minced
½   teaspoon ground cloves
¼   teaspoon ground ginger
3   garlic cloves, minced

2   jalapeño chili peppers, seeded and chopped
1   teaspoon paprika
Juice of 1 lime
Salt to taste
2   cups all-purpose flour
1   tablespoon salt
1   tablespoon freshly ground black pepper
2   eggs, lightly beaten
Peanut or canola oil for frying

Combine the chicken with the next 11 ingredients and refrigerate for 2 to 3 hours. Combine the flour, salt, and pepper, mix well and set aside. Place approximately 1 cup of the flour mixture into a paper or plastic bag and add the chicken, a few pieces at a time, to the bag and shake to coat. Allow the bag to sit for a few minutes before shaking the chicken a second time to coat well. Remove the chicken from the bag, shaking excess flour back into the bag. Add additional flour mixture to the bag as needed. Dip chicken in beaten egg and return to flour mixture to recoat. Next, on a medium-high burner, heat approximately ¼-inch of the oil in a large skillet. Lightly brown chicken on all sides, reduce heat to medium, and continue frying, turning regularly, until chicken is cooked through. When a fork is inserted into the thickest part of the meat, the juices should run clear. Drain well on paper towels, and serve hot. Seal any unused flour mixture in a plastic bag and refrigerate or freeze for future use. To bake follow the steps up to frying and then place the chicken in a preheated 350° oven and bake for 40 to 50 minutes or until cooked through. The chicken is done when a piece is pierced at its thickest part and the juice runs clear.

Makes 4 servings.

SPICY TOMATO SALAD

12	plum tomatoes	1/4	cup extra-virgin olive oil
1	teaspoon caster sugar	1	teaspoon fresh gingerroot, peeled and grated
	Ground black pepper to taste	2	teaspoons light soy sauce
1	medium-size Bermuda onion, peeled and sliced	2	teaspoons chopped coriander leaves
1	red chili pepper, finely sliced	3	green onions, thinly sliced
1/4	cup lime juice		

Slice the tomatoes and gently toss in a bowl with the sugar and pepper. In a separate bowl, mix together the onion, chili, lime juice, olive oil, and grated ginger. Allow tomatoes to stand undisturbed for 15 minutes before combining them with the lime mixture. Add the soy sauce, coriander and green onion. Chill well before serving with the spicy fried chicken.

Makes 6 to 8 servings.

BUTTERMILK FRIED CHICKEN & HOT BISCUITS WITH FRIED APPLES

2	cups buttermilk	1	3-pound fryer, cut up
1	tablespoon curry powder	1 1/2	cups all-purpose flour
1	tablespoon kosher salt, divided	2	teaspoons chili powder
2	teaspoons ground black pepper	1/2	teaspoon paprika
		1/4	teaspoon onion powder
			Vegetable oil

In a large bowl, combine the buttermilk and curry powder. In a separate bowl, combine the salt and pepper and mix well to blend. Measure three teaspoons of the salt and pepper mixture into the buttermilk. Mix well. Add the chicken and turn to coat. Cover and refrigerate overnight. The next day, combine the flour, 1 teaspoon of the salt and pepper mixture, chili powder, paprika, and onion powder in a shallow dish. Mix well to blend. Remove the chicken from the buttermilk, allowing excess to drip back into the bowl. Dip chicken in the flour mixture and turn to coat, shake excess flour from chicken, and place on a foil-lined baking sheet. Refrigerate 20 minutes. Pour vegetable oil in a cast iron skillet to a depth of ¹/₂ inch. Heat oil over medium-high heat to 375°F. Place chicken in the hot oil, skin side down, and reduce heat to medium-low. Cover the pan with a lid and cook until brown, approximately 12 minutes. Turn chicken over and cook uncovered until the chicken is golden brown and cooked through so that when it is pierced with a fork, the juices run clear.

Makes 4 to 6 servings.

HOMEMADE BUTTERMILK BISCUITS

There is no taste treat better than hot from the oven homemade buttermilk biscuits on a cold winter morning. Just thinking about them, I can almost smell their fragrance and taste the delicious strawberry preserves that my mother served with them. So here's another version to try.

3 cups all purpose flour	³/₄ cup Crisco shortening, well chilled
3 teaspoons baking powder	³/₄ cup buttermilk
³/₄ teaspoon baking soda	
1 teaspoon salt	

Preheat oven to 425°F. In a large bowl, sift together flour, baking powder, baking soda, and salt. Cut shortening into the flour mixture with a pastry blender until the mixture forms coarse crumbs. Add buttermilk, tossing with a fork, until dough holds together and lightly knead, just a few times, until smooth. Next, turn the dough onto a floured surface and form into a ³/₄-inch-thick disk. Then using a biscuit cutter or glass dipped in flour, cut out biscuits and place them approximately 2 inches apart on an ungreased baking sheet. Reform any leftover dough and repeat the process. Place in the preheated oven and bake for about 12 to 15 minutes, until golden brown. Serve piping hot with butter and fried apples.

Makes 12 biscuits.

SOUTHERN FRIED APPLES

1/4 cup butter	1/3 cup sugar
2 pounds tart unpeeled apples, washed, cored, and quartered	2 1/4 teaspoons cinnamon

Melt butter in a heavy skillet over medium heat. Add apples, cover, and cook over medium heat until soft, approximately 5 to 10 minutes.

Combine sugar and cinnamon, mix to blend. Uncover apples and sprinkle with sugar and cinnamon. Cook until lightly browned on underside.

Makes 6 to 8 servings.

TASTY FRIED CHICKEN & HOT BISCUITS WITH APPLE BUTTER

Chicken and biscuits just like your mother used to make!

2 cups flour	1 teaspoon thyme
3 tablespoons dry mustard	1 teaspoon crushed rosemary
3 tablespoons sweet paprika	1 teaspoon dried oregano, lightly crushed
1 1/2 teaspoons onion powder	1 to 2 teaspoons salt, to taste (optional)
1/8 teaspoon red pepper	3 1/2- to 4 1/2- pound broiler-fryer chicken, cut up, washed, and dried
1 1/2 tablespoons celery salt	Peanut oil or canola oil, for pan frying
2 tablespoons fresh ground black pepper	
1 tablespoon Lawry's Seasoned Salt	
1/4 teaspoon poultry seasoning	

Combine the flour and seasoning ingredients, mix well. Place approximately 1 cup of the flour mixture into a paper or plastic bag and add the chicken, a few pieces at a time, to the bag and shake to coat. Add additional flour mixture to the bag as needed. Allow the bag to sit for a few minutes before shaking the chicken a second time to coat well. Remove the chicken from the bag, shaking excess flour back into the bag. Next, on a medium-high burner, heat approximately $1/4$ inch of the oil in a large skillet. Lightly brown chicken on all sides, reduce heat to medium, and continue frying, turning regularly, until chicken is cooked through. When a fork is inserted into the thickest part of the meat, the juices should run clear. Drain well on paper towels, and serve hot. Seal any unused flour mixture in a plastic bag and refrigerate or freeze for future use. Serve with hot biscuits and apple butter just like Mom used to do on cold winter afternoons. Apple butter is available in most grocery stores, but why not make your own, just like mom's! For delicious biscuits, see recipe on page 246.

Makes 6 to 8 servings.

APPLE BUTTER

8 pounds ripe apples (Jonathan, Winesap, or other flavorful apple)	1 teaspoon ground cloves
4 cups sweet cider	$2^1/_4$ teaspoons ground cinnamon
3 cups firmly packed dark brown sugar	$1/4$ teaspoon ground allspice
	Zest of 1 lemon

Wash the apples. Remove their stems, core and peel, and quarter them. In a large pot, over medium heat, cook the apples in the cider until they are soft. Remove the pot from the heat and allow mixture to cool before pressing the apples into a puree. To each cup of puree, add $1/2$ cup sugar at a time, up to three cups, depending on taste. Add the spices and lemon zest. Return the fruit to the pot and continue to cook over low heat, stirring constantly, until the sugar is dissolved and the mixture thickens. Test doneness by placing a small amount of the mixture on a cold saucer. The outside surface of the portion tested should show a light sheen upon standing. When no rim of liquid separates from around the edge of the butter, it is done. Pour into sterilized jars and seal according to the manufacturer's directions.

Makes 3 to 4 pints.

FRIED CATFISH & HUSHPUPPIES

JIMMY STINSON'S CATFISH

The succulent sweet and mild flavor of today's farm-raised catfish is perfectly show-cased by the ingredients in this recipe. One of my favorites, it first appeared in *The African-American Heritage Cookbook.*

2	pounds whole catfish	1	cup blackened catfish seasoning
4	cups Louisiana hot sauce	2	tablespoons salt
2	cups yellow cornmeal	$^1/_4$	cup black pepper
2	cups all-purpose flour		

Marinate catfish in hot sauce for 2 hours. Meanwhile, mix the meal, flour, and spices together and use it to coat the fish. Heat shortening to approximately 350 degrees F., and fry fish until golden brown. You may have to lower temperature if fish is frying too fast.

Makes 4 servings.

HUSHPUPPIES

$2^1/_2$	cups self-rising white cornmeal	$^1/_4$	teaspoon ground cayenne pepper
$^1/_3$	cup chopped green pepper	$^1/_2$	teaspoon ground black pepper
$^1/_4$	cup chopped onion	1	cup buttermilk
1	teaspoon salt	2	large eggs
1	teaspoon sugar		Vegetable oil
$^1/_4$	teaspoon nutmeg		

Combine the first eight ingredients in a large mixing bowl and mix well to blend. Form a well in the center of the cornmeal mixture and set aside. In a separate bowl combine the buttermilk and eggs, mix well and pour into the well of the cornmeal mixture, stirring until just blended. Allow the mixture to stand at room temperature for 30 minutes. Pour oil in a Dutch oven or cast-iron skillet to a depth of 2 inches. Heat the oil to 375°F and drop the cornmeal batter by heaping teaspoonfuls into the hot oil.

Fry in batches for 2 to 3 minutes on each side or until golden. Drain on brown paper bags or paper towels and pile onto a plate with fried catfish. Serve family style with cole slaw and lots of family fun and laughter.

Makes 18 to 24 hushpuppies, depending on size.

FRIED CATFISH & CHEESY GRITS

6	4- to 6-ounce catfish filets		2	teaspoons pepper
2	cups buttermilk		3/4	teaspoon onion powder
2	cups yellow cornmeal		1/2	teaspoon garlic powder
1/4	cup flour			Salt and pepper to taste
1	tablespoon seasoned salt			Vegetable oil

Place catfish filets in a single layer in a shallow dish; cover with the buttermilk and chill for 1 hour. While the fish are chilling, combine the cornmeal and the next 5 ingredients in a shallow dish. Remove the filets from the refrigerator and allow them to stand at room temperature for 10 minutes before removing them from the buttermilk. Allow the excess buttermilk to drip off the fish back into the bowl. Season fillets with salt and pepper to taste and dredge in flour. Fry in oil that has been poured to a depth of 1 1/2 inches and heated to 350°F. Cook in batches for about three to four minutes on each side or until golden brown. Drain on brown paper bags or paper towels.

Makes 3 to 4 servings.

CHEESY GRITS

Hominy grits are a Southern institution. The process of making hominy grits begins when corn kernels, dried on the cob, are removed by soaking the cobs in a special solution to soften the kernels. Next, the kernels are hulled and degermed using friction and dried. The coarse whitish grains we enjoy as grits are then ground from hominy.

4	cups boiling water		$^1/_2$	cup butter
1	teaspoon salt		1	cup grated cheddar cheese
1	cup hominy grits (do not use instant)		2	eggs
			Up to 1 cup milk	

Preheat oven to 350 degrees. In a large pot, bring water to a rolling boil; add salt and grits. Reduce to a simmer and stir and cook grits for 3 to 4 minutes, or until grits thicken. Remove grits from heat and stir in butter and cheese; mix well. In a large measuring cup combine eggs and sufficient milk to make 1 cup. Add the milk mixture to the grits and mix well to combine. Pour into casserole and bake in the preheated oven for approximately 45 minutes. Cut the grits into squares and serve hot.

Makes 6 servings.

ALMOST ANY FRIED FISH WITH JUST GRITS

This recipe works equally well with bream, crappie, and the perennially popular catfish.

$^3/_4$	cup yellow cornmeal		$^1/_2$	teaspoon onion powder
$^1/_4$	cup all-purpose flour		$^1/_4$	teaspoon salt
2	teaspoons salt		8	4-ounce catfish fillets
1	teaspoon cayenne pepper			Salt and pepper
1	teaspoon paprika			Peanut or canola oil for frying
$^1/_4$	teaspoon garlic powder			

Combine first 8 ingredients in a shallow dish. Salt and pepper fish to taste. Dredge fish in cornmeal mixture, coating evenly. Shake off excess cornmeal mixture, place on a plate in a single layer, and refrigerate for 20 minutes before frying. Place approximately $1^1/_2$ inches oil into a deep cast iron skillet. Heat over a medium to medium-high burner until the oil just begins to smoke. Add fish and fry in batches, 5 to 6 minutes or until golden brown. Adjust heat as necessary to prevent burning. Drain fish on paper towels.

Serve piping hot with tartar sauce, hot sauce, or mustard. We eat fish and grits for breakfast most often, but it is served almost as often for dinner. If you drop in for dinner, it's more than likely that you will receive Cheesy Grits (recipe on previous page). If you are serving fried fish with fries or hushpuppies and slaw, don't forget the mustard, hot sauce, or tartar sauce. The recipe for homemade tartar sauce follows.

JUST GRITS

I know I can share this secret with you, and only you; so, when asked what you put in your grits to make them so flavorful, smile like a Cheshire cat and respond, "Just grits."

5 cups water	2 eggs well beaten
1/2 teaspoon salt	2 tablespoons butter
1 cup hominy grits (do not use instant)	

In a large pan add salt to water, bring to a boil. Stir in hominy grits slowly. Reduce heat and stir until thickened, approximately 5 minutes. Cook for 15 minutes longer, stirring occasionally to keep from sticking. During the last 10 minutes of cooking time, stir rapidly while adding your eggs and butter.

Makes 8 servings.

TARTAR SAUCE

1 1/4 cups finely chopped onion	1/4 cup sweet pickle relish
2 3/4 cups celery, chopped	3 cups mayonnaise
1 cup dill pickle relish	

Drain the juices from the onions, celery, and relish or the onion juice especially will make your tartar sauce bitter. Combine with the mayonnaise and mix well. Refrigerate to chill before serving with your hot fish.

SHRIMP & GRITS

A new Southern favorite, this fast flavorful dish will soon become a favorite of your family as well.

1 medium onion, minced	2 tablespoons Worcestershire sauce
1 green bell pepper, minced	1 pinch cayenne pepper
3 cloves garlic, minced	2 cups hot cooked grits
2 tablespoons vegetable oil	2 tablespoons softened butter, divided
1 pound medium-size shrimp, shelled and deveined	

Cook onion, pepper, and garlic in oil over moderately low heat, stirring, until onion is translucent and limp. Add shrimp and cook mixture over moderately high heat, stirring, for 3 minutes, or until shrimp are cooked through. Shrimp should be pink and the tails slightly curled. Stir in Worcestershire sauce and cayenne pepper. Spoon hot grits onto platter, top with dots of butter, and arrange the shrimp mixture around and over grits.

Makes 4 servings.

SPICY SHRIMP & RICE

6 tablespoons olive oil, divided	Salt and freshly ground black pepper to taste
1 large onion, finely sliced	1/4 teaspoon ground allspice
3 cloves of garlic, finely minced	1/8 teaspoon chili powder
2 very ripe medium tomatoes, peeled	1 cup long-grain or Basmati rice
2 bay leaves	1 pound medium shrimp, shelled and deveined
1 teaspoon dried parsley leaves	1 tablespoon minced parsley
1/4 teaspoon saffron	

Slowly simmer the onions in 2 tablespoons of the oil until they are golden. Add the garlic, tomatoes, bay leaves, parsley, and saffron. Cover and simmer for 15 minutes.

Next season the dish with salt, pepper, allspice, and chili powder. Boil the rice according to package directions until it is just done. Strain rice into a sieve and keep warm over a pot of boiling water. Add the shrimp to the tomato mixture and cook, covered, over high heat for 3 minutes. Stir in the remaining 4 tablespoons of oil and parsley into the rice. Serve immediately. Arrange the rice in a ring on plates and place the shrimp in the middle.

Makes 2 to 4 servings.

ROAST PORK IN PEACH SAUCE

This recipe first appeared in *A Taste of Freedom: A Cookbook with Recipes and Remembrances from The Hampton Institute.* However, the recipe was too delicious not to reintroduce it in this recipe book from Georgia, the Peach State!

	5-pound pork loin roast	$1/4$	teaspoon ground allspice
3	garlic cloves, quartered	$1/2$	teaspoon ground black pepper
3	tablespoons vegetable oil	$1/8$	teaspoon ground cloves
$1^1/2$	teaspoons salt	2	medium onions, sliced
1	teaspoon onion powder	4	bay leaves

Wash the pork roast, pat it dry, and pierce it in several places with a two-prong fork. Force a garlic quarter into each hole. If necessary, use a paring knife to widen the hole. Rub the roast with vegetable oil and set aside. Combine the next 5 seasoning ingredients, mix well, and rub into the roast. Refrigerate for 3 hours, or if possible, overnight. Preheat the oven to 325°F. Combine the Spiced Peach Syrup ingredients (see below) and set aside. Place the onions and bay leaves in the bottom of a roasting pan. Place roast on bed of onions, fat side down. Roast the pork loin, allowing 35 minutes' cooking time per pound. Baste occasionally with Spiced Peach Syrup (see Spiced Peach Syrup recipe below). During the last 15 to 20 minutes of cooking time, cover the roast with peaches, attaching them with toothpicks.

Makes 10–12 servings.

SPICED PEACH SYRUP

1 large can peach halves in
   heavy syrup
1/2 teaspoon ground allspice

1/2 teaspoon ground cinnamon
1/8 teaspoon ground cloves

Combine the peaches and syrup with the remaining ingredients, and use to baste and dress the roast according to the above directions.

Makes approximately 1/2 cup syrup.

CRANBERRY-ORANGE GLAZED HAM

Ring in the holidays and dazzle your guests with this beautiful ham, which looks absolutely festive on any holiday table!

1 7- to 8-pound smoked, fully
   cooked ham half
1 cup cranberry concentrate
1/2 cup orange juice
1/2 cup ginger ale
1/2 cup firmly packed brown
   sugar
2 tablespoons vegetable oil

1 tablespoon white vinegar
2 teaspoons dry mustard
1/2 teaspoon ground ginger
1/2 teaspoon ground cloves
1/8 teaspoon ground nutmeg
   Orange slices
   Fresh cranberries

Trim the skin away from the ham, leaving a quarter inch of fat. Place the ham in a large roasting bag. Combine the remaining ingredients and pour over the ham. Tie the bag tightly, place in large bowl that allows the glaze to form around the ham without being too tight. Refrigerate the ham 8 hours or overnight, turning occasionally. Remove the ham from the bag, reserving the marinade. Preheat the oven to 325°F. Place the ham on a rack in a shallow roasting pan. Insert a meat thermometer into the ham without allowing it to rest on the bone, which could cause a false reading. Baste the ham with the reserved marinade every 15 to 20 minutes. Bake at 325°F for 2 to 2¹/₂ hours or until the meat thermometer registers 140 degrees. If you do not have a meat thermometer, bake the ham at 325°F, allowing 18 to 24 cooking minutes per pound. Garnish ham with orange slices held in place with a toothpick. Hide each toothpick by spearing a cranberry on it.

Makes 12 servings.

SOUTHERN-STYLE BARBECUED PORK SANDWICHES

A delicious recipe that can also be used on your grill or with your smoker!

6–8   pound Boston butt, trimmed   Southern Rub (recipe follows)
      of excess fat to ¹/₄ inch   Mop Sauce (recipe follows)

Prepare the Mop Sauce and refrigerate. Combine the Southern Rub ingredients. Using a little more than half of the rub mixture, coat meat on all sides, place the roast in a plastic bag, seal tight, and refrigerate it overnight. The next day, remove the roast from the refrigerator and allow it to rest at room temperature for 45 minutes. Preheat the oven to 350°F, remove the plastic bag, and bake the roast uncovered for 45 minutes. Reduce temperature to 300°F and cook for an additional 6 to 7 hours or until the pork roast is very tender. Mop the pork with the mopping sauce every 1¹/₂ to 2 hours. When roast is cooked through and reaches an internal temperature of 180 degrees, remove it from the baking pan, wrap it tightly in aluminum foil, and allow it to rest for at least 30 minutes. Remove the roast from the foil, and roughly chop or "pull" the pork. Add a small amount of your favorite BBQ sauce, mix well, and serve on hamburger buns with coleslaw on the side (some people garnish their sandwiches with the coleslaw) and icy cold beer.

Makes 8 to 10 servings.

MOP SAUCE

$^3/_4$ tablespoon salt
$^3/_4$ tablespoon dry mustard
$^1/_2$ tablespoon garlic powder
$^1/_2$ tablespoon chili powder
$^1/_4$ tablespoon bay leaf powder
$^3/_4$ tablespoon paprika
$^1/_2$ tablespoon hot sauce (or to taste)

1 cup Worcestershire sauce
$^1/_2$ cup apple cider vinegar
1 tablespoon liquid smoke
4 cups beef broth
$^1/_2$ cup vegetable oil

Combine all ingredients and simmer together for about 15 minutes in a large saucepan. Cool slightly and use as a delicious grilling mop for beef or pork.

Makes approximately 6 cups.

SOUTHERN RUB

2 tablespoons salt
2 tablespoons chili powder
$^1/_2$ tablespoon coarse black pepper

$^1/_2$ tablespoon garlic powder
1 teaspoon cayenne pepper
2 teaspoons dry mustard
$^1/_4$ cup turbinado sugar

Combine the above ingredients and use as a rub for pork or beef.

Makes about $^1/_2$ cup.

OVEN-ROASTED HONEY BARBECUED CHICKEN

2	3-pound fryers, cut up	2	large onions, chopped
$3/4$	teaspoon salt	2	8-ounce cans tomato sauce
$3/4$	teaspoon black pepper	$1/2$	cup cider vinegar
$1/4$	teaspoon cayenne pepper	$1/2$	cup + 1 tablespoon honey
$1^3/4$	teaspoons paprika	$1/4$	cup Worcestershire sauce

Wash chicken under warm running water, drain, and pat dry. Place chicken skin side down in an ungreased baking dish. Combine salt and pepper and use to season the chicken. Combine the remaining ingredients, mix well, and pour over the chicken. Bake uncovered in preheated oven for 30 minutes. Turn chicken and bake an additional 20 minutes basting occasionally, or until when pierced with a fork, the chicken juices run clear.

Makes 8 servings.

The following recipes are part of our soul food heritage, which should never be forgotten. More than just Southern cooking, soul food was survival food. Slaves would cleverly prepare dishes using the beef, chicken, and pork sections discarded by their masters, and serve them up with ingredients transplanted with them from their homeland, such as yams, goobers, and black-eyed peas, to make a soul-satisfying meal. Following slavery these foods continued to be served in celebrated soul food restaurants such as Paschals in Atlanta, where Dr. Martin Luther King, Jr., and others met during the 50s and early 60s to plan civil rights strategy. Through the generations, soul food has become black America's national dish. As we sit down to break bread at our homecoming tables, it is a communal offering that recognizes our common ancestral roots. However, now, rather than eating it every day, we often choose to serve soul food on special occasions to celebrate our history and heritage.

COLLARD GREENS WITH SMOKED NECK BONES

2	tablespoons bacon drippings or 5 slices of bacon		$^1/_2$	teaspoon salt
1	large onion, sliced thin		1	teaspoon black pepper
2	pounds smoked pork neck bones		2	teaspoons crushed red pepper
			1	teaspoon thyme leaves
1	quart water		2	bay leaves
2	beef bouillon cubes		5	pounds collard greens

Heat bacon drippings or render fat from bacon over medium-high heat. Once fat has been rendered from bacon, remove and discard or dice and return to the pot when the collard greens are added. Sauté onion in the drippings until they are translucent. Wash neck bones, removing all gritty bone and other residue from the meat. Add the meat, water, and remaining seasoning ingredients. Bring meat to a quick boil, reduce heat, cover, and simmer over low heat for 1 hour.

While neck bones are cooking, prepare the collard greens by removing thick stalks and discarding any yellowed or badly blemished leaves. Wash greens under cold running water and rinse any remaining sand from the sink. Fill sink with cold water, add greens, and plunge up and down several times to wash any remaining sand and sediment from the greens. Several washings may, but are not usually, necessary with store-bought greens. Stack several leaves, roll them cigar fashion and slice into horizontal segments slightly smaller than $^1/_4$ inch.

When the neck bones have simmered for an hour, remove all but one quart of the juice from the pot and reserve. Gradually stir in the greens, allowing each batch to wilt before adding more greens. Bury the neck bones in the simmering greens. Cover and reduce the heat to medium-low. Continue cooking the greens an additional 30 minutes. Uncover the pot and cook an additional 15 to 30 minutes, or until the greens are tender to personal taste, stirring occasionally. Younger greens will require less cooking time; older greens will require more. Add reserved pot juices as necessary to prevent sticking and scorching. Cook until the greens are tender and the meat nearly falls off the bones. Add additional seasoning to taste.

Serve this delicious country dish with hot buttermilk cornbread, fresh field peas if you've got 'em, and some garden fresh tomatoes and cucumbers with a sprinkling of hot pepper vinegar and some salt and pepper. You know what I'm talkin' 'bout! I'm huuunnnngrrrry *now!* What about you?

Makes 6 to 8 servings.

SMOKED TURKEY NECKS & COLLARD GREENS

1 pound of smoked turkey necks (or whatever parts are available in your part of the woods)	1 medium onion, coarsely chopped
1½ quarts water	2 stalks celery, coarsely chopped
2 chicken bouillon cubes	1 large green pepper, coarsely chopped
2 or 3 jalapeño peppers (optional)	1 tablespoon sugar
4 large cloves garlic, minced	1 tablespoon bacon drippings or vegetable oil (optional)
4 pounds of fresh collards	Salt and black pepper to taste

Wash turkey parts and place them in a Dutch oven. Add water, chicken bouillon cubes, jalapeño peppers, and garlic. Replace the cover and bring mixture to a rapid boil. Reduce the heat to low and simmer 30 minutes. While the turkey is boiling, prepare the collard greens by removing thick stalks and discarding any yellowed or badly blemished leaves. Wash greens under cold running water and rinse any remaining sand from the sink. Fill sink with cold water, add greens, and plunge up and down several times to wash any remaining sand and sediment from the greens. Several washings may be, but are not usually necessary with store-bought greens. Roll leaves cigar fashion and slice into horizontal segments slightly smaller than ¼ inch.

Next, gradually stir in the greens with the turkey, allowing each batch to wilt before adding more greens. Add onion, celery, green pepper, sugar, drippings or oil, and seasonings to the pot. Bury the smoked turkey in the simmering greens. Cover and reduce the heat to medium-low. Continue cooking the greens an additional 30 minutes. Uncover the pot and cook 15 to 30 minutes more, or until the greens are tender to personal taste, stirring occasionally. Younger greens will require less cooking time; older greens will require more. Add additional liquid as necessary to prevent sticking and scorching. Add additional seasoning to taste.

Makes 6 servings.

PIG'S TAILS & TURNIP GREENS

2 to 3 pounds of pig's tails cut into 2-inch pieces	1 large bell pepper, chopped
³/₄ teaspoon salt	2 large cloves of garlic, minced
2 large onions, chopped	¹/₈ teaspoon red pepper or to taste
	¹/₄ cup bacon drippings

Wash pig's tails by grasping each tail near its base. Next dip a scrub brush in water and scrub the tail vigorously to remove all traces of scum and particles of dirt. Then wash the tails under cold, running water before patting them dry and placing them in a large, heavy pot with sufficient water to cover.

Bring the water to a boil, add the salt, and cook tails for 30 to 45 minutes. While pig's tails are cooking, prepare greens by removing thick stalks and discarding any yellowed or badly blemished leaves. Wash greens under cold running water and rinse any remaining sand from the sink. Fill sink with cold water, add greens, and plunge up and down several times to wash any remaining sand and sediment from the greens. Several washings may be, but are not usually necessary with store-bought greens. Stack several leaves, roll stacked leaves cigar fashion and slice into horizontal segments slightly smaller than ¹/₄ inch.

Remove and set aside all but one quart of the liquid and add additional liquid as required to yield one liquid quart. Next, gradually stir in the greens, allowing each batch to wilt before adding more greens, the celery, onion, green pepper, sugar, oil and seasonings to the pot. Bury the pigtails in the simmering greens. Cover and reduce the heat to medium-low. Continue cooking the greens an additional 30 minutes. Stir in bacon drippings, uncover the pot and cook an additional 15 to 30 minutes, or until the pig's tails are tender to personal taste or fork tender (approximately 1 hour) and the greens are tender to personal taste, stirring occasionally. Younger greens will require less cooking time; older greens will require more. Add additional liquid as necessary to prevent sticking and scorching. Add additional seasoning to taste. (For pig's tails and cabbage, substitute approximately two large heads of cabbage for the turnip greens and proceed according to instructions.)

Makes 6 servings.

PIG'S TAILS & LIMA BEANS

2 to 3	pounds of pig's tails cut into 2-inch pieces	1	pound dried lima beans, washed and soaked overnight
³/₄	teaspoon salt	¹/₂	teaspoon dry mustard
2	large onions, chopped		Salt and freshly ground pepper to taste
1	large bell pepper, chopped		
2	large cloves of garlic, minced		
¹/₈	teaspoon red pepper or to taste		

Pick over the peas to remove any foreign objects and soak overnight in sufficient water to cover by 2 to 3 inches. The next day, wash each pig tail by grasping it near its base. Next dip a scrub brush in water and scrub the tail vigorously to remove all traces of scum and particles of dirt. Wash the tails under cold, running water before patting them dry and placing them in a large, heavy pot with sufficient water to cover.

Bring the water to a boil, add the salt and cook the pig's tails for 30 to 45 minutes. Skim away any scum during cooking. Add lima beans and all remaining ingredients. Cook for another 1 to 1¹/₂ hours until tender. Add additional water as necessary to prevent the beans from scorching.

Makes 8 servings.

"CHITLINS" & HOG MAWS

The hog maws (stomach) are added to stretch the more expensive chitterlings (intestines) in this recipe. However, you may substitute chitterlings for the maws if you prefer and disregard the directions for cooking and cleaning maws.

Twenty to 30 pounds of "chitlins," or "chits," if you are in a hurry or feeling particularly refined, is a good start in my family, with the exception of my husband who refrains from the enjoyment of this Southern delicacy. Classified as American soul food, and once prepared by slaves as survival food, they are eaten in many other parts of the world, including Great Britain and even China, as my daughter and I discovered while wandering through L.A.'s China Town. You know we tried them. They were fried with Chinese seasonings and tasted delicious.

10	pounds of pork hog maws
10	pounds pork chitterlings
6	quarts water
1	tablespoon salt
1/2	teaspoon red pepper or to taste
2	large yellow onions, quartered
2	large green peppers, seeded, quartered, and cut up

3	cloves sliced garlic
1	large white potato, peeled
1/2	lemon, seeded and quartered
5	whole cloves
3	bay leaves
3/4	cup of fresh lemon juice, divided

Cleaning Hog Maws: First, thaw the maws, if frozen. Under running water, remove the fat and debris from maws. Cut maws into 2-inch pieces. Rinse in fresh water several times and set aside.

Cleaning Chitterlings: If frozen, thaw chitterlings overnight. Reserve the bucket for collecting and disposing of the debris. Hold a piece of the chitterling in one hand so that the smooth side faces away from you and the fatty membranous lining is clearly visible to you. Take the other hand, or use a knife as my mother did, to remove the three Fs: fat, feed, and feces from the lining. (Oh hush! You sausage eaters partake of chitterling too, as they are still sometimes used as sausage casings.) Proceed carefully, segment by segment, rinse and repeat. When performed correctly, it's a time-consuming task. (I don't eat everyone's chitterlings.) Even pre-cleaned chitterlings should be cleaned again, whether they need it or not. Place waste in the bucket and the cleaned chitterling in a sink full of cold water. After all of the chitterlings have been cleaned in this manner, plunge the chitterlings up and down a few times, drain water from the sink, rinse in this manner several times. Next remove the chitterlings a segment at a time. Wash each segment under cold running water while checking again for the three Fs. Using kitchen shears, cut them in two-inch slices right into a large non-reactive bucket or pot to which a half-cup of lemon juice and two quarts of cold water has been added. (Or as my mother used to do, you can cook them first and cut them up using a large cooking fork to hold them in place and a large knife to cut them.) After all of the chitterlings have been rinsed in this manner, add sufficient water to cover them and allow them to set for two hours before cooking.

Cooking: The hog maws are the thickest and must be cooked first. Place the maws in a large pot with three quarts of water. Take into consideration the 10 pounds of chitterlings, which must be added, and use two pots if necessary. Add the onion, green pepper, and salt. Bring the mixture to a boil and allow the maws to cook for an hour and twenty minutes before adding the chitterlings and remaining ingredients. Cover and simmer 4 to 5 hours or until chitterlings are tender. Watch carefully and add additional water as necessary to prevent burning. Remove the top during the last 30 minutes of cooking to allow the juices to cook down and form gravy. Continue to watch closely and add additional water, if required, to prevent scorching. Stir occasionally. Remove and discard the bay leaf, using a fork or spoon. If desired mash the potato against the side of the pot and stir to further thicken the gravy or remove and discard.

As you can see, cleaning chitterlings is a time-consuming process. As in days of old we most often eat them around Thanksgiving and Christmas. My sister-in-law, Erie, has huge family dinners in Chicago and she begins cleaning, cooking, and freezing her chitterlings months ahead of time!

My parents owned a soul food restaurant in Plattsburgh, New York, called "The House by the Side of the Road." Almost every Sunday, I sat in the dining-room with my brother, listening to the band's "Jam Session" while eating chitlins over rice, with a side of collard greens, a mound of my mom's homemade potato salad, a slab of cornbread and some red (cherry) Kool-Aid or sweet tea.

In the summer, if they were barbecuing on the open pit which stood in a screened building on the side of the road, you could add a barbecued rib or two to that meal. As the band's singer crooned the Impressions' "It's All Right," all I could do was lick my fingers and nod my head in agreement.

Makes 10 to 12 servings (depending on the appetites of your guests).

Fried Chitterlings & Hog Maws

10   pounds of pork hog maws

10   pounds pork chitterlings
6   quarts water

1   tablespoon salt
1/2   teaspoon red pepper or to taste
1/4   stick of butter

Clean and cut up the maws and chitterlings according to the directions on page 263. The hog maws are the thickest and must be cooked first. Place the maws in a large pot with three quarts of water. Consider the 10 pounds of chitterlings, which must be added, and use two pots if necessary. Add the onion, green pepper and salt. Bring the mixture to a boil and allow the maws to cook for an hour and twenty minutes before adding the chitterlings and remaining ingredients. Cover and simmer an additional hour and twenty minutes or until chitterlings are tender. Watch carefully and add additional water as necessary to prevent burning.

Drain hog maws and chitterlings from the pot and discard the liquid and onions. Place ¼ stick of butter in large skillet and melt over medium high heat. Stir in maws and chitterlings in small batches and stir until lightly browned. Remove to a paper-towel lined plate to drain and repeat the process until all are cooked. Reheat and serve hot with plenty of hot sauce or a jalapeño pepper on the side.

Makes 8 to 10 servings.

PIG'S FEET IN SPICY TOMATO SAUCE

6	medium pig's feet, split, cleaned, and rinsed	3	stalks of celery, finely chopped
6	quarts of water	2	jalapeño peppers, seeded and chopped (optional)
2	teaspoons salt	½	cup vinegar
3	large onions, coarsely chopped	¼	teaspoon ground allspice
3	large cloves of garlic, minced	¼	teaspoon ground cloves
2	large green peppers, stemmed, seeded, and chopped	¼	teaspoon ground nutmeg
		5	bay leaves
		3	12-ounce cans tomato sauce
		½	teaspoon

Wash pig's feet under cold running water. In a large pot (eight quarts or more) bring six quarts of water and salt to a rapid boil. Add pig's feet, onions, garlic, green peppers, and celery to the boiling water; reduce heat and gently simmer for 1 hour. Add the remaining ingredients and simmer an additional two to three hours or until the pig's feet are fork-tender, the meat falls readily from the bones, and the succulent sauce thickens.

CHICKEN FEET STEW

My mother, in sharing stories of her childhood, often told me that on Sundays when the preacher came to dinner the best part of the chicken went to him, followed by her father. It was then apportioned according to age, with the youngest children receiving the disappointing feet. I am sure that with so many preachers living in Atlanta during the time period of this book, someone can relate to my mom's story.

2	pounds skinned chicken feet	1	cup green beans, slice into 1-inch sections
3	cubes chicken bouillon cubes	3	bay leaves
10	new potatoes halved	4	cloves of garlic, minced
4	onions, quartered		Salt and pepper to taste
1½	cups baby carrots		

If the tough outer skin of the chicken has not been removed, first loosen the skin by passing it through a flame until the skin is blistered all over. Next, use a paper towel to pull off the pieces of parched skin and then discard them. Remove the nail from the base of each toe with kitchen shears or a sharp, heavy knife. Wash the feet and then place them in a stockpot with sufficient water to cover, bring to a boil and cook for ½ hour, skimming any sediment from the top as it cooks.

Add bullion cubes, potatoes, onions, carrots, green beans, bay leaves, garlic, salt, and pepper to taste. Simmer until tender, approximately an additional 30 to 45 minutes. Remove bay leaves before serving. The chicken broth can be thickened by combining 2 tablespoons of flour with ¼ cup of cold water. Mix thoroughly to remove any lumps and drizzle into the simmering mixture while constantly stirring. Add additional salt and pepper to taste and serve hot.

Makes 6 to 8 servings.

BAKED TURKEY LEGS

When chicken feet just won't do, try these meaty turkey legs. If you know your day at home will be busy and you don't have the time or inclination to stand over a hot stove, pop these into the oven and by dinnertime your neighbors will be knocking at your door in hopes of receiving a dinner invitation.

4 turkey legs Seasoned salt and pepper to taste 4 cloves of garlic, crushed	1 bell pepper, seeded and coarsely chopped 1 onion, coarsely chopped

Preheat oven to 250°F. Wash turkey legs under cold running water, place in baking dish and season according to taste. Add remaining ingredients and seal tightly with aluminum foil. Place in a preheated oven and allow to cook 4 hours or until meat falls easily from the bones. Remove bones and discard. Serve with rice, mashed potatoes, or a mixture of broccoli, cauliflower, and carrots. If you desire thicker gravy, pour pan drippings into a saucepan. Combine 3 tablespoons of flour with 1 cup of water, mix well to remove any lumps, and rapidly stir into your pan drippings while stirring. Serve over rice, if desired, or with a salad and hearty homemade bread. You choose!

Makes 4 large servings or 6 small servings.

African-American culture and heritage is the blending of many cultures, including Caribbean. It stands to reason that Caribbeans of African descent would be attracted to Atlanta as a major center of black culture. They studied and taught at the AUC and owned businesses on Auburn Street. They also brought their food with them. With its common root in Africa, it's not surprising that it soon found its way to African American tables. The Caribbean food influence remains strong in Atlanta. Its presence is strongly felt to this day with the plethora of Caribbean restaurants that surround the AUC campus. At lunchtime there is usually a long line. With these recipes, there is no wait.

ROAST TURKEY WITH JERK SEASONING

1 12½-pound turkey	¼ cup soy sauce (low sodium may be substituted)
¼ cup jerk seasoning spices (see recipe on page 24)	3 cups chicken broth (low sodium is acceptable)
½ cup honey	Vegetable oil
3 tablespoons lime juice	

Remove neck and giblets from the turkey, rinse under cold running water, and pat dry. Use fingers to carefully loosen skin over breast and tops of legs without tearing the skin. Combine jerk spices, honey, lime juice, and soy sauce and rub this mixture onto the turkey. Refrigerate to marinate overnight.

Prepare stuffing (recipe follows) and allow it to cool completely before filling the turkey cavity just before roasting. Place turkey in roasting pan and add chicken broth. Brush top evenly with vegetable oil and bake at 350 F for 30 minutes, then reduce temperature to 325°F for 3½ hours. After one hour, cover turkey with foil to prevent skin from burning. The turkey is ready when it is golden brown and the juice runs clear when pierced in the drumstick joint with a fork. This is also delicious when served with spicy sausage stuffing and Jamaican rice and peas. See recipe below.

Makes 12 to 15 servings.

SPICY SAUSAGE STUFFING

3½ pounds lean ground pork (not sausage)	1 teaspoon hot pepper sauce
3 cloves garlic, minced	¼ teaspoon nutmeg
¼ cup minced parsley	1 teaspoon black pepper
1 teaspoon salt	1¼ teaspoons thyme
	1 tablespoon rum

Combine the above ingredients, blend well, and fill the neck and cavity of the turkey. Skewer cavity closed and bake according to the above directions.

Makes 6 servings.

JAMAICAN RICE AND PEAS

1   cup dried kidney beans,
    rinsed
    Approximately 5 cups water,
    divided
1   13$\frac{1}{2}$-ounce can coconut milk
5   green onions, finely chopped
1   jalapeño pepper, seeded and
    chopped fine

3   cloves garlic, peeled and
    minced
2   teaspoons dried thyme
2   cups long-grain white rice
1$\frac{1}{2}$ teaspoons salt
$\frac{1}{2}$ teaspoon black pepper

Place the beans and 4 cups cold water in a 4-quart pot. Cover, bring to a boil, remove from the heat, and allow to stand for 1 hour. Drain, and return the beans to the pot. Add the coconut milk, onion, jalapeño pepper, garlic, thyme, and 1 cup cold water. Cover and simmer for 30 minutes until the beans are just tender. Drain the beans, reserving the liquid, return them to the pot, and add the rice, salt, and pepper; measure the reserved liquid and add enough cold water to make 4 cups total. Add the liquid to the pot. Cover, bring to a boil, and reduce the heat to low. Simmer for 15 minutes until the liquid is absorbed. Add more salt and pepper if desired.

Makes 8 to 10 servings.

OXTAIL STEW WITH SAFFRON RICE

3   pounds of oxtails, trimmed of
      excess fat and washed
     Salt and black pepper
2   medium onions, sliced thin
1/4   cup flour
1/2   teaspoon salt
1/2   teaspoon black pepper
1/3   cup vegetable oil
2   tomatoes, coarsely chopped

1   Scotch bonnet pepper, chopped
4   garlic cloves, minced
1   large green pepper, seeded and
      coarsely chopped
6   cups hot beef broth
3   tablespoons tomato purée
1/2   teaspoon dried thyme
     Salt and black pepper to taste

Place oxtails in a large bowl and season to taste with salt and black pepper. Add approximately half the onions, garlic, and Scotch bonnet pepper, refrigerate for at least 2 hours or overnight. Combine flour, salt, and black pepper in a bowl and dredge the oxtail pieces in flour mixture, making sure all sides are well covered.

Heat oil over medium-high heat and lightly brown the oxtails. Remove meat from pan, drain off all but 1 to 2 tablespoons of the oil. Add remaining onion, tomato, green pepper, Scotch bonnet, and garlic to pan and sauté lightly. Add hot broth and tomato purée, stir well. Place in an ovenproof dish with meat and thyme, and cook in a medium oven until tender, about 1 1/2 hours. Serve with saffron rice (recipe follows).

Makes 4 servings.

SAFFRON RICE

1   clove garlic
1/4   cup diced onion
1/4   cup diced green bell pepper
1   diced pimento
3   tablespoons olive oil
1/4   teaspoon salt (optional)

     Pinch of fresh ground black
       pepper
     Pinch of turmeric
1/4   teaspoon saffron
1 3/4   cups chicken broth
1   cup long-grain white rice

Over medium-low heat, sauté the garlic, onion, green bell pepper, and pimento in the olive oil until the vegetables caramelize. You may substitute pimento juice or chicken broth for the olive oil and simmer until the onions are transparent and the green bell peppers are soft. In a two-quart saucepan bring broth to a boil and add the rice and remaining ingredients. Add additional salt and pepper to taste. Cover the saucepan and cook over low heat for about 20 minutes.

Makes 4 servings.

JAMAICAN CURRIED GOAT

Delicious when served over a big mound of rice or rice and peas.

2 pounds goat meat	2 cloves garlic, crushed
2 teaspoons salt or to taste	2 tablespoons butter
3 tablespoons curry powder	¹/₄ cup vegetable oil
¹/₂ teaspoon cumin	3 cups beef broth
¹/₂ teaspoon black pepper	2 tomatoes, chopped
4 green onions, chopped	2 onions, sliced
1 or 2 Scotch bonnet peppers, chopped, with or without seeds	4 to 5 potatoes, peeled and cut into bite-size pieces
	Lemon juice

Cut the goat meat into small pieces; place them in a bowl. Combine the salt, curry powder, cumin, and black pepper; mix well and use to season the goat meat. Stir in the green onions, Scotch bonnet peppers, and garlic, and set aside to marinate for at least 1 hour but preferably overnight. Brush onions, peppers, and garlic from the meat and fry it in the butter and oil over medium to medium-high heat until it is lightly browned.

Add enough broth to cover the meat and bring to a boil. Reduce the heat, cover the pan, and simmer until the meat is tender, adding more broth as necessary to permit the meat to boil freely without sticking. Add the sliced onions, potatoes, and stir in the seasonings in which the meat was marinated. Taste, adjust seasonings, cover the pot again, and allow goat to simmer another 15 to 20 minutes or until the broth approaches a stew-like consistency. However, it should not be too thick. Traditionally, the gravy is fairly thin so that you have lots to pour over the rice. Once the potatoes are cooked through, add a tablespoon or two of lemon juice.

Excellent when served with white rice, mango chutney, or fried plantains.

Makes 4 to 6 servings.

CONCH STEW

This tasty island stew is even better the second day. If you have difficulty finding conch meat, chicken, lobster, or shrimp may be substituted.

2¹/₂ pounds of conch meat	2 tablespoons olive oil
¹/₂ cup white wine vinegar	2 tomatoes, peeled, seeded, and
1 large onion, finely chopped	chopped
1 medium-size green pepper,	¹/₂ cup chicken broth
finely chopped	Dash of Tabasco sauce
2 cloves garlic, minced	1 tablespoon Maggi seasoning
2 tablespoons butter	

Clean, peel, and pound the conch well to tenderize. Next, wash it with the vinegar, cut it into bite-size pieces, and set aside.

Sauté the onions, green peppers, and garlic in butter and olive oil. Add the tomatoes, chicken broth, Tabasco, and Maggi seasoning. Simmer for approximately 20 minutes before adding the conch; cover and continue to cook until meat is tender, about 10 to 15 additional minutes.

Makes 4 to 6 servings.

EXCELLENT PORK STEW

3 tablespoons vegetable oil
2 pounds pork tenderloin, cut into 1¹/₂-inch pieces
1 large onion, chopped
2 tablespoons all purpose-flour
2 14¹/₂-ounce cans beef broth
2 cups dry white wine
4 large potatoes cut lengthwise into quarters
1 large green bell pepper, chopped
3 large garlic cloves, chopped

1 tablespoon chopped fresh parsley
1 teaspoon thyme
1 teaspoon cumin
¹/₄ teaspoon chili powder
4 bay leaves
3 large carrots cut into ³/₄-inch pieces
¹/₂ pound green beans, trimmed, halved
Salt and pepper to taste
Chopped fresh parsley

Heat the oil in heavy large pot or Dutch oven over high heat. Add pork and onion and cook while stirring until the pork is brown on all sides and the onions begin to caramelize. Add flour and stir. Add beef broth and wine. Bring to a quick boil, reduce heat to a simmer and cook down until stock is reduced by half. Add remaining ingredients and continue to cook until meat is tender and the vegetables soft. Serve with a hearty homemade bread and salad.

Makes 4 to 6 servings.

CLARK-ATLANTA UNIVERSITY

If you're not living on the edge, you're taking up too much room.

—African proverb

BREADS AND DESSERTS

On July 11, 1988, academic powerhouses Atlanta University and Clark College merged to form Clark Atlanta University (CAU). With this union CAU became the largest university in the Atlanta University System and the only one to grant graduate degrees. In addition, it became one of only two private, historically black universities in the United States to award doctorate degrees in more than five disciplines. Although traditionally identified as a historically black institution, today CAU is widely recognized as a national university as indicated by its classification as a Doctoral/Research–Intensive University by the Carnegie Foundation for the Advancement of Teaching in 2000 and its ranking as a national university by *U.S. News and World Report* in 2003. The only private historically black university in the nation to receive such a classification, Clark Atlanta University was also ranked as a "Top College for African Americans," in the January 2001 issue of *Black Enterprise.*

These honors, especially its recognition as a national university, come as no surprise given its rich legacy of academic excellence from its parent institutions. Accepting as its mandate the motto of Atlanta University—"I'll Find a Way or Make One"—and that of Clark College—"Culture for Service"—Clark Atlanta stands alone as the nation's oldest historically black graduate institution.

Clark and Atlanta University have been strengthened both by the challenges they confronted individually and the partnership, which they formed in 1988. This dynamic union set Clark Atlanta University apart as one of the premiere universities of the twenty-first century. Justifiably proud of its past accomplishments, it continues to write new history and set even higher standards while charting a "Bold New Future."

Atlanta University—"I'll Find a Way or Make One"

"It is generally conceded that the period immediately succeeding the 'Civil War' in this country was one of the most interesting and critical in its history. The ruin and devastation that abounded in the South, the destitution and ignorance among the black people who had been recently declared 'free forever,' called for noble men and heroic women to rehabilitate the South."

—*The Atlanta University Bulletin,* January 1915

At the close of the Civil War, while Atlanta lay in ruins, the American Missionary Association (AMA) purchased two adjoining lots in the city and appointed the Reverend Fredrick Ayer, an aged home missionary, and his wife to start a school. They arrived in the city in November 1865, and within three weeks were joined by two sisters, Misses Rose and Lucy Kinney.

According to Miss Caroline Gordon, a teacher of the first normal class and preceptress for the first three years of Atlanta University, "A small dwelling house on the corner lot served as a home for teachers and a long low building was used as a chapel and a school room. The house was so open, that several of the teachers were 'obliged to wear their cloaks, hoods and mittens to keep warm in the winter.' " —Miss Caroline Gordon, *The Bulletin of Atlanta University,* January 1909.

The school filled up so rapidly that an overflow school was held in an old dilapidated church on nearby Jenkins Street. The AMA purchased an old box car in Ohio for $310 and sent it to Atlanta, where it was named the Walton Street School but was popularly known as the "car-box." Teaching continued in the Jenkins Street church and the car-box, with Mr. Ayers and one of the sisters teaching in one location while Mrs. Ayers and the other sister taught in the other location. Other missionaries followed. In addition to teaching, home visits were made and Sunday school teachers organized to serve the growing spiritual needs of the freed community.

In 1866 the AMA appointed Mr. Edmund A. Ware, a 29-year-old graduate of Yale College, superintendent of schools in Georgia and the Freedmen's Bureau appointed him superintendent of building school houses in the state, headquartering him in Atlanta. Ware soon determined that none of the sites then in use were suitable for a school. In the summer of 1866 a building located in the northern part of the city and formerly used as a Confederate Commissary was obtained for use as a school building. Ware immediately made plans to build a two

President Edmund Asa Ware
*(Archives and Special Collections:
Robert Woodruff Library at the Atlanta
University Center)*

story addition with four rooms in front. The new school building became what is even today known as the Storrs School, in recognition of a gift of nearly one thousand dollars from the Storrs Congregational Church in Cincinnati.

By around Christmas 1866, teachers and students from the Jenkins Street Church and the car-box moved into the new building. Ware served as the school's first principal. By 1867, however, the school was full. A small building near Storrs was secured to serve as a school.

Teacher Caroline Gordon described that period: "Dear old Billie, a veteran war horse, and an old army ambulance did duty in conveying the teachers to and from the Summer Hill School. In the rainy season the wheels sank to the hubs in the mud. The home was a curiously furnished house for Northern and Western teachers, graduates from Holyoke, Oberlin, Yale, etc. Army blankets served for carpets. Iron bedsteads three feet wide from army stores and mattresses made from corn husks, were obtained in various ways. Dressing cases, wardrobes, wash stands, clothes presses, in short all the furnishings necessary were supplied by the teachers and helpers. The chairs, many of them were made from barrels upholstered with cotton and calico. All this time the strength, and talents of the workers were put upon the scholars and people who were so anxious to learn. No one thought of discomforts. Mr. Ware preached, taught and visited schools that were organized and organized others in various parts of the state." —Miss Caroline Gordon, *The Bulletin of Atlanta University,* January 1909

Others teaching at the school were Miss Jane Twichell, who would later become Mrs. Ware, and Miss Amy Williams, who would eventually become the school principal. Ware and Ayers were among the eleven signers of the charter, approved in 1867, to establish Atlanta University. Ware served as president of the Board of Trustees, and in 1869 was appointed the first president of the University, a position he retained until his death in 1885. Under his leadership, the educational program was established, including a grammar school to train students not ready to enter the preparatory and college programs.

The University, chartered for the "Christian education of youth," was part of the move-

President Horace Bumstead
*(Archives and Special Collections:
Robert Woodruff Library at the Atlanta
University Center)*

ment, spearheaded by freedmen and abolitionists, to educate Negroes at the end of the Civil War. The educational efforts were supported by black and white churches and organizations such as the American Missionary Association and the Freedmen's Bureau. Atlanta University would become the first school in the state of Georgia to offer courses leading to a college degree for African-American students.

In an address commemorating the semi-centennial of the charter of Atlanta University, former President Horace Bumstead recalled, "When Atlanta University was chartered in 1867, the motto chosen for its seal was 'I'll find a way or make one.' It had previously been the motto of the class of 1863 at Yale College, in which the elder President Ware and two of his classmates [Bumstead and Francis] were given their training and inspiration for long years of service to this institution."

The first students of the University began classes in April 1869 and by October 1869, 89 students were enrolled. In later years Dr. Bumstead would recall viewing the property with Dr. Ware before the first building was erected. Ware "brought me out to 'Diamond Hill,' as it was then known, and pointing out the spot, 'Here, in a few weeks, we shall lay the cornerstone of the first building of Atlanta University.' I looked around and what did I see? No grass, no trees, no shrubbery—a battle-scarred hill, whose red clay soil had been turned up in the erection of a fort on the very site of Stone Hall where we are now assembled, and entrenchments running from the fort on either side; and, scattered here and there a few dilapidated shanties which had been the homes of some of the freed people." —Horace Bumstead, in an address to commemorate the semi-centennial of the charter of Atlanta University, May 30, 1917

The completion of the large building on Diamond Hill provided for the opening of the second session, with enlarged facilities on the university grounds. Among those first students was Lucy Craft Laney.

Lucy, one of ten children born to former slave parents, learned to read and write by the

Horace Bumstead and family.
(Archives and Special Collections: Robert Woodruff Library at the Atlanta University Center)

age of four, and was able to translate difficult Latin passages such as Julius Caesar's *Commentaries on the Gallic War* by age twelve. In 1869 she entered the first class at Atlanta University, graduating from the normal department (teacher's training) in 1873. At that time, women were prohibited from taking the classic course at Atlanta University. "Miss Lucy" taught in Macon, Savannah, Milledgeville, and Augusta for ten years, before beginning her own school in 1883 in the basement of Christ Presbyterian Church in Augusta.

Haines Normal and Industrial Institute

The school, the Haines Normal and Industrial Institute, was originally intended as a girls' school. However, when several boys appeared in search of an education, Laney could not refuse them. After addressing a meeting of the General Assembly of the Northern Presbyterian Church in Minneapolis in 1886 to appeal for funds, she received only her fare home. She did, however, attract the attention of lifetime benefactor, Mrs. Francine E. H. Haines, for whom her school was named. Within thirty years of its founding, Haines Institute had 900 students enrolled, 34 teachers, and offered a fifth year of college preparatory high school where Laney taught Latin to male and female students. Her students were well prepared to enter schools such as Howard, Fisk, Yale, and other prestigious colleges.

Haines served not only as an educational center but also as a cultural center for the African-American community. It hosted orchestra concerts, lectures by nationally famous guests, and various social events. Laney would go on to open the first kindergarten and create the first nursing training programs for African-American women in Augusta. She also helped to found Augusta's local NAACP chapter in 1918, and she was active in the Interracial Commission, the National Association of Colored Women, and the Niagara Movement. She also helped to integrate the community work of the YMCA and YWCA. Among her many friends and students were notables such as Mary McLeod Bethune, W.E.B. Du Bois, Joseph Simeon Flipper, John Hope, Richard R. Wright, Sr., and Langston Hughes.

Langston Hughes reception at Atlanta University, 1946.
(Archives and Special Collections: Robert Woodruff Library at the Atlanta University Center)

President Edward Twichell Ware, son of Edmund Asa Ware (first president of Atlanta University), became the University's third president.

(Archives and Special Collections: Robert Woodruff Library at the Atlanta University Center)

An AUC Accolade

Lucy Craft Laney, the Reverend Henry McNeal Turner, and the Reverend Martin Luther King, Jr., were the first African-Americans to have their portraits hung in the Georgia state capitol; they were selected by Governor Jimmy Carter in 1974. Laney's portrait bears tribute to "the mother of the children of the people," a woman who knew that "God didn't use any different dirt to make me than the first lady of the land."

By the late 1870s the university had begun granting bachelor's degrees and supplying black teachers and librarians to public schools across the South. Following Dr. Ware's death in 1855, three acting presidents, including Dr. Bumstead, served from 1886 until 1887. Finally, Dr. Bumstead was named as the University's second president in 1888.

In 1895, while Bumstead was president, an event of sweeping importance occurred: "The Cotton States and International Exposition was held in Atlanta from September 18th to December 31st. For many in the state it was a symbol of the New South emerging after reconstruction." For African Americans it was seen as an opportunity to showcase their many accomplishments since the abolition of slavery in hopes that they would be seen worthy of receiving the one thing they most wanted—full civil rights. The impact of one speech given would be far-reaching and long-lasting.

THE ATLANTA EXPOSITION

"The Cotton States and International Exposition will furnish ample opportunity for the colored people of the South to exhibit whatever progress they have made during the short period of freedom. It is to be hoped that they will avail themselves of this opportunity and make a creditable display; as this will be helpful to the race in many ways. It will place it in a favorable light before the world, the greater part of which is still very skeptical with reference to the future of the Negro, especially in this country. If we are faithful to our trust, and then invite the largest number to come and see. There is nothing that convinces like the facts." —William H. Crogman, LL.D 76, chief commissioner of the Negro Exhibit. *The Bulletin of Atlanta University,* May 1895.

The exposition's board of directors invited Booker T. Washington, principal of Tuskegee University and considered by many to be the most influential black leader of his time, to speak at its opening exercises. He addressed the "Negro problem"—the question of what to do about the abysmal social and economic conditions of blacks—by arguing that blacks should temporarily forgo pursuing social equality and political rights in favor of pursuing economic parity. In this regard he urged black ownership of businesses and property and felt that all other rights would follow. Others advocated an immediate movement or struggle for civil rights, specifically the right to vote, on the theory that economic and social rights would follow. This group advocated the use of violence, if necessary, to achieve their goals.

Dr. W.E.B. Du Bois and other like-minded civil rights advocates began publicly demand-

70th birthday celebration for Dr. W.E.B. Du Bois at Atlanta University,
February 23, 1938.
(Archives and Special Collections: Robert Woodruff Library at the Atlanta University Center)

ing that all black citizens be granted: 1) the right to vote, 2) civic equality, and 3) the education of Negro youth according to ability. In 1905, Du Bois helped found the Niagara Movement, a radical civil rights protest organization whose membership consisted predominately of Northern, urban, college-educated black men—the "Talented Tenth"—which became a forerunner of the National Association for the Advancement of Colored People, then a predominately white organization Du Bois helped to found in 1909.

The NAACP began planning tactics in an intensive campaign to enforce the Fourteenth and Fifteenth Amendments. Major court battles against segregation and discrimination were initiated by this bold new organization.

In 1929–30, Atlanta University began offering graduate education in the liberal arts as well as the social and natural sciences. Gradually professional programs in social work, library science, and business administration were added. During the same period Atlanta University affiliated with Morehouse and Spelman colleges to form the Atlanta University System. The campus was moved to its present site, where the modern organization of the Atlanta University Center emerged, with Clark College, Morris Brown College, and the Interdenominational Theological Center joining the affiliation later.

Rufus Early Clement became the sixth president of Atlanta University. Elected in 1937, he would become the longest serving president, holding the position until his death in 1967.

President Rufus E. Clement and Atlanta's Mayor Hartsfield.
(Archives and Special Collections: Robert Woodruff Library at the Atlanta University Center)

Committee on Appeal for Human Rights, March 26, 1961.
(Archives and Special Collections: Robert Woodruff Library at the Atlanta University Center)

During his administration the Atlanta School of Social Work, a self-supporting professional school affiliated with the University and the Schools of Library Service, later known as the School of Library and Information Services, was established in 1941. The School of Education was established in 1944, and the School of Business Administration was established in 1946. In 1947 the Atlanta School of Social Work integrated with the school and in 2001 it was renamed the Whitney M. Young, Jr., School of Social Work.

Atlanta University and the other colleges of the Atlanta University Center would play a vital role in the pending civil rights movement. The confluence of these universities' students and faculty, black businesses, and the institutions of Sweet Auburn Avenue created a citadel for civil rights activism in the city. Within the Atlanta University Center, Stone Hall (now known as Fairchild-Stone Hall), would become an early focal point of university activities.

South Hall, Stone Hall, and North Hall.
(Archives and Special Collections: Robert Woodruff Library at the Atlanta University Center)

Breads, Biscuits, and Rolls

CORNMEAL YEAST BREAD

Cornmeal isn't just for muffins and pan breads anymore.

2 packages dried yeast	1 teaspoon salt
¹/₂ cup warm water (105–115°F)	1 egg, lightly beaten
³/₄ cup warm evaporated milk (105–115°F)	1 cup all-purpose flour
¹/₃ cup butter, softened	³/₄ cup yellow cornmeal
¹/₃ cup sugar	3 to 3¹/₂ cups all-purpose flour

Lightly oil two 8¹/₂ × 4¹/₂ × 3-inch loaf pans and set aside. Place yeast in a bowl with warm water and dissolve. Allow the yeast to proof for five minutes. Add the next four ingredients and stir until the butter melts. Next, add the egg, cornmeal, and flour. Use an electric mixer to beat at medium speed until the mixture is well blended. Gradually stir in sufficient flour to form a stiff dough.

Turn the dough out on a lightly floured surface and knead until the dough is smooth and elastic, approximately 10 minutes. Place in a lightly oiled mixing bowl, turning to grease the top. Cover the bowl with a clean tea-towel and allow the dough to rise in a warm (85°F) draft-free place for one hour or until doubled in bulk. Punch dough down and divide in half. Shape dough into two loaves and place into bread pans, cover with a clean tea-towel, and allow to rise until double in bulk, approximately 45 minutes. While bread is rising, preheat oven to 350°F. Bake bread at 350°F for 30 to 35 minutes or until the loaves sound hollow when lightly tapped with knuckles. Remove bread from the pans and cool on wire racks.

Makes 2 loaves.

YAM YEAST BREAD

2	packages dry yeast		¹/₈	teaspoon nutmeg
1¹/₂	cups very warm (110–115°F) water		¹/₈	teaspoon mace
³/₄	teaspoon sugar		2	tablespoons butter, softened
5 to 6	cups unbleached white flour		1	cup cooked yam purée (from 1 to 2 yams)
3	teaspoons salt		1	egg, well beaten
¹/₂	teaspoon white pepper			

Grease and flour two 9 × 5-inch loaf pans and set aside. Place the yeast, warm water, and sugar in bowl and allow the yeast to dissolve. Combine 5 cups of the flour with the spices and gradually stir the flour mixture into the yeast mixture. Add the butter, yam purée, and additional flour, as necessary, to form a moist dough. Knead the dough for 10 to 15 minutes before placing it in a buttered bowl to rise. Cover the bowl with plastic and allow it to rise in a warm (75 to 80°F) draft-free place until doubled.

Punch dough down and let rise again about 45 minutes. Punch down, divide between the two prepared loaf pans, and allow dough to rise for another 45 minutes. Prepare the glaze by combining the egg with a teaspoon of water and mixing well. Brush the top of the bread with the glaze mixture before baking it in a preheated 425°F oven for 30 to 40 minutes or until the bottom of the loaf sounds hollow when rapped with knuckles. Cool on a rack at least an hour before slicing.

Note: If your room is drafty and your bread is having difficulty rising, place it on a heating pad set on low.

Makes 2 loaves.

CORNMEAL ROLLS

With their unique Southern flair, the heady aroma of these fresh baked dinner rolls will beckon your family to the dinner table faster than you can say, "Dinner time."

1¼	cups flour	2	tablespoons shortening
¾	cup cornmeal	1	egg
1	tablespoon sugar	½	cup milk
½	teaspoon salt		Melted butter
1	tablespoon baking powder	1	egg + 1 tablespoon water

Preheat oven to 450°F. Sift together the flour, cornmeal, sugar, salt, and baking powder. Rub in the shortening with your fingertips. Add egg and milk, mix well, and roll out to a ¼-inch thickness. Cut into rounds with a large cutter and brush with melted butter. Fold in half like a parker house roll, brush tops with egg white mixture, and dust with cornmeal. Press the fold gently and bake in preheated oven for 12 to 15 minutes.

Makes 16 rolls.

SOUR CREAM ROLLS

So deliciously light, they practically melt in your mouth. Almost impossible to resist, set them out and watch as they disappear.

2$\frac{1}{4}$	cups all-purpose flour, divided	$\frac{3}{4}$	cup sour cream
2	tablespoons sugar	$\frac{1}{4}$	cup water
1	envelope yeast	2	tablespoons butter
$\frac{3}{4}$	teaspoon salt	1	large egg
			Melted butter

In a large bowl, combine 1 cup of the flour, sugar, undissolved yeast, and salt. Heat the sour cream, water, and butter to 120 to 130°F. Gradually add the sour cream mixture to the flour mixture and beat with an electric mixer set at medium speed for two minutes. Add egg and remaining flour to form a soft batter. Spoon evenly into greased 2$\frac{1}{2}$-inch muffin pans. Brush with melted butter, cover, and allow dough to rise until double in bulk, approximately 1 hour.

Bake in a preheated 400°F oven for 25 to 30 minutes.

Makes 12 rolls.

SOUR CREAM FAN ROLLS

1	cup warm water (110 to 115°F)	2	eggs, lightly beaten
2	tablespoons sugar	$\frac{1}{4}$	cup + 2 tablespoons melted butter
2	tablespoons active dry yeast	1$\frac{1}{2}$	teaspoons salt
$\frac{1}{2}$	cup sugar, divided	$\frac{1}{4}$	teaspoon baking powder
2	cups warm sour cream (110 to 115°F)	7 to 8	cups all-purpose flour

Grease 18 muffin pan cups and set aside. Combine warm water with 2 tablespoons of sugar in a large mixing bowl and dissolve yeast in the sugar water. Allow yeast mixture to stand for 5 minutes. In a separate large bowl, combine the sour cream, eggs, butter, salt, and remaining sugar. Stir in the baking powder, yeast mixture, and four cups of flour until smooth. Mix in enough of the remaining flour to form a soft dough. Turn dough out onto a floured surface and knead the dough until it is smooth and elastic, approximately 7 to 8 minutes. Place the dough in a greased bowl, turning once to grease the top. Cover the bowl with a clean tea towel and allow to rise in a warm place until double in bulk, approximately 1 hour.

Punch dough down, turn out onto a lightly floured surface, and divide in half. Roll each half of dough into a 23-inch × 9-inch rectangle. Cut into 1-1/2-inch strips. Stack 5 strips together and cut the stacked strips into 1½-inch pieces. Place each piece cut side up in a greased muffin cup. Cover with a clean tea towel and allow to rise until doubled in bulk, approximately 20 minutes. Preheat oven to 350°F. Bake in preheated oven for 20 to 25 minutes or until golden brown. Cool on wire racks.

Makes 2½ dozen rolls.

POTATO ROSEMARY ROLLS

Fragrant rosemary is the secret to these delicious dinner rolls that will have your friends and family asking for more.

2 to 2½	cups all-purpose flour, divided		1	cup milk
1½	tablespoons sugar		¼	cup water
1	envelope quick rise yeast		½	cup instant potatoes
1¼	teaspoons salt		2	tablespoons vegetable oil
1	teaspoon dried rosemary, crushed		1	egg, lightly beaten
				Rosemary for topping

In a large bowl combine ⅔ cup of flour, sugar, undissolved yeast, salt, and rosemary. Heat the milk, water, potato flakes, and oil to between 120 and 130°F. Gradually add the flour mixture to the milk mixture.

Use an electric mixer to beat at medium speed for approximately 2 minutes. Stir in enough of the remaining flour to make a soft dough. Turn dough out onto a lightly floured surface and knead lightly until smooth and elastic, approximately 8 to 10 minutes. Cover and allow the dough to rest 10 minutes before dividing the dough into 12 equal pieces. Roll each piece into a 10 inch rope. Coil each rope, tucking the end under the roll. Place rolls two inches apart on a greased baking sheet. Cover and permit the rolls to rise in a warm (85°F) draft-free place for 1 hour or until doubled in bulk. Brush tops with egg mixture and sprinkle with additional rosemary. Bake at 375°F for 15 to 20 minutes or until done.

Makes 12 rolls.

WHOLE WHEAT ROLLS

$3/4$ cup milk	1 package dry yeast
$1/4$ cup table cream	1 egg, well beaten
$1/4$ cup + 1 tablespoon sugar	2 cups whole wheat flour
1 teaspoon salt	$1^1/2$ cups all-purpose flour
$1/4$ cup shortening	Melted butter
$1/4$ cup warm water (105–110°F)	

Preheat oven to 400°F. Grease a baking sheet and set aside. Scald milk and table cream; stir in sugar, salt, and shortening. Set aside and allow the milk mixture to cool to a lukewarm temperature. In a small bowl, combine warm water, yeast, and sugar; stir until the yeast and sugar are dissolved and set the yeast mixture aside to proof. Allow mixture to cool to lukewarm. Add the egg to the milk mixture and mix well. Add the proofed yeast and whole wheat flour; beat until the mixture is smooth. Next, add the all-purpose flour and mix until smooth. Place dough into a large greased bowl. Grease the top of the dough, cover with a clean tea towel, and allow it to rise in a warm (75 to 80°F) draft-free place until doubled. Punch dough down. Divide dough into two equal parts. Turn $1/2$ of the dough onto a lightly floured board and roll into a circle approximately 10 inches in diameter. Cut the circle into 12 equal pie-shaped wedges. Roll each wedge tightly. Beginning at the widest end, roll the wedge toward the point and seal the points by wetting your finger tip and dampening the underside of the point. Gently press the point in place, rewet your finger, and rub it over the point until it seals. Place each crescent on the prepared baking sheet with the point beneath the roll. Curve each roll into the shape of a crescent and allow the rolls to rise 1 hour or until they double in bulk. Place rolls in preheated oven and bake for approximately 10 minutes or until the rolls are lightly browned. Serve with honey butter (see recipe below).

Makes 2 dozen rolls

HONEY BUTTER

¹/₂ cup butter, softened	¹/₃ cup honey

Combine butter and honey and beat until creamy. Serve at room temperature.

Makes 6 to 10 servings.

TEA BISCUITS

2 cups all-purpose flour, sifted	¹/₂ cup shortening
3 teaspoons baking powder	1 egg, beaten
1 teaspoon salt	³/₄ cup milk

Preheat oven to 450°F. Sift together the flour, baking powder, and salt; cut in the shortening until the mixture resembles coarse cornmeal. Combine the egg and milk, mix well. Add to the flour mixture and mix until a smooth dough is formed. Turn the dough out onto a lightly floured surface and knead lightly. Roll out to a thickness of ¹/₂ inch and cut with a biscuit cutter. Place biscuits on an ungreased cookie sheet and bake in a 450°F oven for 12 to 15 minutes.

Makes 12 biscuits.

SWEET POTATO PECAN BISCUITS

Serve these delicious biscuits piping hot, slathered with butter and sorghum syrup.

$^3/_4$ cup cold mashed sweet
potatoes
$^1/_2$ cup butter, melted and
cooled

$^1/_3$ cup light brown sugar
$^1/_2$ cup buttermilk
2 cups self-rising flour
$^1/_2$ cup chopped pecans

Preheat oven to 400°F. Combine sweet potatoes, butter, and brown sugar until well blended, and then stir in buttermilk. Stir the mixture until it is smooth. Add flour and stir until just moistened. Add the pecans to dough and turn it out on lightly floured surface. Knead the dough a few times until it holds together. Roll dough to $^1/_2$-inch thickness and cut with floured 2-inch biscuit cutter. Bake on lightly greased baking sheet for 15 to 18 minutes.

Makes about 18 biscuits.

Henry Ossian Flipper

Soldier, engineer, and author Henry Ossian Flipper was born to slave parents in 1856 in Thomasville, Georgia. Henry would attend Atlanta University for one year before becoming the fifth African American to receive an appointment to West Point, the U.S. military academy. He endured the inhospitable and often hostile treatment of white cadets to become the first African American to successfully graduate from the academy.

After graduation, he was commissioned as a second lieutenant and assigned to the all-Negro 10th Cavalry Regiment, serving at various forts in the southwest. In 1881 while at Fort Davis, Texas, white officers framed him and he was charged with embezzling funds. At a general court-martial, he was acquitted of the embezzlement charge but found guilty of conduct unbecoming an officer and a gentleman. He was dishonorably discharged from the army in 1882 and fought to clear his name for the remainder of his life.

As a civilian, Flipper distinguished himself in several positions, as a mining engineer, special government agent, and translator and interpreter of Spanish. In 1923, after a brief stint as assistant secretary of the interior, he accepted an engineering position with a Venezuelan petroleum company and translated that country's law on hydrocarbons and other combustible minerals. During his lifetime he published three books and a number of journal and newspaper articles. His autobiography, *The Colored Cadet at West Point*, was published in 1878. In 1963, *Negro Frontiersman: The Western Memoirs of Henry O. Flipper* was published posthumously. He died in Atlanta in 1940.

Flipper's descendants continued his lifelong fight to clear his name. In 1976 the army rectified the record and granted him an honorable discharge. A bust of Flipper was unveiled at West Point in the same year. In 1999 President William Jefferson Clinton granted him a full pardon. West Point now gives an award in his honor to the graduating senior who has displayed "the highest qualities of leadership, self-discipline, and perseverance in the face of unusual difficulties while a cadet."

Henry O. Flipper, ca. 1875.
*(Archives and Special Collections: Robert Woodruff
Library at the Atlanta University Center)*

Atlanta University faculty, 1890.
(Archives and Special Collections: Robert Woodruff Library at the Atlanta University Center)

James Weldon Johnson, Atlanta University '94

Poet, composer, novelist, historian, lawyer, diplomat, and civil rights activist James Weldon Johnson is best remembered for penning the words to "Lift Every Voice and Sing," adopted by the NAACP as the Negro National Anthem. His equally talented brother Rosamond wrote the music for the now famous song.

Following graduation from Atlanta University, Johnson returned home to Jacksonville, Florida, and became principal of Stanton Elementary School, the school where his mother had taught. While principal he added a ninth and tenth grade to the school and also earned a law degree, becoming the first black lawyer admitted to the Florida bar. In 1895, just one year after graduating from college, he started the *Daily American,* considered by some to be the first black newspaper in the United States.

When his brother graduated from the New England Conservatory of Music in 1897, the two began collaborating on musical theatre. In 1902 the two brothers moved to New York and collaborated on songs for more than 200 Broadway musicals. Disillusioned with the racial stereotypes propagated by popular music, in 1903 he began graduate studies in literature at Columbia. He then moved on to serve a consulship in Venezuela and then in Nicaragua, where he continued to write and finished a novel, *The Autobiography of an Ex-Coloured Man,* which was published anonymously in 1912 in hopes that readers would think it nonfiction.

In 1913, Johnson resigned his consulship and eventually moved back to New York where he became an editorial writer for the *New York Age,* a position that gave him a public platform as an ardent champion for equal rights. In 1917 he published his first collection of poetry, *Fifty Years and Other Poems;* the title poem received considerable praise when it first appeared in the *New York Times.*

In 1916, he joined the NAACP and became the organization's general secretary in 1920. During his 15 years of service he initiated the drive behind the Dyer Anti-Lynching Bill and led the fight against all-white primaries in the South. During this period he also produced three groundbreaking anthologies: *The Book of American Negro Poetry* (1922), *The Book of American Negro Spirituals* (1925), and *The Second Book of Negro Spirituals* (1926).

His second collection of poetry, *God's Trombones: Seven Negro Sermons in Verse,* appeared in 1927. In 1930 he began teaching creative literature at Fisk University in Nashville. In 1938 he died near his summer home in Wiscasset, Maine, when the car he was driving was struck by a train. He was buried in Brooklyn wearing his lounging robe and holding his favorite book of poetry, *God's Trombones.* His funeral in Harlem was attended by more than two thousand people.

SWEET CORNBREAD

1 cup all-purpose flour	$^1/_8$ teaspoon nutmeg
1 cup yellow cornmeal	2 large eggs
$^1/_3$ cup granulated sugar	1 cup buttermilk
$2^1/_2$ teaspoons baking powder	$^1/_4$ cup cooled, melted butter,
$^1/_2$ teaspoon salt	divided

Preheat oven to 400°F; butter an 8-inch square baking pan and set aside. Combine flour, cornmeal, sugar, baking powder, salt, and nutmeg in a bowl and mix well. In separate bowl, lightly beat eggs. Add buttermilk and ¼ cup butter to the eggs and beat to blend. Combine the buttermilk mixture with the flour and mix until just moistened. Spoon the batter into a buttered baking pan and spread smooth.

Bake in the preheated oven for approximately 20 to 25 minutes or until the golden brown bread springs back when lightly pressed in the center and begins to pull from the sides of the pan. Cut bread into nine squares.

Makes 9 servings.

Adrienne Herndon

In 1895 Adrienne McNiel Herndon joined the faculty of Atlanta University. Although she was married to Alonzo Herndon, the city's wealthiest and most influential black businessman, at five feet tall, the "creamy" skinned, wavy-haired, blue-eyed beauty stood on her own credentials.

May Day party.
(Archives and Special Collections: Robert Woodruff Library at the Atlanta University Center)

Atlanta University alumni tea, 1960.
(Archives and Special Collections: Robert Woodruff Library at the Atlanta University Center)

Adrienne ambitiously pursued a career on the American stage, which was at that time closed to blacks. When she made her Boston debut in a recital of *Antony and Cleopatra,* she was billed as Ann Du Bignon, a member of an old South Carolina family of French and Creole descent. She studied at Boston's School of Expression over a seven-year period to perfect her craft, often enduring extended absences from her family. Her debut met with rave reviews, but then inexplicably, offers of assistance from movers and shakers in the business were never carried out. She then turned her attention to Atlanta University and creating a stage for black talent in Atlanta. During the 1904–05 school year, she directed the school's first Shakespearean production—*The Merchant of Venice.* Adrienne's heart was loyal to the theater. When she and Alonzo designed their mansion, which still stands in Atlanta, it is said that she designed it with a flat roof as an open-air theatre for her productions. She died at age 40 of Addison's disease shortly after moving into the home she and Alonzo had spent many year planning.

RED CORNBREAD

1	cup all-purpose flour		1	tablespoon paprika
1	cup yellow cornmeal		2	large eggs
$1/3$	cup granulated sugar		1	cup buttermilk
$2^1/_2$	teaspoons baking powder		$1/4$	cup cooled, melted butter
$1/2$	teaspoon salt		$1/2$	cup canned roasted peppers

Preheat oven to 400°F. Butter an 8-inch square baking pan and set aside. In a bowl, mix flour, cornmeal, sugar, baking powder, salt, and paprika. In separate bowl, lightly beat eggs. Add buttermilk, butter, and roasted peppers to the eggs and beat to blend. Combine the buttermilk mixture with the flour and mix until just moistened. Spoon the batter into a buttered baking pan and spread smooth.

Bake in the preheated oven for approximately 20 to 25 minutes or until the golden brown bread springs back when lightly pressed in the center and begins to pull from the sides of the pan. Cut bread into nine squares.

Makes 9 servings.

Walter White, Atlanta University '16

Civil rights leader Walter White served as chief executive of the NAACP from 1929 until his death. Fair-skinned and blue-eyed, he could comfortably have "passed" but chose instead to devote his life to the fight for civil rights.

After graduating from Atlanta University in 1916, he worked for the Standard Life Insurance Company. Incensed by Atlanta's Board of Education plan to discontinue public education for blacks after completion of sixth grade, he actively worked toward forming an Atlanta branch of the NAACP. His efforts so impressed fellow alum James Weldon Johnson, then the organization's field secretary, that in 1918 White was invited to join the national organization in New York as assistant secretary. In 1931, he succeeded Johnson as executive secretary.

Under White's leadership the legal arm of the NAACP was strengthened, and he successfully directed civil rights campaigns for federal anti-lynching laws, voting rights, laws

Old Atlanta University Campus Building, ca. 1910.
(Archives and Special Collections: Robert Woodruff Library at the Atlanta University Center)

banning poll taxes and discrimination in the U.S. armed forces, and laws to desegregate and equalize the nation's schools.

In 1937 White received the Spingarn Medal for his investigative work and lobbying for an anti-lynching bill, which was narrowly defeated in 1938. Instrumental in forming the Joint Committee on National Recovery to fight discrimination in the New Deal programs, he served as an adviser to President Roosevelt on the executive order for Fair Employment Practices during World War II, and opened relations with labor unions. In 1945 and 1948, he was named as a consultant to the U.S. delegations to the newly formed United Nations.

White wrote numerous articles, two syndicated newspaper columns, and several books: two novels, *The Fire in the Flint* and *Flight;* two nonfiction works: *Rope and Faggot* and *How Far the Promised Land?;* and an autobiography, *A Man Called White.*

BASIL CORNBREAD

1	cup all-purpose flour		2	large eggs
1	cup yellow cornmeal		1	cup buttermilk
$^1/_3$	cup granulated sugar		$^1/_4$	cup cooled, melted butter
$2^1/_2$	teaspoons baking powder		1	$8^1/_2$-ounce can creamed corn
$^1/_2$	teaspoon salt		$^1/_3$	cup chopped fresh basil

Preheat oven to 400°F.; butter an 8-inch square baking pan and set aside. In a bowl, mix flour, cornmeal, sugar, baking powder, salt, and paprika. In a separate bowl, lightly beat eggs. Add buttermilk, melted butter, corn, and chopped basil to the eggs and beat to blend. Combine the buttermilk mixture with the flour and mix until just moistened. Spoon the batter into a buttered baking pan and spread smooth.

Bake in the preheated oven for approximately 20 to 25 minutes or until the golden brown bread springs back when lightly pressed in the center and begins to pull from the sides of the pan. Cut bread into squares.

Makes 9 servings.

George A. Towns

Educator, author, and community activist George Alexander was affiliated with Atlanta University for most of his life. He entered Atlanta University as a 15-year-old student. He and his close friend James Weldon Johnson were both members of the class of 1894 and corresponded regularly until Weldon's untimely death. Towns went on to earn a degree from Harvard University in 1900 and immediately returned to Georgia and joined the faculty of Atlanta University, where he would remain for the next 40 years. He founded and edited the *Crimson and Gray,* the AU Alumni Association monthly newsletter.

In addition to his academic endeavors, Towns was a tireless civil rights advocate. An active member of the NAACP, he strongly encouraged black voter registration, and he rejected segregation in public transportation by choosing to ride a bicycle to work. Following his retirement from Atlanta University he continued to advocate for civil rights

Atlanta University commencement, 1920s.
(Archives and Special Collections: Robert Woodruff Library at the Atlanta University Center)

but died in Atlanta in 1960 before he could see his work come into full fruition. However, his dreams would be realized in part during his daughter's lifetime.

Grace Towns Hamilton, Atlanta University '27

Civil rights activist and politician, Grace A. Towns was the first African-American woman elected to the Georgia General Assembly. She, and seven other African Americans sent to the state legislature in a special election in 1965, represented the first African-American legislators to enter the lower house since the end of Reconstruction. Hamilton represented her district in mid-Atlanta for the next 18 years and earned the respect of her peers, who considered her "the most effective woman legislator the state has ever had."

Her father was educator and civil rights activist George Alexander Towns, and she was brought up in the racially sheltered environs of Atlanta University, where her father was a professor of English and pedagogy. She was her father's daughter in every way, having been taught by him at an early age that she had a duty to serve her race. Grace was educated from grade school through college at Atlanta University, where she received an undergraduate degree in 1927. She then earned her master's degree in psychology at Ohio State University in 1929.

Following graduation she began teaching psychology at Clark College and the Atlanta School of Social Work. She married Henry Cooke Hamilton, a teacher at LeMoyne College in Memphis, gave birth to their daughter, taught psychology at LeMoyne, surveyed black workers for the Works Progress Administration, and developed interracial programs on numerous college campuses for the YWCA. In 1941 the couple returned to Atlanta when her husband was named head of Atlanta University's high school program.

In 1943 Grace was appointed executive director of the Atlanta Urban League (AUL), one of the first, if not the first woman to hold such a position. Under her leadership the organization redirected its focus from employment issues to other racial issues, waging intensive campaigns for advances in schooling, health care, housing, and voting rights for African Americans. However, sidestepping the issue of segregation eventually caused her to lose her post in 1961. She worked as a private consultant until 1965 when she was elected to the Georgia legislature. For the next 20 years she worked tirelessly to expand political representation for blacks in city, county, and state governments. She was a principal architect of the 1973 Atlanta City Charter, which provided for African-American representation on the Atlanta City Council in numbers that were, for the first time in the city's history, commensurate with their proportion of the population.

As a result of her leadership in the congressional and legislative reapportionment battles, Andrew Young became the first black to represent Atlanta's Fifth District in Congress in 1972 and credited Hamilton with making his election possible.

In a reapportionment battle following the 1980 census of the Fifth District, however, Hamilton sided with white leadership against militant young African Americans who wanted Atlanta redistricted to the advantage of blacks. As a result of this stance, she was defeated in her bid for reelection to the legislature in 1984.

From 1985 till 1987 she served as adviser to the U.S. Civil Rights Commission. She died in 1992.

Atlanta University Women's Lounge
(Archives and Special Collections: Robert Woodruff Library at the Atlanta University Center)

CURRY CORNBREAD

1 cup all-purpose flour	1 tablespoon curry powder
1 cup yellow cornmeal	2 large eggs
$^1/_3$ cup granulated sugar	1 cup buttermilk
$2^1/_2$ teaspoons baking powder	$^1/_4$ cup cooled, melted butter
$^1/_2$ teaspoon salt	

Preheat oven to 400°F; butter an 8-inch square baking pan and set aside. In a bowl, mix flour, cornmeal, sugar, baking powder, salt, and curry powder. In separate bowl, lightly beat eggs. Add buttermilk, melted butter, and roasted peppers to the eggs and beat to blend. Combine the buttermilk mixture with the flour and mix until just moistened. Spoon the batter into a buttered baking pan and spread smooth.

Bake in the preheated oven for approximately 20 to 25 minutes or until the golden brown bread springs back when lightly pressed in the center and begins to pull from the sides of the pan. Cut bread into nine squares.

Makes 9 servings.

Dr. Ralph David Abernathy

The son of a farmer, Ralph Abernathy was born in 1926 in Lindon, Alabama. He became an ordained Baptist minister in 1948 and two years later graduated with a B.S. in mathematics from Alabama State University. In 1951, he earned his M.A. in sociology from Atlanta University. He accepted a pastorate at First Baptist Church in Montgomery, where he met Dr. Martin Luther King, Jr. Their relationship would be solidified by unfolding civil rights events in a deeply segregated city.

South Hall—Boy's Parlor
(Archives and Special Collections: Robert Woodruff Library at the Atlanta University Center)

On December 1, 1955, Rosa Parks, a tired tailor's assistant, refused to give up her seat to a white man and move to the back of the bus. Following her arrest, Abernathy and King organized the year-long Montgomery bus boycott. For more than a year 17,000 black citizens of Montgomery either walked to work or received rides from the few members of the black community who owned cars. Loss of revenue and a decision by the Supreme Court affirming the U.S. District Court's ruling that segregation on buses was unconstitutional brought the boycott to an end on December 20, 1956.

Following the boycott's successful conclusion, Abernathy and King continued working together and in 1957, together with Fred Shuttlesworth and Bayard Rustin, they created the Southern Christian Leadership Conference (SCLC) to organize nonviolent protest. King served as president and Abernathy as secretary-treasurer. In 1961, Abernathy moved to Atlanta and was also appointed vice-president of the SCLC. In May 1968, he directed the Poor People's March in Washington and that same year helped organize the Atlanta sanitation workers' strike. Over the next few years Abernathy was arrested 19 times. He continued working closely with King until the latter's assassination in 1968.

In 1977 Abernathy resigned from the Southern Christian Leadership Conference and

Atlanta University System baccalaureate, 1950.
(Archives and Special Collections: Robert Woodruff Library at the Atlanta University Center)

served as a pastor of a Baptist church in Atlanta. He later made an unsuccessful run for a Georgia congressional seat. His autobiography, *And the Walls Came Tumbling Down*, was published in 1989, the year before he died.

SOUR CREAM CORNBREAD

Cornbread, any way you make it, is a tasty companion to any meal, but it is especially tasty with soups and stews.

1	cup all-purpose flour		1	cup sour cream
³/₄	cup yellow cornmeal		¹/₄	cup table cream
¹/₄	cup + 1 teaspoon sugar		1	egg, slightly beaten
¹/₂	teaspoon salt		2	tablespoons melted butter
¹/₂	teaspoon baking soda			

Preheat oven to 425°F. Lightly grease an 8-inch square pan and set aside. In a large mixing bowl combine the dry ingredients and mix well to blend. In a separate bowl combine the remaining ingredients and mix well. Fold into the dry ingredients and mix well to blend. Pour into the pan and bake in preheated oven for 20 minutes or until golden brown and a toothpick inserted in the center comes out clean. Remove from oven, cut into 9 squares, and serve warm.

Makes 9 squares.

CAKE CORNBREAD

1¼ cups sugar
¼ cup honey
2 eggs
½ cup butter, softened
1¼ cups half and half
¾ cup water

2 cups white cornmeal
2 cups flour
1 tablespoon baking powder
¾ teaspoon salt
Pinch of nutmeg

Preheat oven to 375°F. Butter a 9 × 13-inch baking pan and set aside. Combine sugar, honey, butter, eggs, half and half, and water in a large bowl and mix to blend. In a separate bowl mix together the cornmeal, flour, baking powder, salt and nutmeg. Add the milk mixture and stir thoroughly. The mixture should be slightly lumpy. Pour into the buttered baking pan. Bake for 25 to 30 minutes or until golden brown on top. Serve piping hot, with butter.

Makes 12 servings.

Atlanta University commencement, 1961.
(Archives and Special Collections: Robert Woodruff Library at the Atlanta University Center)

Whitney Young

"We must support the strong, we must give courage to the timid, we must remind the indifferent and we must warn the opposed. Civil rights which are God-given and constitutionally guaranteed are not negotiable in 1963."

—Whitney M. Young, March on Washington for Jobs and Freedom, March 28, 1963

Educator, social engineer, and civil rights leader Whitney Moore Young, Jr., was born in Lincoln Ridge, Kentucky, in 1921 to a family considered part of the black educated elite. His father presided over Lincoln Institute, the black boarding school where his mother taught and that his son attended. The family lived in a simple two-story wooden house on the campus until Young was 15 years old.

In 1944, after studying engineering for two years at MIT, he enlisted in the army and was sent to Europe, where he joined an all-black regiment led by a white captain. Often called upon to diffuse racial tension between the captain and his troops, Young honed his legendary skills as a mediator between the races. He later said, "It was my Army experience that decided me on getting into the race relations field after the war. Not just because I saw the problems, but because I saw the potentials, too. I grew up with a basic belief in the inherent decency of human beings."

After the war Young entered the University of Minnesota where he earned an MSW and became a university lecturer. In 1954 he was named dean of the School of Social Work at Atlanta University, in which position he supported an alumni-led boycott of the Georgia Conference of Social Welfare, which had a poor record of placing African Americans in good jobs. At the same time, he joined the NAACP and rose to become state president.

In 1960, Young received a Rockefeller grant to study for a year at Harvard University. Subsequently, he was appointed to succeed Lester B. Ganger as president of the National Urban League. He immediately began revitalizing the Urban League, turning it from a relatively passive civil rights organization into one that aggressively fought for justice. He infused the organization with money, through his connections with funding sources like the Rockefeller family. Its annual budget increased from $325,000.00 to $6,100,000; the number of employees increased from 38 to 1600. He also initiated alternative education programs such as Street Academy, to prepare dropouts for college, and New Thrust, directed at empowering local black leaders to identify and solve community problems. In addition to pushing for federal aid to cities, Young also participated in all major civil rights demonstrations, including the March on Washington on August 28, 1963, which he was instrumental in bringing to fruition. A close adviser to Presidents Kennedy and Johnson, in 1968, he was honored by President Johnson with the nation's highest award, the Presidential Medal of Freedom.

In 1971, Young suffered a heart attack while swimming with friends and died in Lagos, Nigeria, where he was attending a conference for black leaders.

Clarence A. Bacote

Distinguished historian, scholar, social and political activist, Professor Clarence A. Bacote joined the faculty of Atlanta University as an assistant professor of history in 1930 at age 24. In 1933 while still on the faculty at Atlanta University, he became the first director of the NAACP citizenship schools created to better acquaint African Americans with the role of government. Bacote was promoted to a full professor in 1939. A specialist in Reconstruction history, he was also the university's official historian.

Following the Supreme Court's 1946 decision declaring the white primary unconstitutional, the Atlanta All-Citizens Registration Committee (ACRC) was formed to consolidate various voter registration groups under one umbrella. Bacote chaired the committee, which increased the number of black registered voters from 6,976 to 21,244. In 1952 he successfully managed the campaign that elected Atlanta University president Rufus Clement to the Atlanta School Board. Bacote was also elected vice-president of the Fulton County Democratic Club that same year. Six years later, he and Atlanta attorney J. C. Daugherty were the first blacks elected to the Fulton County Executive Committee from the Third Ward. An authority on Georgia political history and barriers to black political participation within the state, in 1962 he received an appointment to the Georgia State Advisory Committee to the U.S. Commission on Civil Rights. In 1963 he was appointed to department chair, a position that he held until his retirement in 1977. Three years later he was appointed to a seat on the Fulton County Jury Commission. In later years he served as a political consultant for local television stations where he analyzed city, state, and national elections. Following his retirement from Atlanta University, he went on to teach at Morehouse College until his death in 1981.

JALAPEÑO CORN MUFFINS

1	cup all-purpose flour	2	large eggs
1	cup yellow cornmeal	1	cup buttermilk
1/3	cup granulated sugar	1/4	cup cooled, melted butter
2 1/2	teaspoons baking powder	1/2	cup jalapeño jelly
1/2	teaspoon salt		
1/4	teaspoon paprika		

Preheat oven to 400°F; butter 12 2 1/2 inch muffin cups. In a bowl, mix flour, cornmeal, sugar, baking powder, salt, and paprika. In separate bowl, lightly beat eggs. Add buttermilk and melted butter to eggs; beat to blend. Combine the buttermilk mixture with the flour and mix until just moistened.

Evenly divide half of the batter into the buttered muffin cups. Top the batter with 2 teaspoons of jalapeño jelly. Evenly divide the remaining batter amongst the cups and place in the preheated oven. Bake for approximately 20 to 25 minutes or until a golden brown muffin springs back when lightly pressed in the center and begins to pull from the sides of the muffin pan.

Makes 12 muffins.

PEACH AND POPPY SEED MUFFINS

2/3	cup puréed peaches	1 1/4	cups flour
1	teaspoon baking soda	1/4	teaspoon salt
10	tablespoons butter, softened	1/2	teaspoon vanilla extract
1	cup sugar	3	tablespoons poppy seeds
2	eggs		

Preheat oven to 350°F. Grease muffin tins for a dozen muffins. Stir baking soda into puréed peaches. They will foam up. In a separate bowl, cream butter with sugar. When mixture is smooth, add eggs, one at a time. Alternately add flour and peach purée to the butter mixture, then add salt, vanilla extract, and poppy seeds.

Fill each muffin cup nearly to the top. Bake 20 to 25 minutes or until a toothpick or cake tester inserted in one of the muffins comes out clean.

Makes 12 large muffins.

BLUEBERRY MUFFINS

Blueberries are a great source of vitamin C, iron, and fiber, and they contain only 80 calories per cup. The harvest season in Georgia is late May through mid-July. When shopping for blueberries look for plump, firm blueberries that are a light powdery blue-gray color.

2	cups all-purpose flour		2	cups milk
2	cups quick oats		2	eggs, lightly beaten
1	cup dark brown sugar		3	tablespoons vegetable oil
1	teaspoon salt		4	cups blueberries
2¹/₄	teaspoons cinnamon			

Preheat oven to 425°F and line large muffin tins with paper muffin cups. In a large measuring bowl, combine the dry ingredients. Combine the liquid ingredients in a separate bowl and mix to blend. Add to the dry ingredients, and stir just until dry ingredients are moistened. Fold in blueberries. Fill muffin cups ³/₄ full. Bake 25 minutes. These muffins may be frozen after they have cooled.

Makes 16 large muffins.

John Hope

Nationally recognized educator and race relations leader John Hope served as the fifth president of Atlanta University from 1932 until his death in 1936. His professional career began at Atlanta Baptist College (now Morehouse College) in 1898. Eight years later he was elected president of the college, a position he held for 25 years. He was the first African American to serve these schools as president.

Instrumental in establishing the cooperative plan among Atlanta University, Morehouse, and Spelman Colleges in 1929, he was unanimously selected as the first leader of the Atlanta University Center. For a time, he continued to preside over Morehouse College.

John Hope was born in Augusta, Georgia, in 1868 and earned a B.A. from Brown University in 1894. He returned to the South to begin his career of furthering liberal education for African Americans and fighting for social equality among the races.

In December of 1897 he married Lugenia Burns, a woman who was his equal in every way. By the spring of 1898 they had moved to Atlanta where John had accepted a position at Atlanta Baptist College. A civic leader, his interest and activism extended

John Hope
*(Archives and Special Collections: Robert Woodruff Library
at the Atlanta University Center)*

beyond the parameters of the college campus. As a result, he was active in local and national organizations such as the NAACP, the National Urban League, and the YMCA, and presided over both the Commission on Interracial Cooperation and the Association for the Study of Negro Life and History. In his wife he had a partner who was equally committed to the community beyond the campus.

Lugenia Burns Hope

Nationally recognized social reformer and community leader Lugenia D. Burns Hope was born in 1871 in St Louis. From an early age, she worked, often full-time, for several charitable and settlement organizations. She attended the Chicago Art Institute, the Chicago School of Design, and the Chicago Business College from 1890 to 1893.

In 1898, a year after their marriage, she and her husband moved to Atlanta, where she immediately became active in community work. Her initial involvement was with a group that eventually evolved into the Neighborhood Union, the first female-run social welfare agency for African Americans in Atlanta. The Neighborhood Union was founded by Hope in 1908 as a response to the impoverished conditions of neighborhoods surrounding Morehouse College where her husband, John Hope, now served as president.

With its motto "Thy Neighbor as Thyself" serving as its guide, the organization promoted child welfare issues, cultural heritage, and the abolition of slums and vice among other objectives as a means of improving the community. In a grassroots effort, they divided neighborhoods into districts that were canvassed by students conducting surveys to identify conditions in need of improvement and aid. They then began working with other social service agencies to provide services such as kindergarten, day care, medical assistance, health education, temporary shelter for the homeless, vocational training for youth, and classes in child and elder care. At her suggestion, a concerted campaign for improving unsanitary and overcrowded schools for blacks was organized among the women in the city.

During World War I when black soldiers were barred from recreational activities readily available to white soldiers at base canteens and the United Service Organization (USO), the Union ran the Atlanta Young Women's Christian Association's (YWCA's) War Work Councils to serve black soldiers. The program was so well received that Hope was approached to coordinate a nationwide network of Hostess Houses that eventually provided black and Jewish soldiers and their families with a wide variety of services from recreation to relocation counseling.

In addition they initiated a campaign for equality in the Atlanta Public School system, demanding more schools and better pay for African-American teachers. As a result of their efforts, Atlanta's first high school for African-American students, Booker T. Washington, opened in 1924.

Active also in civil rights organizations, Hope was a member of the Association of Southern Women for the Prevention of Lynching and a founding member of the Atlanta Branch of the National Association of Colored Women's Clubs, which involved itself with national reform activities. As first vice president of the Atlanta chapter of the NAACP, she organized citizenship schools. With the assistance of Morehouse College students, six-week classes were offered on voting, democracy, and the U.S. Constitution. Her schools served as a model for other chapters of the NAACP and were later modified for use in the early days of the civil rights movement.

For more than 30 years Mrs. Hope would organize community services and civil rights programs that improved the quality of life for blacks in Atlanta.

Other Atlanta University Graduates

Other distinguished Atlanta University graduates include: **Judge Horace T. Ward,** the first black student in the Deep South to legally challenge segregation in higher education; **Marva Collins,** educator and founder of Chicago's Westside Preparatory School, who received international recognition for her innovative approach to teaching at-risk youth; **Reatha Clark King,** former president of the General Mills Foundation; author **Pearl Cleage;** and actor **Kenny Leon,** former artistic director of Atlanta's Alliance Theatre.

"When the heart overflows, it comes out through the mouth."

—African proverb

Clark University: Culture for Service

Clark was established in 1869 by the Freedmen's Aid Society of the Methodist Episcopal Church, which later became the United Methodist Church. The university was named for Bishop David W. Clark, who visited Atlanta shortly after the war to organize the Southern work and was the first president of the Freedmen's Aid Society.

The school, which was started by Reverend J. W. Lee and his wife as a primary school for newly freed slaves, first met in a sparsely furnished room in Clark Chapel, a Methodist Episcopal Church in Atlanta's Summerhill section. D. W. Hammond served as the first principal for the school, which would later serve to train teachers and preachers. Following the purchase by the Methodist Church Freedmen's Society of a schoolhouse that accommodated 200 students, the school moved to its new home later that year with Miss Lou Henley serving as its next principal.

In the fall of 1870 when Mr. Uriah Cleary took charge of the school, the title of the administrative officer had changed from "principal" to "president." One hundred and thirty students, all of whom were in the grammar grades, were enrolled. According to the Third Annual Report

A view of the campus from the front gate.
(Archives and Special Collections: Robert Woodruff Library at the Atlanta University Center)

Chrisman Hall
(Archives and Special Collections: Robert Woodruff Library at the Atlanta University Center)

of the Freedmen's Aid Society: "Clark University is located in Atlanta, Georgia, and although humble in its appearance with only its preparatory department in operation, its friends have determined that it shall be the nucleus of a full-orbed university."

An early benefactor, Bishop Gilbert Haven, visualized Clark, strategically located in the gateway to the South, as the "university" of all the Methodist schools founded for the education of freedmen. Haven was instrumental in acquiring 450 acres in South Atlanta, where in 1880 Chrisman Hall was completed, due in large part to a $10,000 contribution toward the $30,000 building cost donated by Mrs. Eliza Chrisman. That year the school conferred its first degree.

Located a mile outside of corporation limits, the school had no pavement, no regular means of communication, and limited transportation. When students arrived in the city an old bus was dispatched to meet them at the station. Supplies arrived on a mule-drawn cart. Water was in short supply, and when it rained the unpaved Georgia clay roads turned slick and almost impassable and the drinking water took on its red hue to the extent that food cooked in it was often tinged red. Detractors complained that the school could never survive in its inconvenient location. Unmoved, Haven would respond, "It is not necessary to carry the school to the pupils; they will come to it." And they did.

The Carriage and Wagon Room
(Archives and Special Collections: Robert Woodruff Library at the Atlanta University Center)

While Bishop Haven was the genius behind securing the property for the school, Bishop Henry W. Warren, a supporter of industrial training, developed the initial core curriculum and built the facilities. The industrial curriculum was so developed that at one point it was said that the best carriages, hearses, express wagons, and other vehicles were made at Clark. The university also maintained a farm that produced abundant milk, eggs, pork, potatoes, grain, and vegetables for the use of the boarding department.

Reverend E. O. Thayer was named the seventh president in 1881 and during his administration the Reverend W. P. Thirkield would join the faculty and later become dean of the school of theology, a department of the University. Later the school of theology became Gammon Theological Seminary and Dean Thirkield became its first president. President Thirkield and Bishop Warren worked in conjunction with President Thayer to establish a home for girls where they would be trained in household arts and homemaking. Eight other presidents served with distinction between 1890 and 1924.

Gradually less emphasis was placed upon industrial training as the school turned toward offering a more classical education. The year before Clark was chartered, classical scholar Dr. William Henry Crogman (M.A., Atlanta University), the first African American employed by

William H. Crogman
(Archives and Special Collections:
Robert Woodruff Library at the
Atlanta University Center)

the Methodist Episcopalian Church as a professor in any of its colleges, was appointed to the faculty of Clark College. In 1906 Dr. Crogman became the first African-American president of Clark College and successfully served in this position until 1910. On the occasion of his eightieth birthday Crogman was quoted as saying, "No nobler or more responsible work was ever assigned to the lot of man or angel. I say this with deliberation after 51 years in the classroom as student and teacher, and I say it with the hope that many of the young men and women of

The Printing Room
(Archives and Special Collections: Robert Woodruff Library at the Atlanta University Center)

my race . . . may possibly be attracted to the teaching profession" *(Atlanta University Bulletin,* 1921). To his students he was a "living teacher" who demanded punctuality, accuracy of thought, and thoroughness in work and in this way remained an inspiration and an example.

> *"Clark has more to show for its half century of labor than a beautiful campus and a group of substantial and useful buildings. To call the roll would take some time, for the list of the graduates includes college presidents, professors, teachers, district superintendents, ministers, laymen, business men, doctors, lawyers and many others."*
>
> —Dr. William Henry Crogman

In 1924 Matthew Simson Davage became the school's second African-American president, and during his presidency Clark joined the affiliation previously entered into by Atlanta University, Morehouse, and Spelman College.

The Blacksmith and Repairing Room
(Archives and Special Collections: Robert Woodruff Library at the Atlanta University Center)

Following Davage's seventeen years of service, Dean James Philip Brawley was elected to the presidency in 1941. Three years later the school celebrated its 75th anniversary and issued a fundraising challenge to students and faculty. With the slogan "seventy-five nickels for seventy-five years," the school raised an unprecedented $1,300 in fourteen days. The freshman class led the way with an overall contribution of $202.38.

Fruit Breads

BANANA BREAD

5	tablespoons butter (no substitutes)	$1^3/_4$	cups all-purpose flour
$^1/_2$	cup sugar	1	teaspoon baking soda
$^1/_2$	cup firmly packed dark brown sugar	$^1/_2$	teaspoon salt
1	large egg	$^3/_4$	teaspoon ground cinnamon
2	egg whites	$^1/_8$	teaspoon allspice
$1^1/_2$	teaspoons vanilla extract	$^1/_4$	teaspoon baking powder
$1^1/_2$	cups mashed very ripe bananas	$^1/_2$	cup heavy cream
		$^1/_3$	cup chopped walnuts

Preheat oven to 350°F. Grease and flour a 9 × 5-inch loaf pan and set aside. Place the butter in a large bowl and beat it with an electric mixer set at medium speed until light and fluffy. Gradually add the sugars, beating well after each addition. Next, add the egg, egg whites, and vanilla extract; beat until well blended. Add the mashed bananas and beat on high speed for 30 seconds. In a separate bowl, combine the flour, baking soda, salt, spices, and baking powder, mix to combine before adding the flour mixture to the banana mixture alternately with cream, ending with flour. Add the walnuts and mix well. Spoon mixture into the prepared loaf pan and bake in the preheated oven for 1 hour and 15 minutes or until a tester inserted into the center comes out clean. Allow bread to sit for 10 minutes before turning it out on a wire rack to cool.

Makes 1 loaf.

The Paint and Varnish Room
(Archives and Special Collections: Robert Woodruff Library at the Atlanta University Center)

PEACH LOAF

1¹/₂ cups all-purpose flour	¹/₂ cup vegetable oil
¹/₂ teaspoon salt	1¹/₂ cups peeled and pitted peaches,
¹/₂ teaspoon baking soda	coarsely chopped
¹/₄ teaspoon cinnamon	1 teaspoon vanilla extract
1 cup sugar	¹/₂ cup chopped pecans
2 eggs, well beaten	

Preheat oven to 350°F. Grease and flour a 9 × 5-inch loaf pan and set aside. Combine the flour, salt, baking soda, cinnamon, and sugar and mix well. Form a well in the middle of the flour mixture and add the eggs and oil to it. Mix just until the dry ingredients are moistened. Add the peaches, vanilla extract, and nuts. Mix to combine and pour into prepared baking pan. Place in the preheated oven and bake for 1 hour and 30 minutes or until a tester inserted in the center comes out clean. Allow the loaf to rest for 10 minutes before turning it out on a wire rack to cool.

Makes 1 loaf.

The Foundry

(Archives and Special Collections: Robert Woodruff Library at the Atlanta University Center)

PUMPKIN BREAD

3	cups sugar	1	teaspoon salt
1	cup vegetable oil	1	teaspoon baking powder
4	eggs, beaten	1¼	teaspoons nutmeg
1	teaspoon vanilla extract	1	teaspoon allspice
1	16-ounce can pumpkin purée or pie filling	¼	teaspoon cloves
3½	cups flour	1¼	teaspoons cinnamon
2	teaspoons baking soda	⅔	cup water

Preheat oven to 350°F. Grease and flour two 9 × 5 loaf pans and set aside. Cream the sugar and oil together. Add the eggs, vanilla extract, and pumpkin purée and mix well. Sift together the remaining dry ingredients and add them to the pumpkin mixture alternately with the water. Spoon mixture into the prepared pans and bake in preheated oven for 1½ hours or until a tester inserted in the center comes out clean. Allow the bread to rest for 10 minutes before removing it from the pan to cool.

Makes 2 loaves.

PUMPKIN RAISIN PECAN BREAD

2 cups all-purpose flour, sifted	1 cup sugar
2 teaspoons baking powder	1/2 cup evaporated milk
1/2 teaspoon baking soda	1 teaspoon vanilla extract
3/4 teaspoon salt	1/8 teaspoon almond extract
1 teaspoon ground cinnamon	2 eggs, beaten
1/2 teaspoon ground nutmeg	1/4 cup butter, softened
1/8 teaspoon allspice	1/2 cup chopped pecans
1 cup canned pumpkin	1/2 cup raisins

Grease and flour a 9 × 5-inch loaf pan and set aside. Preheat oven to 350°F. Combine flour, baking powder, baking soda, salt, and spices in a large bowl. In a separate bowl, combine the pumpkin, sugar, milk, extracts, and eggs and mix well. Add the pumpkin mixture and the butter to the dry ingredients and mix until well blended. Add pecans and raisins and mix to combine. Spoon the mixture into the prepared loaf pan and bake in the preheated oven from 45 to 55 minutes or until a tester inserted into the center comes out clean.

Makes 8 servings.

STRAWBERRY NUT BREAD

3 eggs, well beaten	3/4 teaspoon salt
2 cups sugar	3/4 teaspoon cinnamon
1 1/2 cups oil	Pinch of allspice
1 1/4 teaspoons vanilla extract	2 cups strawberries, and juice
3 cups flour	1 cup chopped pecans
1 teaspoon baking soda	

Cheerleading.
(Archives and Special Collections: Robert Woodruff Library at the Atlanta University Center)

Combine the eggs, sugar, oil, and vanilla extract; mix well. In a separate bowl, sift together the dry ingredients. Add the strawberries, strawberry juice and nuts, mixing well after each addition. Bake in 2 or 3 loaf pans at 350°F for 1 hour or until a tester inserted in the center comes out clean.

Makes 2 to 3 loaves.

Professor William H. Crogman

Professor William H. Crogman, Litt.D., was born in the West Indies in 1841. Orphaned at age 12, he left the islands at 14 with B. L. Boomer, at that time first mate on a sailing vessel. Soon after arriving at Boomer's home in Massachusetts, young Crogman was enrolled in the district school, where he performed well. However, Crogman soon returned to the sea, following Boomer and his brother, who was the ship's captain, on their sea voyages around the world for the next ten years.

In 1866, Boomer, aware that Crogman possessed a strong intellect, suggested that he save his money to pursue an academic education. Following that advice, Crogman entered Pierce Academy, in Middleboro, Massachusetts, two years later. Professor J.W.P. Jenks, the principal of the academy, wrote: "Beginning with me in the elementary English branches, I may safely say, in them all, he accomplished in one quarter as much as the average student did in two, mastering almost intuitively, and with equal facility, both mathematical and linguistic principles. So rapid was his progress in his classes that I formed him into a class of one, lest he should be hindered by the dullness of other students. . . . I need say no more, except that his record since leaving the academy, taking all the extenuating circumstances into account, has reflected greater honor upon me as its principal, and his almost sole instructor while connected with it, than any other alumnus."

After completing his studies at the academy, he went south and devoted the remainder of his life to the elevation of his people. He entered Atlanta University in the fall of 1873, where he met his future wife, and graduated with the university's first class in 1876.

William H. Crogman Chapel
(Archives and Special Collections: Robert Woodruff Library at the Atlanta University Center)

That September, 1876, he accepted a position on the faculty of Clark University, where he taught Latin and Greek, eventually chairing the department. He served as the only secretary of the Boards of Trustees of Gammon Theological Seminary and of Clark University for many years. He served as president of Clark University for seven years, growing the school in numbers and strength. He was the superintendent of the Sunday school at Clark for 29 years, in which position he is reputed to have never been tardy. The author of several books, Crogman was also a much sought-after speaker. Dr. Crogman was the first individual to receive the degree of Doctor of Letters from Atlanta University. So esteemed was Professor Crogman that on his fiftieth birthday a reception was held by Dr. Thirkield. Gifts arrived from all over the country, among them: "an elegant gold watch, a set of beautiful Carlsbad china, nine handsomely bound volumes of ancient classics, along with a large ornamental inkstand, from which rolled one hundred dollars in gold. The china was especially appropriate, as it recognized the merit of Mrs. Crogman, who is the queenly helpmeet of the noble subject of this sketch, and presides over one of the most cultured homes of this land." —Dr. E. R. Carter, *The Black Side of Atlanta*

At the 1921 commencement season, when Dr. Crogman retired from active teaching, the Carnegie Foundation awarded him a lifetime pension.

William H. Crogman Cottage
(Archives and Special Collections: Robert Woodruff Library at the Atlanta University Center)

Hot from the Oven: Desserts

PEACH CAKE

2 cups sugar
3 eggs, well beaten
1½ cups vegetable oil
3 cups cake flour
1 teaspoon baking soda
¾ teaspoon salt

2 teaspoons ground cinnamon
⅛ teaspoon nutmeg
Pinch of allspice
1 teaspoon vanilla extract
3 cups slightly firm ripe peaches, peeled and sliced thin

Preheat oven to 350°F. Grease and flour a 10-inch bundt pan and set aside. Combine sugar, eggs, and vegetable oil in a large mixing bowl and beat well. In a separate bowl sift together the flour, baking soda, salt, and remaining spices. Stir flour mixture 1 cup at a time into the sugar mixture. Beat well after each addition. Stir in the vanilla and peaches. Spoon the mixture into the bundt pan and bake for 1 hour or until a tester inserted into the center comes out clean. Allow cake to rest 10 minutes before turning out on a cake rack to cool. Drizzle glaze (recipe follows) over cooled cake.

Makes 10 to 12 servings.

GLAZE

¼ cup melted butter
2 cups powdered sugar, sifted

2 tablespoons heavy cream
¼ teaspoon almond extract

Combine the powdered sugar and melted butter; mix well. Add remaining ingredients and stir until the mixture is smooth and satiny.

Makes about 2 cups.

Louis Tompkins Wright, Clark University, '11

Louis Tompkins Wright, born in La Grange, Georgia, in 1891, received his elementary, secondary, and college education at Clark University in Atlanta. His father, a graduate of Meharry Medical College, died when Louis was four years old, leaving the family destitute. His mother secured work at Clark College in the girl's dormitory.

In 1911 Louis graduated from Clark as the class valedictorian and entered Harvard Medical School, where he faced racial discrimination throughout his tenure at the school. Denied the opportunity to deliver babies as an obstetrics student at the Boston Lying-In Hospital, he argued that he had paid his tuition and therefore was entitled to the same educational opportunities as any other student. As a result, the practice of having black students deliver babies with a black physician, separate from the rest of the class, was abolished. In 1915 he graduated cum laude, fourth in his class. Despite his sterling academic credentials, race prevented him from obtaining internships at hospitals such as Massachusetts General Hospital or Peter Bent Brigham Hospital. Instead, he completed an internship at a black hospital, Freedman's Hospital, in Washington, D.C.

Wright would practice in Atlanta for one year before entering the U.S. Army as a First Lieutenant in the Medical Corps in 1917. While on active duty, he introduced the intradermal method of vaccination for smallpox, later adopted by the U.S. Army Medical Corps. His skills quickly recognized, he became the youngest surgeon to be given responsibility for a base hospital in France. Following his discharge, he opened a surgery practice in New York City. In 1919, after being appointed to Harlem Hospital, which at the time was all white, four white doctors resigned in protest. After 23 years of service, including five years as director of surgery, he became president of the medical board of Harlem Hospital.

In 1934 he became the first black in 21 years to be admitted to the American College of Surgeons. In 1939, he became a diplomate of the American Board of Surgery and the 25th recipient of the Spingarn Medal.

Wright attacked prejudice wherever he saw it, within the medical field and throughout society. He was the first physician anywhere to experiment with the new antibiotic aureomycin, now considered a miracle drug, on human beings. He also experimented with terramycin. From 1948 to 1952, Wright had 89 scientific publications to his credit.

With grants from the National Cancer Institute and Damon Runyon Fund, Wright founded the Harlem Hospital Cancer Research Foundation, where he dealt with the effectiveness of chemotherapeutic agents and published fifteen papers dealing with his research. Today chemotherapy is widely used in the treatment of cancer.

Wright died of a heart attack at the age of sixty-one. His two daughters, Jane Wright Jones and Barbara Wright Pierce, are both doctors.

PECAN SPICE CAKE

1 cup shortening	1/2 teaspoon ground cloves
2 cups sugar	Pinch of nutmeg
4 eggs, beaten	1 cup buttermilk
3 cups sifted flour	2 cups chopped pecans
1 teaspoon baking powder	Powdered sugar
3/4 teaspoon ground cinnamon	

Preheat oven to 350°F. Grease and flour a bundt or tube pan and set aside. Beat shortening with an electric mixer for 2 to 3 minutes before gradually adding the sugar and beating until the mixture is light and fluffy. Slowly add the eggs while continuing to beat the mixture until well blended. In a separate bowl sift together the dry ingredients 3 times before adding it to the shortening mixture. Alternate flour mixture with buttermilk and beat after each addition. Stir in the pecans and pour the batter into the prepared baking pan. Place pan into the oven and bake for 1 hour or until a tester inserted into the center comes out clean. When cake is sufficiently cool, lightly dust it with powdered sugar.

Makes 12 servings.

SWEET POTATO CAKE WITH PINEAPPLE FILLING

1½   cups vegetable oil
2   cups sugar
4   eggs, separated (reserve whites)
4   tablespoons hot water
2½   cups cake flour
3   teaspoons baking powder
¼   teaspoon salt
1¼   teaspoons ground cinnamon

¾   teaspoon ground nutmeg
    Pinch ground allspice
1½   cups peeled and grated raw sweet potato
1½   teaspoons vanilla extract
⅛   teaspoon almond extract
½   cup coarsely chopped pecans
    Cream cheese frosting
    Grated coconut

Preheat oven to 350°F. Grease and flour three 8-inch cake pans and set aside. Combine the oil and sugar in a large mixing bowl and beat until well blended. Add egg yolks one at a time and beat well after each addition. Add hot water and mix well. In a separate bowl sift together the dry ingredients and gradually add to the egg mixture while continuing to beat. Stir in the potatoes, pecans, and extracts. Beat egg whites until stiff peaks form and gently fold into the batter. Place cake in the oven and bake for 25 to 30 minutes or until a tester inserted into the center comes out clean. Allow cakes to cool slightly before removing them from pans. While cakes are still slightly warm, spread the pineapple filling (recipe follows) between the layers. Allow the cake to cool completely and frost with cream cheese frosting (recipe follows). Garnish top of cake with coconut.

Makes 8 to 10 servings.

PINEAPPLE FILLING

3   tablespoons cake flour
½   cup sugar
1   20-ounce can crushed pineapple, undrained

⅛   teaspoon salt
2   tablespoons butter

Combine flour and sugar in a small saucepan; mix until flour dissolves and no lumps are present; add pineapple, salt, and butter. Cook over medium heat, stirring constantly, until mixture is thickened. Cool. Cover to prevent skin from forming on top of filling and cool before using to fill the cake.

Makes 2²/₃ cups.

CREAM CHEESE FROSTING

³/₄ cup unsalted butter, softened at room temperature

1 12-ounce package cream cheese, softened at room temperature

6³/₄ cups confectioner's sugar

2 teaspoons vanilla extract

16 ounces grated coconut

Cream together the butter and cream cheese until the mixture is light and fluffy. Gradually add powdered sugar while continuing to beat. Stir in the vanilla extract and coconut, and mix well.

Makes about 4 cups.

Founder's Day, 1960.
(Archives and Special Collections: Robert Woodruff Library at the Atlanta University Center)

PEANUT BUTTER CAKE WITH CREAMY CHOCOLATE AMARETTO FROSTING

$^3/_4$ cup butter, softened at room temperature
$^3/_4$ cup creamy peanut butter
2 cups firmly packed brown sugar
3 eggs, at room temperature
$1^1/_2$ teaspoons vanilla extract

$2^1/_2$ cups cake flour
1 tablespoon baking powder
1 teaspoon salt
1 cup evaporated milk
$^1/_2$ cup chopped peanuts without skins
$^1/_2$ cup miniature chocolate chips

Preheat oven to 350°F. Grease a 13 × 9 × 2-inch baking pan and set aside. Remove butter and eggs from the refrigerator approximately three hours before use. Combine butter and peanut butter and beat until well blended. Add sugar and cream the ingredients together until light and fluffy. Next, add the eggs, beating well after each addition. Add extract. Sift together flour, baking powder, and salt; add to butter mixture by alternating with additions of milk. Beat well after each addition. Spoon the batter into the prepared baking pan and bake for 40 to 45 minutes or until a tester inserted into the center comes out clean. Cool cake at room temperature before frosting with Creamy Chocolate Amaretto Frosting (recipe follows) and sprinkling with chopped peanuts and chocolate chips.

Makes 12 servings.

CREAMY CHOCOLATE AMARETTO FROSTING

1 6-ounce package semisweet chocolate morsels
$^1/_3$ cup table cream

$1^3/_4$ cups confectioner's sugar
3 tablespoons amaretto liqueur

Combine chocolate morsels and table cream in a medium-size saucepan and heat on low, stirring constantly, until the morsels are melted. Allow to cool 5 minutes before stirring in the powdered sugar, and amaretto and beat until the mixture is smooth.

Makes about 2 cups.

BUTTERMILK POUND CAKE

2	sticks butter, softened	3	cups flour
3	cups sugar	$^1/_2$	teaspoon baking powder
5	large eggs	$^3/_4$	cup buttermilk
$1^1/_4$	teaspoons vanilla extract		

Preheat oven to 325°F. Grease and flour a 12-cup Bundt or tube pan and set aside. In a large bowl cream the butter until light and fluffy. Gradually add the sugar and continue beating until light and fluffy. Add the eggs one at a time, and beat well after each addition. Add vanilla extract and mix to blend. In a separate bowl sift together the flour and the baking powder. Alternate between gradually adding the flour mixture and the buttermilk to the butter mixture, and beat after each addition. Pour into the prepared pan and bake for one hour.

Makes 10 to 12 servings.

COCONUT CREAM CAKE WITH LEMON FILLING

3	cups sugar	1¼	teaspoons vanilla extract
½	pound butter (2 sticks)	3	cups cake flour
6	eggs	2	teaspoons baking powder
2½	teaspoons vanilla extract	1	cup whipping cream

Cream the butter and sugar until light and fluffy. Add eggs one at a time, beating well after each addition. Add vanilla extract. In a separate bowl, sift together cake flour and baking powder. Add the flour mixture to the butter mixture alternately with the whipping cream, beating well after each addition. Divide batter among the three prepared 9-inch cake pans, place in a preheated oven and bake for 25 minutes or until a tester inserted into the center comes out clean. Spread lemon filling (recipe follows) between slightly warm layers; allow the cake to cool before frosting with cream cheese frosting (recipe follows).

LEMON FILLING

1	tablespoon grated lemon zest	6	tablespoons butter
½	cup fresh lemon juice	¾	cup white sugar
1	tablespoon cornstarch	4	egg yolks, beaten

Combine lemon zest, lemon juice, and cornstarch in a medium-sized saucepan and mix until smooth. Add the butter and sugar, and bring mixture to boil over medium heat. Boil for 1 minute, stirring constantly to prevent scorching. Remove from heat and set aside. In small bowl, beat egg yolks with a wire whisk until smooth. Whisk in a small amount of the hot lemon mixture. Pour the egg mixture into the saucepan and return to heat while beating the hot lemon mixture rapidly. Reduce heat to low; cook, stirring constantly, for 5 minutes, or until thick (but do not boil).

Pour mixture into medium size bowl and press plastic wrap onto the surface of the lemon filling mixture to keep skin from forming as it cools. Cool to room temperature. Refrigerate 3 hours.

Makes about 1½ cups.

Luncheon at Kresge Hall.

(Archives and Special Collections: Robert Woodruff Library at the Atlanta University Center)

BANANA NUT CAKE

¹/₂ cup softened butter	2 cups flour
1¹/₂ cups sugar	1 teaspoon baking powder
3 eggs (reserve the whites)	¹/₄ teaspoon salt
1 teaspoon vanilla extract	¹/₄ teaspoon ground nutmeg
1 cup mashed bananas	1 teaspoon baking soda
¹/₄ cup boiling water	¹/₄ cup buttermilk
¹/₂ cup chopped pecans	

In a large bowl cream together the butter and sugar until light and fluffy. Add egg yolks one at a time, beating after each addition. Add vanilla extract and the mashed bananas; mix well. Pour boiling water over the pecans and set aside. In a separate bowl sift together the flour, baking powder, salt, and ground nutmeg and set aside. In a separate bowl, combine baking soda and buttermilk. Add the flour mixture to the banana mixture alternately with buttermilk mixture. Beat well after each addition. Add the pecans. Beat egg whites until stiff peaks form and fold into the batter. Bake for 30 to 35 minutes and allow it to cool completely before spreading it with banana filling and frosting (recipe follows).

Makes 8 to 12 servings.

BANANA FILLING

$^1/_2$ cup softened butter	$^1/_2$ cup chopped pecans
1 pound powdered sugar	1 tablespoon pineapple juice
$^1/_2$ cup mashed bananas	

Mix butter and powdered sugar until creamy. Add bananas, nuts, and juice. Mix well and spread between cooled cake layers.

Makes about 3 $^1/_2$ cups.

CREAM CHEESE FROSTING

$^3/_4$ cup unsalted butter, softened at room temperature	$6^3/_4$ cups confectioner's sugar
1 12-ounce package cream cheese, softened at room temperature	2 teaspoons vanilla extract
	16 ounces grated coconut

Cream together the butter and cream cheese until the mixture is light and fluffy. Gradually add confectioner's sugar while continuing to beat. Stir in the vanilla extract and mix well. Garnish the top and sides of the cake with grated coconut.

Makes about 5 cups.

GEORGIA PEACH AND PRALINE PIE

1   9-inch unbaked pie shell
1   teaspoon all-purpose flour
$^1/_3$ cup all-purpose flour, divided
$^1/_4$ cup sugar
$^1/_4$ teaspoon salt
$^1/_3$ teaspoon ground nutmeg
$^1/_8$ teaspoon cinnamon
$^1/_8$ teaspoon allspice
$^1/_2$ cup light corn syrup

3   eggs
3   cups fresh peach slices,
      chopped
$^1/_4$ cup butter, melted
$^1/_4$ cup firmly packed brown sugar
2   tablespoons butter, softened
$^1/_2$ cup coarsely chopped pecans
      Whipped cream (optional)

Sprinkle 1 teaspoon flour over pie crust; set aside. Combine 3 tablespoons flour, sugar, salt, spices, corn syrup and eggs in a mixing bowl; beat at medium speed with an electric mixer for 1 minute. Fold in peaches and the melted butter. Pour mixture into pie crust. Mix together the remaining flour and brown sugar in another bowl. Using a pastry blender, cut in 2 tablespoons of the softened butter until the mixture resembles coarse crumbs; add chopped pecans and stir. Sprinkle crumb mixture evenly over peach filling. Bake at 375°F for 45 to 50 minutes or until center of pie is set (cover crust edges with foil after 35 minutes to prevent overbrowning).

Eat it warmed, with a dollop of whipped cream, and it's a small slice of heaven!

Makes 8 servings.

PEACH CRUMB PIE

One of the many pleasures of summer in the South is the abundance and variety of fresh fruit. Treat your family to this summer delight any time of year. Preserved peaches allow you to enjoy delicious peach pie year 'round, well after the season has passed.

$3/4$	cup sugar		1	canned peach halves, reserve the syrup
2	tablespoons butter			
$1/4$	cup flour		$1/4$	cup peach syrup
1	teaspoon ground cinnamon		2	tablespoons lemon juice
	Unbaked pie shell			

Combine the sugar and butter and mix well. In a separate bowl combine the flour and cinnamon and mix well. Add the butter mixture to the bowl containing the flour, and cut it into the flour until a crumbly mixture resembling cornmeal is formed. Sprinkle half of this mixture on the bottom of the pie shell. Combine the peaches, syrup, and lemon juice, mix well, and pour over the crumb mixture in the pie pan. Cover with the remaining crumbs. Place in preheated 375°F oven and bake until the crust is well browned, approximately 1 hour.

GEORGIA PECAN PIE

Georgia will be on your mind and on the mind of everyone who samples this delectable pie.

3	eggs		1	teaspoon vanilla extract
2	tablespoons sugar		$1/4$	teaspoon salt
2	tablespoons flour		$1\,1/4$	cup pecan halves
2	cups dark Karo syrup		1	unbaked pie shell

Beat the eggs until light and set aside. In a separate bowl, combine the sugar and flour, mix well, add to the eggs, and beat to combine. Add the Karo, vanilla, salt, and pecans, mix well, and pour into the uncooked pie shell. Bake at 425°F for 10 minutes, reduce heat to 325°F, and continue baking for an additional 45 minutes.

Makes 8 servings.

GEORGIA PECAN PIE II

3 eggs, whole	1 teaspoon vanilla
1 cup dark Karo syrup	1 pinch salt
1 cup granulated sugar	1 unbaked pie shell
1 to 2 cups chopped pecans	
6 tablespoons butter, room temperature	

Mix ingredients and pour into unbaked pie shell. Bake until filling is set, pecans look toasted, and pie crust is nicely browned. Serve pie either cold or slightly warm.

Makes 8 servings.

APPLE CRUMB PIE

Nothing makes one's home feel quite as cozy as the fragrance of apples, cinnamon, and vanilla wafting through it on a crisp, autumn day.

2	quarts apples, peeled, cored and thickly sliced	$1/2$	cup brown sugar
1	teaspoon salt	$1/2$	cup flour
1	teaspoon cinnamon	1	teaspoon cinnamon
1	teaspoon nutmeg	$1/4$	cup butter
2	teaspoons vanilla extract		unbaked pie shell

Preheat oven to 425°F. Combine the apples and the next 4 ingredients and mix well and set aside. In a separate bowl, combine the remaining ingredients except the pie shell and mix to form crumbs. Spoon apples into the pie shell, mound slightly higher in the middle. Spread crumb mixture evenly over the top of the pie, and place in the preheated oven. Bake until apples are softened, approximately 1 hour.

Makes 8 servings.

COCONUT CREAM PIE

1	cup white sugar	2	teaspoons vanilla extract
$1/2$	cup all-purpose flour	$1/8$	teaspoon almond extract
$1/4$	teaspoon salt	1	cup flaked coconut
3	cups milk	1	9-inch pie shell, baked
4	egg yolks, lightly beaten		Whipped cream
3	tablespoons butter		

Combine sugar, flour, and salt in a medium-size saucepan. While constantly stirring over a medium heat, gradually add the milk. Continue cooking and stirring over medium heat until the mixture is thick and bubbly. Reduce heat to low and cook 2 minutes more. Remove the pan from heat.

Gradually stir 1 cup of the hot milk mixture into the beaten egg yolks, then return this mixture to the saucepan and recombine with the rest of the milk mixture. Bring to a gentle boil. Cook and stir 2 minutes before removing the pan from heat.

Add butter, vanilla extract, almond extract, and coconut into the hot mixture, and stir to combine. Pour the hot filling into the baked pie crust. Thoroughly chill and garnish with whipped cream prior to serving.

Makes 8 servings.

Fresh Strawberry Pie

As beautiful to look at as it is to eat. Serve up a delicious slice of summer with this rich, luscious strawberry filled pie. Strawberries do not ripen after they are picked, so be sure to select fully ripened, ruby red berries with fresh looking caps.

1¹/₂ quarts fresh strawberries, washed and hulled	2 tablespoons lemon juice
3 tablespoons cornstarch	1 9-inch baked pie shell
1 cup sugar	Whipped cream

Separate out approximately half of the best strawberries. In a large mixing bowl, mash the remaining strawberries, add the cornstarch and sugar to the mashed strawberries, place mixture in a saucepan, bring to a boil and cook until the liquid is thick and clear, approximately 3 minutes. Remove from the heat and stir in the lemon juice. Cool the strawberry mixture and add the reserved strawberries, cutting the larger ones in half if necessary (save a few to garnish your pie). Pour into pie shell, and chill thoroughly. Garnish with whipped cream immediately before serving.

Makes 8 servings.

JAMAICAN RUM CAKE

1 pound butter or margarine, softened	2 teaspoons baking powder
1 pound dark brown sugar	2 teaspoons baking soda
1 dozen eggs	1¼ teaspoons ground cinnamon
1 pound flour	¼ teaspoon ground nutmeg
2¼ teaspoons vanilla extract	⅛ teaspoon ground allspice
2 teaspoons burnt sugar (found in Caribbean markets)	2 cups fruit mixture (recipe follows)
	Rum

Prepare the fruit mixture one month in advance. Preheat oven to 350°F. Butter and flour a bundt pan and set aside. In a large bowl, cream butter and sugar together until light and fluffy. Add eggs 2 at a time, beating well after each addition. Add vanilla and burnt sugar. In a separate bowl, sift together the remaining dry ingredients. Add slowly to the large bowl, mixing well. The batter will be very heavy. Add

Andrew Young at Clark College commencement, 1975.
(Archives and Special Collections: Robert Woodruff Library at the Atlanta University Center)

approximately 2 cups of the fruit mixture (or less according to taste). Mix well. Pour into well-greased and -floured cake pans. Bake at 350°F for about 1 hour or until a knife inserted in the middle comes out clean.

Once the cake is cooled (do not remove it from the tin), pour approximately $1/4$ cup of rum over it. Cover tightly with aluminum foil. Check the cake every 2 to 3 days. If it becomes dry, add some more rum. Continue in this manner for 1 month. (You might not have to add any rum to it after 2 weeks, but keep checking it.)

Makes 8 servings.

FRUIT MIXTURE

1 pound seeded dates, coarsely chopped	1 pound currants, coarsely chopped
1 pound raisins, coarsely chopped	1 pound cherries, coarsely chopped

Approximately one month in advance of making the cake, place fruit in a jar that can be tightly sealed. Cover the fruit with rum, cover tightly, and store in a cool, dark place.

Makes 4 pounds.

A Taste of Home for Jailed Protestors

Jailed student protestors were not forgotten by the community. Like many others, Reverend C. A. Ivory visited Diane Nash and Ruby Doris Smith every day, bringing with him delicious homemade baked goods sent by the members of his congregation. Ruby would later write to her sister of receiving the "cookies" along with a letter. "Yum, yum," she exclaimed while promising to watch her diet.

Tell Them We Are Rising

Following the Civil War, General O. O. Howard visited Storrs School, where Mrs. Caroline D. Scott taught. In a letter to Richard R. Wright, Atlanta University Class of 1876, Mrs. Scott recounted, he "came into our Sunday-school. We had just had a stirring Sunday-school hymn sung when General Howard said: 'What message shall I give my Sunday-school boys from you when I get back to Washington?' (He was a great Sunday-school worker.) There was a dead silence when for a second time the question was asked.

"I can see your face now, as you sprang up from the far corner of the room. 'Tell them we are rising,' rang out. Nothing ever pleased President Ware more, and although it was the Sabbath day there was loud applauding. General Howard wept. I was just as pleased as President Ware and General Howard, for you were one of my boys. On the General's return to Washington he wrote to the poet Whittier of the incident. Whittier wrote a short poem and mailed it to General Howard."

—Mrs. Caroline D. Scott, *The Atlanta University Bulletin,* July 1911

HOWARD AT ATLANTA

RIGHT in the track where Sherman
Ploughed his red furrow,
Out of the narrow cabin,
Up from the cellar's burrow,
Gathered the little black people,
With freedom newly dowered,
Where, beside their Northern teacher,
Stood the soldier, Howard.

He listened and heard the children
Of the poor and long-enslaved
Reading the words of Jesus,
Singing the songs of David. . . .

And he said: "Who hears can never
Fear for or doubt you;
What shall I tell the children
Up North about you?"
Then ran round a whisper, a murmur,
Some answer devising:
And a little boy stood up: "General,
Tell 'em we're rising!"

O black boy of Atlanta!
But half was spoken
The slave's chain and the master's
Alike are broken.
The one curse of the races
Held both in tether
They are rising—all are rising,
The black and white together!

—John Greenleaf Whittier, 1869

Truly as a result of the fight for freedom and equality the chains that had bound both black and white were broken. On the front lines of this new battle for the South were black students Ruby, Julian, and Lonnie. They were inspired and led by civil rights heroes and generals such as John Wesley Dobbs, Dr. Martin Luther King, Jr., and the King family dynasty, W.E.B. DuBois, Whitney Young, and Walter White. They dedicated themselves to finishing the unfinished work spoken of by Lincoln in Gettysburg—giving their last full measure of devotion. And with them were friends such as Rabbi Joachim Prinz. Their work ensured that the South would rise again, but in unexpected ways as blacks and whites once deeply divided eventually united to raise it up together, creating a very special place that all could claim as home. By making room at the table for all Americans they created and continue to create a New South and new homecoming traditions as each member and each generation brings something unique to the table.

"America must not become a nation of onlookers. America must not remain silent. . . . It must speak up and act, from the President down to the humblest of us. As Jews we bring to this great demonstration, in which thousands of us proudly participate, a twofold experience—one of the spirit and one of our history. . . . Our ancient history began with slavery and the yearning for freedom. Our modern history begins with a proclamation of emancipation. . . . The time, I believe has come to work together—for it is not enough to hope together, and it is not enough to pray together."

—Rabbi Joachim Prinz, at the 1963 March on Washington for Jobs and Freedom

THIS MOMENT IN HISTORY—TIME LINE

February 14, 1867—The Augusta Baptist Institute is founded. With dilapidated infrastructure, no records, and almost no funds, this was one of the first schools for African Americans in the state of Georgia.

March 31, 1867—General John Pope arrives by train to the city of Atlanta, marking the second occupation of both Atlanta and Georgia.

May 28, 1867—Morris Rich opens a dry goods store in Atlanta at 36 Whitehall. Rich's department store would become an important locus of the protest movement in Atlanta, the site where King was arrested with, among others, students Julian Bond and Lonnie King (no relation).

September 9, 1867—Nine soldiers from Fort McPherson roam through Shermantown (a town of freedmen around Wheat St., today's Auburn Ave.), vandalizing homes and beating blacks. Note: Shermantown was a common name for African-American communities in Georgia after the War Between the States (Civil War).

March 2, 1867—The Reconstruction Act, calling for the enfranchisement of former slaves in the South was passed in March 1867 over President Johnson's veto and was strengthened by three supplemental acts passed later the same year and in 1868. Reconstruction begins.

1867—Storrs and Summerhill Grammar Schools are established by the Freedmen's Bureau in Atlanta.

April 20, 1868—Atlanta becomes Georgia's state capital.

May 1868—Impeachment proceedings against President Johnson, who in 1868 is spared conviction and removal from office by one vote in the Senate. Republicans in Congress disapprove of Johnson's dismissal of radical politicians and generals active in Reconstruction and think he is obstructing implementation of the government's Reconstruction policy.

July 28, 1868—The 14th Amendment, passed in June 1866, is ratified. Designed to protect the rights of southern blacks and restrict the political power of former Confederates, the 14th Amendment prohibits the States from denying or abridging the fundamental rights of every citizen and requires them to grant all persons equal protection and due process.

August 11, 1868—Thaddeus Stevens, radical Republican leader in Congress and father of Reconstruction, dies.

November 3, 1868—Civil War general Ulysses S. Grant becomes president of the United States.

February 3, 1870—Congress ratifies the 15th Amendment (passed by Congress February 26, 1869). The 15th Amendment guarantees the right to vote to all male citizens of the United States, regardless of color or previous condition of servitude, opening the door to the election of African-Americans to the U.S. Congress and Southern local and state offices.

1870—The first Public School Act in Georgia provides for separate public schools for black and white students.

January 1870—Hiram R. Revels, the first African-American senator, is elected to the U.S. Senate to fill the unexpired term of former Confederate president Jefferson Davis.

August 1, 1871—Joseph Thomas Robert becomes head of the "Augusta Institute." Originally the Augusta Baptist Institute, it had been renamed shortly before Robert's arrival.

March 1, 1875—Congress approves the Civil Rights Act of 1875, guaranteeing equal rights to black Americans in public accommodations and jury duty and barring discrimination by hotels, theaters, and railroads. In *Civil Rights Cases,* 109 U.S. 3 (1883), the Supreme Court declares the 1875 Civil Rights Act unconstitutional.

March 5, 1875—The first black person to serve a full term in the United States Senate, Blanche K. Bruce, formally enters the Senate, where he is elected to three committees: pensions, manufactures, and education and labor. Not until 1969 does another black American begin a Senate term.

1876—President Grant sends federal troops to restore order during race riots directed at blacks in South Carolina.

1877—During the disputed presidential election between Samuel Tilden (Democrat) and Rutherford B. Hayes (Republican), Hayes makes a deal with Southern Democratic leaders to become president in exchange for withdrawing federal troops from the South and ending federal efforts to protect the civil rights of African-Americans. Reconstruction ends.

January 29, 1879—General William Tecumseh Sherman visits Atlanta, his first visit since setting the city ablaze during the Civil War.

April 11, 1881—The Atlanta Baptist Female Seminary, a college for African-American women, opens in the basement of Friendship Baptist Church on the corner of Mitchell and Haynes Streets. It will become Spelman College.

July 1881—African-American washerwomen in Atlanta organize the Washing Society and launch a strike to demand higher fees for their services. The strike, which rapidly expands from 20 to 3000 women, found broad support within the black community. Organizing meetings are held in Atlanta's black churches.

July 4, 1881—Tuskegee Institute is established by Booker T. Washington in Tuskegee, Alabama. It is the first institute of higher learning to have a black faculty.

August 13, 1881—Atlanta's Spelman College opens the first nursing school for African-Americans.

September 18, 1895—African-American educator and national leader Booker T. Washington delivers his Atlanta Compromise address, at the Cotton States and International Exposition in Atlanta.

February 12, 1909—The NAACP is founded as the American Negro Committee by a group of thirteen activists, of whom W.E.B. Du Bois is the only African American while the others are Jewish. By 1914, there are 6,000 members and 50 branches of the organization.

November 1, 1910—Civil Rights activist and charter member of the NAACP, W.E.B. DuBois begins publishing the NAACP monthly magazine *Crisis*.

1913—White teachers in Atlanta earn $85 a month; black counterparts earn $55.

1922—Booker T. Washington High School, the first black high school in Atlanta, opens under the leadership of C. L. Harper. With an opening enrollment of 1,947 students, the school is already overcrowded. Martin Luther King, Jr., will later become one of the school's most illustrious graduates.

1932—Anticipating that the whites-only primary will eventually be declared unconstitutional, black leaders establish citizenship schools to teach blacks how to register to vote.

1934—Reverend Martin Luther King, Sr., pastor of Ebenezer Baptist Church, leads a voter registration march to City Hall. Retired railroad mail clerk John Wesley Dobbs organizes the Atlanta Civil and Political League to encourage black involvement in politics.

1941—Martin Luther King, Sr., leads four black ministers' associations in petitioning the Atlanta Board of Education (ABE) for equal black and white salaries.

1942—William Reaves files a salary equalization suit on behalf of black teachers.

1943—Samuel L. Davis files a federal suit against Ed S. Cook, president of ABE. At issue is the per-pupil spending on white versus black students: $119.61 for white students as compared to $44.11 for black students.

1944—A plan is implemented to equalize salaries between black and white teachers.

July 4, 1944—Reverend Primus King enters the courthouse in Columbus, Georgia, in an attempt to vote during the "white-only" Democratic primary. Prominent black Atlantans Martin Luther King, Sr., and Professor Clarence Bacote, head of Atlanta University's history department, also fail in their attempt to vote during Georgia's all-white primary. However, they all are registered to vote in the general election.

April 1, 1946—The U.S. Supreme Court rules Georgia's all-white primary unconstitutional in the case of *Primus King v. State of Georgia*. A massive two-month voter drive follows, which raises the number of registered blacks in Atlanta from under 7,000 to over twenty-four thousand.

1947—James and Robert Paschal open a thirty-seat luncheonette on West Hunter Street. During the civil rights movement, the Paschal brothers bond protesters out of jail, serve free meals, and stay open late as a meeting place for those awaiting the release of relatives from jail. The original location, which closed after being sold to Clark Atlanta University, is the focus of a fight by preservationists to save this historic landmark. The Paschal brothers go on to open three more Paschal's restaurants in Atlanta—two at the airport and one at a posh downtown location.

1948—Black parents petition Atlanta Board of Education for equal economic treatment of their children in the Atlanta public school system. Annual white per pupil expenditures equal $139.73, while $59.86 is spent on black pupils. Kindergartens are added to black schools.

April 3, 1948—When the stay order approving the hiring of black policemen in Atlanta is overturned, eight black policemen are hired to patrol black neighborhoods such as Auburn Avenue. They are, however, prohibited from arresting whites and told to report to the Butler Street YMCA rather than police headquarters on Decatur Street.

1948—The U.S. Supreme Court strikes down racially restrictive covenants in the landmark case of *Shelley v. Kraemer*.

1950—Two hundred black children and their parents petition to end segregation in the city schools. The petition is denied.

November 1953—Dr. Rufus Clement (president, Atlanta University) is elected to the Atlanta Board of Education and becomes the first black elected to citywide office since Reconstruction.

1954—On May 17, 1954, the U.S. Supreme Court hands down its landmark decision in *Brown v. Board of Education, Topeka,* which declares public school segregation unconstitutional. Following release of the decision, State Attorney General Eugene Cook issues a statement saying the ruling doesn't apply to Georgia.

1954—The NAACP holds meetings in Atlanta and issues The Atlanta Declaration, calling for school boards to implement *Brown.*

November 2, 1954—Georgia voters approve a Constitutional amendment giving the governor power to close any desegregated school and providing for government subsidies to students who attend private schools.

1955—Rosa Parks disobeys a city ordinance by refusing to move to the back of a Montgomery, Alabama, bus. She is arrested and Montgomery's black citizens organize a yearlong boycott of public transportation. In that same year, the Federal Interstate Commerce Commission bans segregation on interstate trains and buses.

September 12, 1955—The Atlanta NAACP files its fourth petition to the Atlanta Board of Education urging compliance with *Brown v. Board of Education.* On September 23 Governor Griffin and two hundred leading state politicians organize a large meeting at the Biltmore Hotel at which they declare their defiance and intention to defend the status quo.

1956—The General Assembly passes six bills that provide for the opening of private schools (not subject to *Brown)* and the closing of integrated public schools. A new flag is approved and a resolution declaring *Brown* null and void passes the Senate with a 30–0 vote, and the House with a 178–1 vote. Angry Southerners draft the Southern Manifesto, an attack on *Brown v. Board of Education.* It is signed by 19 Senators and 81 representatives from former confederate Southern states—including all of Georgia's congressional delegation. Only three Southern senators refused to sign it: Estes Kefauver, Albert Gore, Sr., and Lyndon Johnson.

1957—The Little Rock Nine are blocked from integrating Little Rock High School when Arkansas Gov. Orval Faubus calls in the National Guard. President Eisenhower sends in federal troops to ensure compliance.

1957—Georgia's General Assembly passes resolutions questioning the legality of 14th and 15th Amendments and calling for the impeachment of Supreme Court justices.

1957—In January, sixty blacks from ten states attend an integration strategy meeting in Atlanta that will eventually evolve into the Southern Christian Leadership Conference.

August 29, 1957—The 1957 Civil Right Act, the first civil rights legislation passed in the United States in 79 years, passes in the Senate by a vote of 60 to 15.

January 11, 1958—Ten parents (with assistance from Thurgood Marshall and Constance Baker Motley of the NAACP Legal Defense Fund, and E. E. Moore, Jr., of Atlanta) file *Calhoun v. Latimer* in federal court, charging the school system with failure to comply with *Brown*. In a later ruling Judge Frank Hooper finds the Atlanta public school system segregated and orders a desegregation plan to be filed within a reasonable time.

1958—The Interdenominational Theological Seminary for the education of African-American ministers is founded at the Atlanta University Seminary.

June 16, 1959—United States District Court Judge Frank H. Hooper rules that although he lacks the power to order integration, he does have the power to end segregation. He orders the Atlanta city schools to desegregate.

January 18, 1960—City of Atlanta approves plan to desegregate schools.

1960—The University of Georgia in Athens is desegregated with the court-ordered admission of Charlayne Hunter and Hamilton Holmes.

1960—Atlanta University students stage a series of sit-ins at government building lunch counters and transportation terminals. The protests lead to several arrests, including that of Martin Luther King, Jr., at Rich's department store.

February 29, 1960—Responding to a filibuster organized by Georgia Senator Richard Russell, Majority Leader Lyndon Johnson announces he will keep the Senate in continuous session until the civil rights bill proposed by the Eisenhower administration is passed. Later that year, a diluted version of the bill is passed.

May 9, 1960—Judge Hooper establishes a May 1, 1961, deadline for the desegregation of Atlanta schools.

January 11, 1961—Charlayne Hunter and Hamilton Holmes attend their first classes at the University of Georgia in Athens (UGA). After the Athens police break up a raucous group leaving a nighttime basketball game and surrounding Hunter's dorm, Hunter and Holmes are suspended "for their own protection."

January 12, 1961—Judge Bootle orders UGA to readmit Charlayne Hunter and Hamilton Holmes and charges Governor Ernest Vandiver with the responsibility of protecting them.

April 7, 1961—Black leadership and white business leaders reach agreement to end SNCC/SCLC protests of white downtown business segregation: businesses promise to desegregate after September 1961, within 30 days of desegregation of Atlanta public schools. Students will end their protests. In addition, all charges against the students are dropped.

April 12, 1963—Dr. Martin Luther King, Jr., representing the Southern Christian Leadership Conference, is arrested in Birmingham for contempt of court and parading without a permit. He had come to Birmingham in an attempt to integrate public facilities in accordance with Supreme Court rulings. While in jail, he composes his "Letter from a Birmingham Jail," responding to a public letter from eight white clergymen who criticize him for breaking the law. King writes: "We have waited 340 years for our constitutional and God-given rights. . . . It is easy for those who have never felt the stinging darts of segregation to say 'wait.' "

June 3, 1963—Vice President Lyndon Baines Johnson advises President John F. Kennedy that "blacks are tired of this patience stuff . . . " and that Kennedy ought to "sit down with [Georgia Senator Richard] Russell" and answer every argument he made against civil rights.

1963—In July, Atlanta area movie theater owners meet and agree to admit six black patrons per performance through August 5, and open to as many who want after that, assuming there are no incidents. But if integration causes trouble, the theaters claim the right to resegregate.

August 28, 1963—After meeting with President John F. Kennedy, Martin Luther King, Jr., gives his "I Have a Dream" speech on the steps of the Lincoln Memorial to a crowd of an estimated quarter of a million people.

November 22, 1963—President John F. Kennedy is assassinated in Dallas.

January 3, 1964—Dr. Martin Luther King, Jr., is honored as *Time* Magazine's "Man of the Year."

1964—Black and white students join forces on the civil rights issue with the formation of the Council of Federated Organizations (COFO); and they initiate massive voter-registration drives in the summer of 1964.

August 4, 1964—Three civil rights workers, James Chaney (black) and Andrew Goodman and Michael Schwerner (both white) are murdered on a trip through Philadelphia, Mississippi.

February 21, 1965—Malcolm X is assassinated in New York City.

March 7, 1965—The Edmund Pettus Bridge incident takes place in Selma, Alabama. Marchers are billy-clubbed, tear-gassed, and whipped with cattle prods as they attempt to cross the bridge and begin their protest march to the state capital in Montgomery.

March 25, 1965—Mrs. Viola Liuzzo, a white mother of five, is murdered while driving black marchers back to Selma.

August 6, 1965—The 1965 Voting Rights Act is signed into law by President Lyndon B. Johnson.

August 11 and 12, 1965—The Watts riots erupt in California, America's worst single racial disturbance. Thirty-five people die; the National Guard is called in to restore order.

March 7, 1966—The U.S. Supreme Court rules poll taxes unconstitutional.

May 16, 1966—Dr. Martin Luther King, Jr., speaks out against U.S. government policy on Vietnam.

June 6, 1966—James Meredith is shot and killed on a 220-mile "March Against Fear" from Memphis, Tennessee, to Jackson, Mississippi.

September 6, 1966—A race riot erupts in the Atlanta neighborhood of Summerhill after a suspected car thief is shot escaping a white police officer. The riot, which lasts from September 6–11, results in 138 arrests and 35 injuries. Student Non-Violent Coordinating Committee's (SNCC's) Stokely Carmichael is indicted for inciting a riot, and Julian Bond resigns from SNCC.

November 8, 1966—Edward Brooke, Republican from Massachusetts, is elected to the United States Senate, the first black senator since Reconstruction.

1967—In June, Stokely Carmichael is arrested in Atlanta; racial unrest follows in which one black dies and three are wounded. Mayor Allen declares a curfew.

1967—Summer riots take their toll: 43 die and 324 are injured in Detroit. Twenty-three die and 725 are injured in the Newark, New Jersey, riots. Dr. Martin Luther King, Jr., Roy Wilkins, and Whitney Young, Jr., make a public appeal to put a stop to the riots.

June 23, 1967—Thurgood Marshall becomes an associate justice and the first black to sit on the U.S. Supreme Court.

April 3, 1968—Dr. King, Jr., goes to Memphis, Tennessee, to lead a march in support of striking sanitation workers. There he delivers his last speech, "I've Been to the Mountaintop."

April 4, 1968—Dr. Martin Luther King, Jr., is assassinated on the balcony of the Lorraine Motel in Memphis.

April 5, 1968—President Lyndon B. Johnson declares Sunday, April 7, 1968, a national day of mourning for Dr. King.

April 9, 1968—Dr. King is eulogized at Atlanta's Ebenezer Baptist Church and laid to rest at the South View Cemetery. More than 300,000 people marched through Atlanta with his horse-drawn coffin.

April 11, 1968—President Johnson signs civil rights legislation banning racial discrimination in the sale and rental of housing to blacks and other minorities.

June 5, 1968—Robert Kennedy, brother of the late President John F. Kennedy, is assassinated in Los Angeles while campaigning for the presidency of the United States.

1969—The Justice Department sues the West Peachtree Corporation for discriminatory rent policy and 80 Georgia school systems for racial segregation, including Decatur's.

November 1970—Jimmy Carter, a former state senator, is elected governor and declares that the time for racial discrimination in Georgia is past.

1971—On behalf of 26 black parents, the ACLU sues nine metro-area school boards (cities of Atlanta, Decatur, Marietta, and Buford, and the counties of Fulton, DeKalb, Cobb, Gwinnett, and Clayton) to develop a desegregation plan.

1972—Andrew Young becomes the South's first black U.S. congressman since Reconstruction.

1972—A settlement in the Atlanta desegregation lawsuit is reached: busing assures at least 30 percent black enrollment in all schools, the black-white faculty ratio will change, and a black superintendent will oversee an integrated board.

1974—Hank Aaron, of the Atlanta Braves, hits 714 home runs, breaking Babe Ruth's record.

1976—Governor Jimmy Carter is elected president.

1979—Three hundred Klansmen hold a cross-burning ceremony at Stone Mountain.

1981—Andrew Young is elected mayor of Atlanta.

November 2, 1983—After initially declining to support the bill, President Ronald Reagan signs into law the establishment of the Reverend Dr. Martin Luther King, Jr.'s, birthday as a national holiday. It is the first new national holiday since 1941, when Congress approved the holiday of Thanksgiving in November.

1987—In January, approximately 20,000 civil rights demonstrators marched through predominantly white Forsyth County, Georgia, a week after a smaller march was disrupted by Ku Klux Klan members and supporters.

July 11, 1988—Clark Atlanta University is founded.

1988—Rev. Jesse Jackson places second in Democratic presidential race, winning 13 primaries and caucuses. U.S. Congress passes a Civil Rights bill vetoed earlier by President Reagan.

1990—Georgia strikes down a law prohibiting Ku Klux Klan members from wearing hooded masks in public as unconstitutional.

1992—Cynthia McKinney, a former member of the Georgia House of Representatives, becomes the first black woman elected from Georgia to the U.S. Congress.

November 16, 2000—Seventy-four-year-old civil rights leader and minister Hosea Williams dies in Atlanta.

2001—H.B. 16 is passed by both houses of the General Assembly and signed into law by Governor Roy Barnes to change the Georgia State flag by decreasing the size of the Confederate emblem.

INDEX OF NAMES

INDEX OF RECIPES